MINISTRY AND MONEY

A Practical Guide for Pastors

Janet T. Jamieson
Philip D. Jamieson

WESTMINSTER
JOHN KNOX PRESS
LOUISVILLE • KENTUCKY

To Bethany and Mark

1st edition
Published by Westminster John Knox Press
Louisville, Kentucky

09 10 11 12 13 14 15 16 17 18—10 9 8 7 6 5 4 3 2 1

Book design by Sharon Adams
Cover design by Pam Poll Design
Cover illustration: David Cutler/Images.com

Library of Congress Cataloging-in-Publication Data

Jamieson, Janet T.
   Ministry and money : a practical guide for pastors / Philip D. Jamieson, Janet T. Jamieson.
      p. cm.
   Includes bibliographical references and index.
   ISBN 978-0-664-23198-9 (alk. paper)
   1. Church finance. 2. Clergy—Finance, Personal. I. Jamieson, Philip D. II. Title.

BV770.J26 2009
254'.8—dc22

2009001909

PRINTED IN THE UNITED STATES OF AMERICA

Contents

Preface   v

Part 1: Developing a Theology of Money
1. The Problem of Money in the Church   3
2. The Bible and Money   11
3. A Short History of the Church's Teachings on Money   19
4. Developing a Theology of Money   38

Part 2: Applying a Theology of Money
5. Church Finance 101: Understanding the Basics of
   Church Accounting   53
6. Church Finance 201: Understanding Church Financial Reports   73
7. Budgeting in the Church   101
8. Financial Transparency in the Church   116
9. Money in the Personal Life of the Pastor   131
10. Experiencing Freedom through Giving   161
11. Expanding the Conversation: How to Talk about Money
    When *Not* Asking for It   176
12. Conclusion   197

Notes   201
Index   217

Preface

Throughout most of our married life the idea of coauthoring a book was not something that we ever contemplated. The vocations of accountant and pastor did not seem to have a great deal of overlap. That began to change when we both took positions at the University of Dubuque. As employees of an institution that trains men and women for both accounting and pastoral ministry (among many other things), we began to look at our work in new ways. In 2003 we were able to develop and teach together a class that we called "Money and Ministry." It was well received by our seminary students and partly filled a void that is common in theological education. Many pastors receive little training in the financial aspects of ministry, and what they often learn is divorced from a theological context. This book is our effort to continue to help fill that void.

We wish to thank the many people who supported us in the process of developing and writing this book. We are grateful to the amazing group of colleagues, led by Neal Johnson and Steve Rundle during the 2007 Calvin College Seminars in Christian Scholarship program on "Business as Ministry," who challenged us to expand our thinking about the church's involvement in this important area.

Our colleagues and students at the University of Dubuque and University of Dubuque Theological Seminary have been both patient and helpful. We particularly wish to thank our student assistants: Mark Hughes, Kelsey Ingalls, Jamie Meyer, Maya Tilyaeva, and Deborah Wise. A special thanks goes to Professor Robin Accinelli for her editing and helpful suggestions on the complex issues surrounding clergy income tax and financial planning, and to Professor Andrea Parrett for providing insight, guidance, expertise, and editing in the area of accounting for churches.

We also are deeply grateful to the trustees, president, and administrators of the University of Dubuque and the University of Dubuque Theological Seminary, along with the Wendt Center for Character and Ethics at the University of Dubuque, for granting us release time from teaching and a sabbatical, during which a significant portion of the book was written.

Finally, we want to thank our parents, Robert and Elaine Turner and Lloyd and Alice Jamieson. They were the first ones to teach us of the abundant life that can only be found in Christ and of the importance of giving in grateful response to God's goodness.

PART 1

Developing a Theology
of Money

1

The Problem of Money
in the Church

Pastor Beth loved the ordained ministry, and she was apparently quite good at it. Her first parish, a small rural church, had flourished under her leadership. Established in 1857, in the intervening years the church had dwindled somewhat in membership but not in spirit. Comprised of several extended families, much of the administrative work just seemed to naturally take care of itself. The building was clean and well maintained. Committees met regularly, and under Beth's leadership the church even grew somewhat in both worship attendance and membership.

Moreover, there always seemed to be enough money to get things done. Pastor Beth remembered fondly the response of the people to her appeal for a group to go on a short-term mission trip. Tornadoes had devastated several communities in the next state, and Beth wanted her people to go and help with the cleanup. Given the fairly tight budget, Beth wondered what the response might be. But leaders assured her, "Don't worry, Pastor. We can have a fund-raiser and get enough together to send a team." And that's exactly what happened.

That was not the only time this sort of thing happened. It always seemed that whenever there was a special need, the people were willing to put on a special dinner or organize an all-church garage sale. Additional money was always raised. All Beth had to do was ask. The lay leadership assured her, "Pastor, you worry about what God would have us do, and we'll worry about how to get the money together to do it."

After five years, Beth began to wonder if God might be calling her to another ministry. After prayer and conversation, she decided that this was the case. The people were sorry to see her go but were very glad to have had her pastoral leadership. Beth moved to a larger suburban parish that was more of a challenge, but it was also more exciting. There was so much more going on and so much more need as well.

Beth remembers well the evening she shared with the Administrative Council her vision of partnering with an inner-city parish in support of a new after-school program. She had been at the church nearly four months and felt that now was the time to broach the topic. She had been told by the pastor of the other congregation that the program would need about $15,000 from Beth's church in order for the ministry to succeed. Summoning her courage, she addressed the members of the council: "Friends, God has provided us a wonderful opportunity to help one of the other congregations in our community. All we need to give them is $15,000." Beth remembers well the initial silence of the leadership and remembers even more clearly the first response. "Well, Pastor Beth, that sounds like an important program and everything, but what are we going to give up in our current budget to support that? Money doesn't grow on trees, you know."

She was at a loss. She had a general understanding of the budget. She knew that it was tight, but she thought that someone in the lay leadership would have an idea. After a lengthy silence and several bad ideas, one of the lay leaders finally said, "Pastor Beth, perhaps you should focus on preaching and let us think about the financial matters of the church." The meeting then moved on to old business.

What Pastor Beth did not understand at the time was that the response of this church to her financial leadership was quite similar to the response of her first congregation. No doubt, the suburban church was less willing to embrace Beth's vision for ministry. But in reality, Beth showed little leadership in the ministry of money in either place. She was completely dependent upon the goodwill of the congregation and its own commitment to ministry. With little knowledge of the financial dynamics of congregational life, Beth was unable to lead in a process of funding ministry. Lacking the ability to talk about funding ministry, Beth ultimately lacked the ability to help make her pastoral vision a reality.

At this point, Beth had one or two options before her. First, she could have taken the advice of the Administrative Council and not worried about financial matters anymore. Of course, in this context, that would mean ignoring any future vision for ministry that would actually help the congregation increase its work in mission. As awful an option as that would be, were Beth to choose it, she would find herself, if not in "good company," at least in a "large company," for this is exactly what many clergy do. As a result of exercising this option, slowly the pastoral imagination shrinks so that ministry is transformed into maintaining the current levels. The missional vision of many clergy and congregations is completely bounded by maintenance: maintain current giving levels in order to maintain current programming.

A second option for Beth was to partially take up the challenge by turning to the church fund-raising literature.[1] Increasingly, many clergy are doing this. Denominational judicatories continuously offer workshops on how to make better givers. Is it any wonder that they do so? Across the Protestant spectrum, but especially in the mainline Protestant denominations, financial concerns increasingly dominate the time of pastors. The lack of funding for many Protestant congregations is reaching a point of crisis.[2] Many smaller churches are finding that they can no longer afford full-time ordained pastoral leadership. Rising health care and pension costs only exacerbate the problem.

At denominational levels the problems are even worse. Citing diminished giving, the Presbyterian Church (U.S.A.) recently eliminated 75 national staff positions and 55 overseas mission coworker positions.[3] These types of statistics are being repeated throughout many denominations. Judicatories continually seek ways to lower administrative costs. Many United Methodist annual conferences are eliminating or combining districts. Actions such as these should help stem the tide of red ink, at least in the short term. But what will be the cost to mission? Will congregations pick up the ministry that is cut at the judicatory level? Many local churches are already barely maintaining their current level of existence. The dominant question for many congregations of all sizes is not "How shall we increase our ministry?" but "How will we maintain our current level of staffing?" There is really no clear end in sight for budget and ministry cuts.

It is our experience that most pastors love the ordained ministry. Most love preaching and teaching, pastoral care, and leading worship. Most pastors do not mind the administrative tasks that are a part of parish ministry. But it is also our experience that most pastors strongly dislike the "money aspect" of parish ministry. Most see it as a necessary evil. The stewardship drive and annual stewardship sermon are terrible chores that must be done. So most pastors do their best to complete those tasks as quickly as possible. In other words, at best most pastors are "reluctant stewards of the church's human, physical, and financial resources."[4]

Why is this? Why are so many clergy reluctant stewards? To answer that question will probably yield the answer to why so many lay leaders have limited expectations for clergy to lead in the ministry of money. Seminaries and schools of theology are not noted for the way in which they prepare clergy for this aspect of pastoral ministry.[5] Still, even a casual survey of seminary curricula will show the paucity of classes devoted to the topic.[6] There are a number of reasons for this.

First, pastoral ministry is a profession for generalists. Pastoral ministry involves competency in many areas—preaching, teaching, pastoral care, and church administration, to name a few. Furthermore, many students bring only a rudimentary knowledge of the content of the classical disciplines. It is not uncommon for many entering master of divinity students to have only a rudimentary understanding of the Bible. Increasingly, the first time many of these students encounter the history of the church or foundational church doctrines is in the introductory classes. In short, one reason why there are so few seminary classes devoted to the ministry of money is that there is simply no time or room to offer them.

But there may be a second reason as well. We shall call this the "filthy lucre" rationale. There still exists among many Protestants a belief that there is something too secular, if not unseemly, about the study of money. The King James Version, following William Tyndale,[7] translates 1 Timothy 3:8 as "Likewise must the deacons be grave, not doubletongued, not given to much wine, not greedy of filthy lucre." This translation can be contrasted with more contemporary ones like the New International Version: "Deacons, likewise, are to be men worthy of respect, sincere, not indulging in much wine, and not pursuing dishonest gain." The New Revised Standard Version renders the verse this way: "Deacons likewise must be serious, not double-tongued, not indulging in much wine, not greedy for money."

In the more modern versions the verse has been better translated to place the emphasis upon the use of money rather than money itself. In other words, what is condemned is not money per se but greed or dishonesty in ministry. Obviously, that is an important distinction. Yet it seems to be the case that for many, the problem remains money itself. Perhaps even though much of the Protestant culture has moved beyond the King James Version, it is still that translation which establishes a common Christian relationship to money. Money is somehow unclean and therefore should not be an object of seminary study. One would imagine then that understanding money should be left to the more secular laity! Perhaps it doesn't really matter what constitutes the layperson's relationship to "filthy lucre"!

And so we are left with a tragic inconsistency. Even as churches focus increasingly upon money, clergy have very little seminary training to aid in that work. It may well be the case that depending upon previous education or vocational background, some clergy may have a solid understanding of finance and economics. But that type of background is still quite different from gaining the ability to adequately reflect theologically about money. Furthermore, there is a great deal of difference between understanding the money dynamics of for-profit industries and nonprofits such as a church. Like Pastor Beth, many clergy are reduced to silence at important times in the lives of congregations because of their inadequate preparation.

This book is an attempt to help clergy more adequately deal with the financial issues of parishes and parishioners. We hope that it will inspire clergy to take seriously the role money plays in congregational life. This book is not primarily intended to make clergy better fund-raisers or more capable money managers. There are quite a few books on the market that already seek to do that. It could well be that this book helps pastors and laity do that, but it is not our primary purpose.

Furthermore, this book is not intended to equip clergy to take over a congregation's financial ministry or to displace lay involvement. Our assumption is that God has placed many gifted laypeople in congregations who are very talented in finance and stewardship. They often function thanklessly as chairs of finance committees and as church treasurers. Without their hard work and dedication, the church's work could not continue. A pastor would be foolish to eliminate such capable and devoted people from positions of influence. So we have no desire to "swing the pendulum" in the opposite direction. Instead, pastors need to find their specific role within the ministry of money and exercise the particular authority that we believe God gives to the ordained.

Therefore, our aim in this book is to help clergy assume their specific role in the ministry of money. We shall do that in two primary ways. First, in part 1 we will attempt to help clergy develop an adequate theology of money. We will begin, in chapter 2, with the biblical foundations for a theology of money. The Bible speaks frequently about the problems and promises associated with money. It speaks of the necessity of stewardship, the blessings of wealth, and the use of money for aiding the poor. Yet many still find it difficult to garner a consistent biblical theology of money. Far too many Christians depend more upon the adages of Benjamin Franklin for their thinking about money than they do the Scriptures.

We are not the first Christians to struggle with a coherent theology of money, so in chapter 3 we will turn to the history of the church to learn what the various traditions have taught concerning money. Beginning with the patristic literature and moving through the medieval period, we will discover that the church's understanding has developed a great deal. Next we will turn to the Reformers, and we should not be surprised that Luther and Calvin have much to say about financial matters. After all, it was a church building project that helped make the selling of indulgences the critical issue that it was! Finally, after briefly examining John Wesley's thoughts on money, we will turn to the American church and review some prominent teaching around money in the modern church.

Building on the biblical and traditional foundations, we will attempt in chapter 4 to develop a basic theology of money. Failing to understand what the Bible affirms about the perils and promises of money, many pastors simply hold either a deep distrust of money or a naive acceptance of our consumerist culture. This lack of understanding is compounded by a lack of theological reflection upon Scripture and the vast resources of the Christian tradition. In this chapter we will attempt to determine how Christians ought to relate to money. Building on the New Testament understanding of money as one of the "powers" or "principalities," we will recommend an approach to money that sees it as a key aspect of faithful Christian discipleship. We will propose that money is neither good, bad, nor neutral. Instead, as a fallen power it has a tendency to lead people away from God. But because of the reality and promise of Christ's lordship, money can and must be brought under the dominion of the triune God. It is our assumption that an adequate understanding of the mission of God implies an acknowledgment that God is at work in our midst. We will seek to better understand how we and our use of money can more faithfully participate in what God is doing.

Having built a foundation for approaching the topic of money, in part 2 we will seek to better equip clergy for dealing with the day-to-day administrative tasks relating to the financial ministries of a church. In chapter 5 we will provide a basic overview of accounting in the church. We will explore the topic of fund accounting in depth and will introduce the common church financial statements and the concept of financial transparency. In this chapter, the pastor will be challenged to develop an understanding of the foundations of church finance that will permit him or her to take authority for this area of administration within the church. Chapter 6 builds upon the foundation set in chapter 5. Many clergy feel inadequate in knowing how to read the financial statements produced by their church. This chapter provides a tutorial that will equip pastors with the basic tools necessary to understand and interpret the basic financial reports.

The next two chapters of this section deal with budgeting in the church and the need for financial transparency. We will explore the topic of internal controls and their importance in maintaining financial integrity and transparency. Last, we will provide guidance as to whether or not a church needs an audit.

It is our belief that faithful financial discipleship must be modeled as well as taught. Therefore, chapter 9 will serve as an overview of the issues surrounding money in the personal life of the pastor. Specifically, we will examine issues concerning clergy income tax, compensation planning, personal spending, and giving. We have known far too many clergy who have lost their ability to lead the financial ministry of a congregation because their own financial lives were chaotic.

Finally, we will turn to two additional points of application. In chapter 10, we will develop recommendations for teaching and preaching about money that will move a congregation beyond the annual stewardship season. Faithful teaching about giving is one of the most important things that the church has to offer people.

In chapter 11 we will seek to expand the money conversation. The only time that money is mentioned in the pulpit for many congregations is during budget-setting time or the annual stewardship drive. We will argue that this is not only insufficient but is also incommensurable with a consistent and faithful theology of money. In contrast, we will offer a vocationally centered vision of business as mission.

Then we will turn to issues of pastoral care and money. This is one of the most important points of failure for many clergy. Underlying many pastoral care issues is the way in which people relate to money. Money is at the center of many individual and marital problems. Thus, this chapter will briefly deal with developing ways to offer spiritual companionship regarding money.

In closing, let us return to Pastor Beth. How might her meeting with the Administrative Council been different if she had had greater confidence and capacity to discuss the financial ministry of her congregation?

Let us imagine a different outcome: Toward the end of her first year at the suburban church, Beth received a phone call from a fellow clergyperson. He was the pastor of an inner-city congregation that was seeking to strengthen its after-school program. He was looking for another congregation with which to partner. The partner would need to help both with volunteers and financial resources. The financial commitment would be about $15,000.

After concluding the phone call, Beth was thrilled. She knew that her own congregation needed another way to participate in ministries of justice and mercy, so for the past several months she had been reviewing the current operating budget as well as the budgets from the last five years. Reviewing the statement of activity, Beth saw that giving had remained stable in relationship to the budget. At the same time, she felt confident that God was now providing a significant opportunity to expand the church's mission work.

That following Monday evening, the Administrative Council had its monthly meeting. The meeting went well, and everyone was in good humor. The chair asked for new business, and Beth said, "I have a matter for us to consider." After summarizing her conversation with the other pastor and explaining what it would entail for them, Beth said, "Friends, God has provided us a wonderful opportunity to help one of the other congregations in our community. All our financial commitment would be is $15,000." Joe, the chairperson of the finance committee, finally said, "Well, Pastor Beth, that sounds like an important program and everything, but what are we going to give up in our current budget to support that? Money doesn't grow on trees, you know."

Beth replied, "You can say that again, Joe! That's why I've spent the last several months looking over our income and operating costs. I have good news! I am convinced that we can save between $3,000 and $4,000 per year by trimming some of our administrative costs. I know that doesn't add up to $15,000, but I'm also certain that the members of this congregation have both the means and the desire to give more, if we give them a reason to do so."

"What we have before us is an opportunity not only to support an important mission project but also to change the money culture of this congregation. I think that we have been making a basic mistake in our approach to stewardship. We have been asking people to subscribe to a budget. We tell them that we need this amount of money in order to pay all the bills and meet our obligations. Reviewing the past statements of activity, I've noticed that the people have done a great job with meeting those obligations but have done little else over the last five years."

"But I want us to change our way of thinking. What if we thought first about what God is doing in our community and then began with this question: What part does God want us to play in God's work? I believe that our thinking about money needs to begin there. What do you think?"

Again, there was a time of quiet. Finally, it was Joe who broke the silence again. "Well, Pastor, I can see that you've done your homework. Frankly, I'm a little amazed; as far as I can tell, you're the first pastor we've had who even looked at the financial statements. And I like your ideas about cutting some of our administrative costs. Now, this new way of thinking about money, I'm not quite so sure about. I'll have to give that some more thought. But I believe that you are right, that we can do better. And I also believe that you are the pastor who can help lead us in that direction." After further positive discussion, the council voted to move ahead and look at ways of financing this new mission initiative.

It will not always be this easy. Sometimes congregations will say "No" or "Not yet." But we are convinced that most churches are looking for clergy who will help lead them in a more faithful way of dealing with money. We offer this book to aid in that work.

2

The Bible and Money

What does the Bible say about money? Actually, the Scriptures teach a great deal about the topic. Much is said about both the promise and the peril of money. There are some commandments about giving and some dire warnings against hoarding wealth. There are both promises of prosperity and statements about the blessedness of poverty for believers. The Bible is definitely not silent on the topic.[1]

This chapter will provide a brief overview of the Bible and money. Additional Scripture references will be cited throughout the rest of the book. We will focus here on three important aspects of biblical teaching: blessing, giving, and the relationship between wealth and idolatry.

BLESSING

Issues of economic abundance and subsequent loss dominate the Old Testament. Beginning with the book of Genesis and the goodness of creation in an agricultural paradise (the garden of Eden), the Old Testament relates a roller-coaster-like ride of upswings and downturns in the economics of the ancient Middle East. Adam and Eve are rich but lose everything. The wealthy Abraham is called to leave his fortune in order to enter a new land. For his faithfulness, he is blessed, and through him all peoples are blessed (Gen. 12:3). His material blessings soon follow ("Now Abram was very rich in livestock, in silver, and in gold," Gen. 13:2). Following him, the fortunes of the other patriarchs and matriarchs ebb and flow until the book ends with Joseph, whose prosperity and power in Egypt is second only to Pharaoh's.

At this point, the bottom falls out. Exodus begins with a terrible economic reversal: God's greatly blessed people have been reduced to slavery. From being possessors of much, they now themselves have become possessions. But God hears their cries and saves them from slavery in order to take them to a land flowing with milk and honey. With this restoration of wealth, one might hope the story would end happily. But, of course, it is only beginning.

Throughout the Old Testament, the ebbs and flows of Israel's economic fortunes are tied to covenant faithfulness. Israel is materially blessed but always with the understanding that the blessing points beyond itself. The prosperity is not an end in itself but a sign of Israel's relationship with God.

This relationship places very important contingencies upon the blessing. First is the contingency of purpose. Israel was created to be a light to the nations (Isa. 60:3), so material blessing is meant to serve the larger purpose of testimony to the one, true God. Israel's prosperity is meant to attract the nations to the reality of God. The queen of Sheba's response to the grandeur of Solomon's reign is a primary example (1 Kgs. 10:6–10).

The queen is truly amazed at Israel's wealth, but of far greater importance, she recognizes the authority of the God of Israel. She even understands the vocational mandate "to execute justice and righteousness" (v. 9) that such blessing implies. And that takes us to the second important contingency.

Material blessing implies justice for the poor. In the Old Testament, this is a rather radical understanding. One of the most important illustrations is the concept of the sabbatical year. Described in both Exodus 23:10–11 and Leviticus 25:2–7, the sabbatical year implied that the land was to remain fallow every seventh year: "For six years you shall sow your land and gather in its yield; but the seventh year you shall let it rest and be fallow, so that the poor of your people may eat" (Exod. 23:10–11). Interestingly, Christopher J. H. Wright comments:

> While the religious aspect of the law may be implicit, then (especially in view of the deep religious significance of anything to do with the land and agriculture), the humanitarian or social aspect is quite explicit. The fallow year was to be for the benefit of the poor, meaning specifically those without land of their own. In the seventh year the natural produce of the land was common and free.[2]

As Wright implies, the religious aspect of Israel's ongoing dependence upon God is not overt here. Allowing the land to go fallow does imply the Israelites' need to trust God for their lives and livelihood. But both the Exodus and Leviticus texts cited above explicitly state the connection of this commandment with caring for the poor.

Deuteronomy 15:1–11 makes the most explicit economic statement of the sabbatical year. There is some uncertainty as to whether or not the debts mentioned in the passage are to be merely suspended for the year or completely canceled. Still, what is certain is that the law is meant to alleviate suffering and show mercy to the poor. The blessings of prosperity ultimately point to and are bounded by God's righteousness and justice.

Concerning this same text, Craig Blomberg states that it "discloses an interesting progression."[3] One sees here the movement from "no poor" in verse 4 to "if there are poor" in verse 7, to finally the assumption in verse 11 that "there will never cease" to be poor in the land. The text perhaps reflects a later stage in Israel's history. Still, what is most important for our purposes is that even growing realism about economic differences does not change the commandment. Economic blessing remains radically attached to justice and mercy for the poor. There is no relaxation of the commandment. If anything, the language is strengthened. Furthermore, note that twice the blessing is referred to as gift: "the land that the LORD your God is giving you" (vv. 4 and 7).

This raises the central issue regarding economic blessing or prosperity. Material blessing in the Old Testament does not imply ultimate ownership. "The land shall not be sold in perpetuity, for the land is mine; with me you are but aliens and tenants" (Lev. 25:23). Here, in very direct terms, the Old Testament states the ultimate relationship between the faithful and the land. It does not belong to them. They are stewards and not owners. Therefore, material goods always imply an ethos grounded in the character of God. We shall return to this central biblical understanding later.

Because material blessings point beyond themselves, there is a third important implication: there is no guarantee of economic prosperity for the righteous. Certain passages from the book of Proverbs might seem to imply that care for the poor ensures one of material blessing.[4] The book of Job counters such a mechanistic relationship.

In the midst of his great pain and suffering, Job reminds his accusers that he has indeed fulfilled God's commandments to care for the poor (29:11–18). In explicit detail, he enumerates the categories of the needy: the poor, orphans, widows, the blind, the lame, and strangers. He has not failed to watch over and share his wealth with them. Yet blessings have not automatically continued to follow for this righteous and wealthy man. Once again, the book of Job, like the rest of the Old Testament, testifies to the penultimate nature of material blessing. Wealth points beyond itself to a relationship with God. That relationship with God implies an ethic of justice and mercy as illustrated in the sabbatical year. Finally, there is no mechanistic relationship between blessing and righteousness. There can be no doubt that sometimes the righteous do prosper, but not at all times, in all places, and in a simple and straightforward manner.[5]

GIVING

As we have already seen, blessing implies giving in the Old Testament. But the question immediately arises: how much? Few would argue against giving, but what exactly is required? Regarding giving, do the Old and New Testaments have the same expectations?

In the Old Testament, giving is mandatory. Various offerings were part of the temple sacrificial system.[6] In addition to these, a tithe was levied on certain agricultural products. In Deuteronomy 14:22–29, one may observe the relational nature of the tithe. The tithe is used to strengthen relations with God, with the Levites, and with the poor. The givers themselves also enjoy the tithe by means of the celebratory feast. No doubt, the feast of the tithe was to help persons recall God's great provision for them. One also sees established here the necessity of caring for the Levites, who did not receive a portion of the land for themselves (see Num. 18:20–32). Finally, because of the abundance of the tithe offering, the poor were also cared for through it.

One other Old Testament reference to the tithe should be mentioned here. Malachi 3:6–12 may well be the best-known reference to the tithe in the Bible. This is due to its constant use in Christian stewardship preaching. But what is most important here is that the tithe is a sign of Israel's trust in God. Again we see that offerings point beyond themselves as signs of an underlying relationship. They do not establish that relationship, but they are indicators of its strength. It is very important to note here that one does not have a principle of reciprocity in this passage. Elizabeth Achtemeier writes:

> Judah has suffered the effects of the covenant curses because she has broken the covenant (v. 9); here her God offers her the blessings that accompany covenant love and trust. But it is not a tit-for-tat arrangement, not a vending machine concept of God, not a bargain by which Judah makes an investment and receives a reward in return. To find in this passage any such legalistic or automatic or materialist understanding is a complete distortion of the covenant relationship with our God.[7]

Throughout the Bible, faithful giving does not bind God. Instead, the opposite is the case. Giving is meant to be a primary sign of a people who are living under God's gracious sovereignty.

Furthermore, verse 12 returns us to an earlier theme: God's desire to bless the nations through Israel's faithfulness. Seeing the fruit of Israel's trusting relationship with God will allow Israel to see the reality of the living God. The recipients of God's blessing extend far beyond the initial receivers. Gentiles will marvel at God's provision for Israel. To them we now turn in discussing giving in the New Testament.

In spite of the teaching of many Christians, there is no New Testament equivalent of the Old Testament's mandatory tithe. The tithe is only mentioned in a few places in the New Testament: Matthew 23:23; Luke 18:9–14; and Hebrews 7:4–10.[8] In both the Matthew and Luke passages, tithing is attached to hypocrisy and the inability to understand what is most important about faithful living. In these passages, not only is tithing not commanded, but there is an explicit warning concerning it. One is able to give in such a way that God's intended blessings associated with giving are completely missed. There can be presumptuous as well as faithful giving among the religious.[9] Finally, the Hebrews passage is a part of the author's larger argument in which Christ is compared to Melchizedek. Abraham's tithe to Melchizedek is very important. However, that importance is a sign of Christ's sovereignty. None of these passages either explicitly commands or forbids the tithe for Christians. To gain an understanding of giving in the New Testament, one should examine Paul's writings.

Throughout the New Testament, one can find examples of the principle that the motivations of the giver are as important, if not more so, than the gift itself. Such examples range from the benign (God's love for a "cheerful giver" in 2 Cor. 9:7) to the truly fearsome (the deadly results of the dishonest giving of Ananias and Sapphira in Acts 5). As we have already seen, the motivation of gift-giving in order to receive blessings from God is not a biblical principle. It was, however, an ancient one. Jouette M. Bassler has argued that the principle of benefaction was a primary motivator both for the asking and the giving of gifts:

> The practice of benefaction, which involved implicit or explicit requests for large-scale gifts of money, sustained the Greco-Roman world at several levels. It was an accepted practice with roots deep in the notion of the reciprocity of gift-giving, yet problems were apparent to those caught up in the process. . . . Requests became expectations, expectations became demands, and demands were accompanied by thinly veiled threats. The voluntary quality of the benefaction was thus seriously compromised.[10]

Bassler's primary interest is in the asking for money. But what is true for the motivation of asking is also true for the motivation of giving. It is an unacceptable practice in the New Testament to give while expecting a reciprocal gift from God. Giving is motivated not out of expectation for future gifts but by gratitude for what one has already received. This is perhaps best illustrated in 2 Corinthians 9:6–15. In this passage, Paul argues that the Corinthian

Christians should understand themselves as part of a "chain of benefaction." That is, because God has so richly blessed them, they should now give in order to aid the poor believers in Macedonia. But unlike the common cultural expectations of benefaction, the Macedonians are not indebted to the Corinthians but to God. Bassler concludes:

> Though convinced that God would provide for them richly, Paul does not allow crass materialism to emerge as a motivating factor. Whatever the Corinthians received would simply enable more generosity. The Corinthians are thus a link in a chain of benefaction, agents of God's generosity. As such they must reflect this divine generosity in their own giving, for they are to be not only recipients of it but also conduits of it.[11]

Here we believe one can perceive the primary principle for giving in the New Testament. Unlike the Pharisee, one does not give in order to show his or her righteousness. And unlike the pagan Roman or Greek, one does not give in order to receive a reciprocal gift. Instead, the primary reason for giving is gratitude for the bounty which one has already received.

THE RELATIONSHIP BETWEEN WEALTH AND IDOLATRY

As we have seen, there are Old Testament texts that speak of God giving material blessings. This blessing is never for the sake of the blessed alone. Blessing implies sharing with the poor and points beyond itself as a witness to the one true God. But if the full purpose is ignored, material blessing or wealth may become perilous. For then, it consistently leads to the twin sins of greed and idolatry.

The prophets consistently denounce those twin sins. Their message is simultaneously ethical and theological.[12] Perhaps most famous is Amos 2:6–8. Here one may see the complete perversion of blessing. Mistreatment of the poor ends in debauchery before the altars of idols. But God will not allow such offenses to occur forever. In Amos 4:1–3 one sees how the blessing is now squandered. By refusing to show care for the poor and faithful witness and trust to God alone, the rich end in terror.

The connection between wealth and idolatry is equally clear in the New Testament. Twice in the Pauline corpus, greed is equated with idolatry. Ephesians 5:5 states, "Be sure of this, that no fornicator or impure person, or one who is greedy (that is, an idolater), has any inheritance in the kingdom of

Christ and of God." In very similar terms, Colossians 3:5 reads, "Put to death, therefore, whatever in you is earthly: fornication, impurity, passion, evil desire, and greed (which is idolatry)." Material blessing, if misused, becomes a competing deity.[13]

The final connection is made by Christ in the Sermon on the Mount: "No one can serve two masters; for a slave will either hate the one and love the other, or be devoted to the one and despise the other. You cannot serve God and wealth" (Matt. 6:24).[14] We believe that the key issue regarding what the Bible teaches about money is here. The issue is the choice between which god we shall serve. In the Sermon, Christ becomes the new lawgiver. One point of continuity between the old and new laws regards the proper use of wealth and its potential to replace service to the true God.[15]

The Corban tradition helps to illustrate the difficulty of faithful giving. Human principles of sound investing practices (as important as they are for maximizing returns) may actually inhibit the authentic giving of disciples and churches. In Mark 7:9–13 Jesus contrasts the keeping of the direct commandment to care for one's parents with a human emphasis on honoring oaths. Churches control significant amounts of wealth that are tied down by rules of preserving principle and underspending interest income. Honoring the rules of foundations and trusts can never be a replacement for caring for those who are in need. Yet how much wealth is sequestered by churches and denominational entities throughout the world? Robert Lupton writes:

> Being wealthy beyond historic comparison, the church is not immune from the influences of contemporary wisdom. We have learned to invest God's resources in inflation-proof real estate and to protect his options with legal documents. It is hard to imagine how much of the assets of the kingdom are reserved in the endowments, dedicated funds, and certificates of deposit of the Western church. The Hebrews called it corban. We call it stewardship.[16]

Even the money set aside for God's purposes can become idolatrous when growth in assets comes before its use for furthering God's mission today. Outperforming the Standard and Poor's 500 Index is no replacement for Christ's standard of feeding the poor. A strong and ever growing portfolio that might help someone, someday, cannot take the place of offering the gospel's good news to the present generation.

Although wealth can be a blessing for Christians, there is certainly no guarantee of it. Furthermore, what does seem to be much more clearly taught is wealth's potential for misuse. To this day it remains the primary competitor to the reign that Christ proclaimed. In the chapters ahead we will continue to highlight this primary biblical theme concerning money. Are we using it to care for others and witness to the kingdom of God? Or is it using us, becoming for us an idol that destroys and ultimately cannot save?

DISCUSSION QUESTIONS

1. Have you ever experienced what you would describe as a "material bless-ing"? Would you connect this with faithfulness?
2. What do you believe about tithing? Should it be mandatory for Christians?
3. Have you ever experienced money concerns or possessions squeezing God out of your life? Is this an ongoing struggle for you?

3

A Short History
of the Church's Teachings on Money

There are many ways to read the history of the church. Often we read it in terms of the development of doctrine. Sometimes we read it in terms of the great historical figures. We also read it in relation to the many voices that have not traditionally been heard, such as women and ethnic minorities. But rarely do we read it in terms of the church's teaching about wealth. When one begins to read church history this way, a startling discovery occurs: it quickly becomes obvious that throughout the history of the church, much has been said about the topic. From the most ancient communities, through the patristic period, the Middle Ages, the Reformation, and into the modern era, many of the most important figures have written about God's remarkable material blessings, the necessity of giving, and the dangers of excessive wealth. If the contemporary church does not know how to think about money, it is not because of the tradition's silence.

THE NEW TESTAMENT COMMUNITY

The giving and sharing of possessions is a key point of emphasis in even the most ancient of Christian communities:

> Awe came upon everyone, because many wonders and signs were being done by the apostles. All who believed were together and had all things in common; they would sell their possessions and goods and distribute the proceeds to all, as any had need. Day by day, as they spent much time together in the temple, they broke bread at home and ate their food with glad and generous hearts, praising God and having

the goodwill of all the people. And day by day the Lord added to their
number those who were being saved. (Acts 2:43–47)

The earliest description of the newly constituted Christian community
includes a reference to the sharing of possessions. Apparently, one of the key
marks of the new activity of the Holy Spirit was the willingness to share in
order that no members of the new community go without. This seems to have
been a natural consequence of the "wonders and signs" being done by the
apostles. The text does not explicitly command that all should give away all
that they have. Possessions and money simply have found their natural place
and natural use within the earliest Christian community.

The displacement of wealth is further illustrated by the following:

> One day Peter and John were going up to the temple at the hour of
> prayer, at three o'clock in the afternoon. And a man lame from birth
> was being carried in. People would lay him daily at the gate of the
> temple called the Beautiful Gate so that he could ask for alms from
> those entering the temple. When he saw Peter and John about to go
> into the temple, he asked them for alms. Peter looked intently at
> him, as did John, and said, "Look at us." And he fixed his attention
> on them, expecting to receive something from them. But Peter said,
> "I have no silver or gold, but what I have I give you; in the name of
> Jesus Christ of Nazareth, stand up and walk." And he took him by
> the right hand and raised him up; and immediately his feet and
> ankles were made strong. Jumping up, he stood and began to walk,
> and he entered the temple with them, walking and leaping and prais-
> ing God. (Acts 3:1–8)

Although the giving of money occupies a central place in the earliest church,
it is not the most important point. The dawning of God's kingdom is marked
by a willingness to share, but money is not the most significant commodity to
be given. The power of God is freely offered in many ways, as shown in this
healing. Money and possessions are of great importance, but they are not the
dominant concern or asset of the ancient Christian community. Of far greater
emphasis is the loving graciousness of this new people.

That may be illustrated further by one of the most troubling passages in the
New Testament: the story of Ananias and Sapphira. The story follows a reit-
eration of the sharing characteristic of the early church:

> Now the whole group of those who believed were of one heart and soul,
> and no one claimed private ownership of any possessions, but every-
> thing they owned was held in common. With great power the apostles
> gave their testimony to the resurrection of the Lord Jesus, and great
> grace was upon them all. There was not a needy person among them,

> for as many as owned lands or houses sold them and brought the pro-
> ceeds of what was sold. They laid it at the apostles' feet, and it was dis-
> tributed to each as any had need. There was a Levite, a native of
> Cyprus, Joseph, to whom the apostles gave the name Barnabas (which
> means "son of encouragement"). He sold a field that belonged to him,
> then brought the money, and laid it at the apostles' feet. (Acts 4:32–37)

Once again, radical sharing is stated as a natural response to God's amazing activity through the work of the apostles. This context causes us to conclude that our primary concern here should not be what caused the sudden deaths of the couple. In relation to that, we would note that there is no other story related to giving that is nearly as dramatic as this one. The harshness of the response is clearly not based upon the gift being too small.

> "Ananias," Peter asked, "why has Satan filled your heart to lie to the
> Holy Spirit and to keep back part of the proceeds of the land? While
> it remained unsold, did it not remain your own? And after it was sold,
> were not the proceeds at your disposal? How is it that you have con-
> trived this deed in your heart? You did not lie to us but to God!" Now
> when Ananias heard these words, he fell down and died. (Acts 5:3–5)

There was never a command to give everything. But by misrepresenting the gift, Ananias showed that he was still in thrall to the power of money. This was the great offense. It is therefore impossible to draw any principle for giving from the passage. Rather, one's motivations for giving and what they reveal about one's relationship to wealth are the central concerns.

Money's potential power to harm Christian community and dampen the mighty signs and wonders of God's activity became a central concern of Christian teaching about money throughout most of the church's history. The story of Ananias and Sapphira is the first recorded instance of a retreat from this core reality of the early church: money shall not be allowed to separate believers from each other. Their surrender to money's domination posed a far greater threat to the earliest Christian community than did the opposition of the Jewish authorities in Jerusalem.

Martin Hengel offers several important points on the earliest church's teaching regarding property and riches:

> We cannot extract a well-defined "Christian doctrine of property"
> either from the New Testament or from the history of the early
> church. . . . By contrast, primitive Christianity contains a radical crit-
> icism of riches, a demand for detachment from the goods of this world
> and a conquest of the barriers between rich and poor through the fel-
> lowship of agape. All this comes about under the shadow of the immi-
> nent coming of the kingdom of God.[1]

What we can learn from the book of Acts is that the earliest Christians were daily making their choice as to which master they would serve. With certain important exceptions, most ancient Christians were choosing "God over mammon." As we will see in a number of authors from the patristic period, that trend did not long continue.

THE PATRISTIC PERIOD

To properly understand the teaching regarding money and property in the ancient church, one must understand the Roman context. Justo González writes:

> In general, little in Latin writing favors common property. On the contrary, it can be argued that one of Rome's most characteristic contributions to the Western world was its understanding of private property. . . . In ancient Rome, where each small farmhouse was surrounded by its farmland, and each dwelling included the altars to one's ancestors, the notion of property developed a sacred quality that it had lacked in ancient Greece. For Romans, ownership in the full sense included the right to use, to enjoy, and even to abuse one's property.[2]

It is this idea of "absolute" property ownership that informed and caused much of the early church's sometimes radical critique of wealth. Once again, we see the choice between God and mammon. No one can serve two absolute masters, nor can one simultaneously accept Christ's lordship over all things and maintain absolute rights to one's property.

This is well illustrated in Clement of Alexandria's treatise *Who Is the Rich That Shall Be Saved?* from the end of the second century. Clement carefully exegetes Matthew 19:24 and answers in the affirmative that it is possible for the rich to be saved from damnation. Their wealth does not automatically exclude them from salvation. However, there is great danger in riches, and they must be properly used. Riches are not meant "to be thrown away" but are "possessions, inasmuch as they are possessed."[3] The ongoing problem with wealth is its tendency not to stay in its properly ordered place.

> But he who carries his riches in his soul, and instead of God's Spirit bears in his heart gold or land, and is always acquiring possessions without end, . . . whence can he be able to desire and to mind the kingdom of heaven,—a man who carries not a heart, but land or metal, who must perforce be found in the midst of the objects he has chosen?[4]

That which is meant to be possessed ends up possessing. Clement warns repeatedly about this tendency of wealth. Yet he remains positive that the rich can be saved "if they are willing to submit their life to God's commandments, and prefer them to transitory objects."[5]

Cyprian of Carthage (d. 258) demonstrates an increasing emphasis upon what became one of the most important aspects of Christian living: almsgiving. In his *Treatise on Works and Alms*, Cyprian carefully explicates the necessity of giving for Christians. Prefiguring the later penitential system, he states:

> Nor would the infirmity and weakness of human frailty have any resource, unless the divine mercy, coming once more in aid, should open some way of securing salvation by pointing out works of justice and mercy, so that by almsgiving we may wash away whatever foulness we subsequently contract.[6]

A change has occurred in that the focus of giving points toward the perfecting of the Christian's soul. Giving is not meant to be a voluntary activity but is necessary for spiritual life:

> You are the captive and slave of your money; you are bound with the chains and bonds of covetousness; and you whom Christ had once loosed, are once more in chains. You keep your money, which, when kept, does not keep you. . . . Divide your returns with the Lord your God; share your gains with Christ; make Christ a partner with you in your earthly possessions, that He also may make you a fellow heir with Him in His heavenly kingdom.[7]

By "almsgiving" Cyprian does not mean the loose change or several dollars with which we might associate the term.[8] Instead, he frequently speaks to the complaints that such giving may jeopardize one's heirs. His answer is that Christians have been incorporated into a new family and questions of patrimony are of minimal importance. Cyprian concludes his argument by speaking of the soundness of the transaction that occurs through Christian almsgiving:

> Let us give to Christ earthly garments, that we may receive heavenly raiment; let us give food and drink of this world that we may come with Abraham, and Isaac, and Jacob to the heavenly banquet. That we may not reap little, let us sow abundantly. Let us, while there is time, take thought for our security and eternal salvation, according to the admonition of the Apostle Paul who says: "Therefore, while we have time, let us labor in what is good unto all men, but especially to them that are of the household of faith. But let us not be weary in well doing, for in its season we shall reap."[9]

Clement and Cyprian represent well the pre-Constantinian church. Their admonitions regarding giving are offered to Christians who are relatively poor themselves. There are few powerful people counted among the Christians. This of course dramatically changes following the conversion of Constantine in the early fourth century. We will examine John Chrysostom and Augustine of Hippo to show in what way the church's rise in prestige shaped its teaching on wealth.

To fully understand the patristic period's teachings about money, one must first comprehend the Aristotelian doctrine that money was among those things that could not be increased.[10] This belief, coupled with several Old Testament texts such as Exodus 22:25 and Deuteronomy 23:19–20, led not only to the condemnation of usury (loans to be repaid with interest) but also caused ancient and medieval Christians to believe in a limited supply of money. Thus, to have more than one needed automatically meant that others would go without what they needed. Ipso facto, the rich robbed from both God and neighbor.

John Chrysostom (349–407) frequently preached on wealth and the power it creates. Made archbishop of Constantinople, he was beloved by the poor while despised by the wealthy of that important city. Weary of his preaching against the greed and extravagance of the wealthy, Empress Eudoxia eventually had him exiled. He died in exile in approximately 407.

The substance of Chrysostom's teaching on wealth can be discovered in a series of sermons that he preached on Luke 16:19–31, the parable of the Rich Man and Lazarus. Originally preached during his priesthood in Antioch, these sermons reveal a certain tension in Chrysostom's thought. On the one hand, he assumes private property. The wealthy are called upon to share their possessions with those who are in need. However, Chrysostom is also quite radical in denouncing the accumulation of great wealth. For him, this is only done at the expense of the poor. Reflecting upon the future sufferings of the greedy, he says:

> You should think the same way about those who are rich and greedy. They are a kind of robbers lying in wait on the roads, stealing from passers-by, and burying others' goods in their own houses as if in cave and holes. . . . If you cannot remember everything, instead of everything, I beg you, remember this without fail, that not to share our own wealth with the poor is theft from the poor and deprivation of their means of life; we do not possess our own wealth but theirs.[11]

Wealth is treated as a great danger, and the only way for ruin to be avoided is through giving to the poor. Referring to accumulated wealth as the cargo upon a trading ship, Chrysostom warns that the rich man is heading toward "shipwreck" because he "refused to unload his cargo with discretion."[12] If not properly used, wealth becomes the greatest danger of all. It eventually contributes to the damnation of souls.[13]

Chrysostom also spends considerable time reminding his congregation about what constitutes true wealth:

> Let us learn from this man not to call the rich lucky nor the poor unfortunate. Rather, if we are to tell the truth, the rich man is not the one who has collected many possessions but the one who needs few possessions; and the poor man is not the one who has no possessions; but the one who has many desires. We ought to consider this the definition of poverty and wealth.[14]

Finally, Chrysostom concludes that true wealth will only be revealed in the final judgment:

> Just as in the theater, when evening falls and the audience departs, and the kings and generals go outside to remove the costumes of their roles, they are revealed to everyone thereafter appearing to be exactly what they are; so also now when death arrives and the theater is dissolved, everyone puts off the masks of wealth or poverty and departs to the other world. When all are judged by their deeds alone, some are revealed truly wealthy, others poor, some of high class, others of no account.[15]

Our final representative of the early church is the important bishop and theologian Augustine of Hippo (354–430). The substance of his teaching on money and possessions is seen in the following:

> I know that we ought to say that a person enjoys what he produces, but merely makes use of practice. The point of this distinction seems to be that a thing enjoyed is related directly to ourselves and not to something else, whereas a thing used is sought as a means to some other end. Thus we say that the things of time should be used (rather than enjoyed) as a means to our enjoyment of the things of eternity. It is a perversion for people to want to enjoy money, but merely to make use of God. Such people do not spend money for the sake of God, but worship God for the sake of money.[16]

Augustine's classic distinction between enjoyment and use sets the pattern for his teaching on money. He is as explicit as any of the early teachers that money in itself is not evil: "So now, listen to me, and I will show you that what is condemned in a rich person is not money, but avarice."[17] The problem with money (like many other things) is that it easily becomes the end rather than a means to the only fitting end to a human life: fellowship with God.[18] Like everything else, the key to money is learning how to properly use it:

> About these riches of yours, which you love to possess, and which all the same you are prepared to give away for the sake of your present

life . . . Do you love them? Send them on ahead where you can follow them; or else, when you are loving them on earth, you either lose them while you are still alive, or leave them behind you when you're dead.[19]

Citing Matthew 25:35–40, Augustine is certain that one sends riches "on ahead" by giving to the poor.[20] In summary, money is not evil, but it is dangerous. What is meant to help facilitate a relationship with God can easily take the place of God.

THE MEDIEVAL PERIOD

Pope Gregory the Great is often understood as a transitional figure between the late patristic and early medieval periods. In his work, one may see more and more a growing emphasis upon the individual's relationship to money. In Gregory one may witness the triumph of the idea that wealth is not itself sinful, but following Augustine, how one uses wealth must be the place of emphasis. Utilizing what Thomas Oden has described as a "dipolar method of pastoral case studies,"[21] Gregory in his *Pastoral Rule* teaches how to care for both the rich and the poor: "Differently to be admonished are the poor and the rich: for to the former we ought to offer the solace of comfort against tribulation, but in the latter to induce fear as against elation."[22]

It is fascinating to contrast Gregory's approach with Chrysostom's. Unlike Chrysostom's thundering denunciations, Gregory discusses a strategy to enable the wealthy person to hear. Citing King David and Nathan the prophet (2 Sam. 12), Gregory suggests the importance of an indirect approach:

> But sometimes, when the powerful of the world are taken to task, they are first to be searched by certain similitudes, as on a matter not concerning them; and, when they have pronounced a right sentence as against another man, then in fitting ways they are to be smitten with regard to their own guilt.[23]

Furthermore, with Gregory there is a strong acknowledgment of the increasing complexity of the Christian life:

> Differently to be admonished are those who already give compassionately of their own, and those who still would fain seize even what belongs to others. For those who already give compassionately of their own are to be admonished not to lift themselves up in swelling thought above those to whom they impart earthly things; not to esteem themselves better than others because they see others to be

supported by them. . . . Differently to be admonished are those who neither desire what belongs to others nor bestow what is their own, and those who give of what they have, and yet desist not from seizing on what belongs to others.[24]

In the second example, one can certainly perceive a stronger doctrine of individual ownership than in the earlier years of the church. There is no longer a sense of the earlier belief that excessive property ownership always implies theft from the poor. What we can see here is that the management of sin in believers has begun. Sins of money such as covetousness and avarice are now anticipated and by means of the penitential system dealt with and hopefully healed.

Further complicating matters is the use of almsgiving in the increasingly systematized penitential manuals:

But if a cleric is covetous, this is a great offense; covetousness is pronounced idolatry, but it can be corrected by liberality and alms. This is the penance for his offense, that he cure and correct contraries by contraries.[25]

The sin of avarice is often and explicitly corrected through the giving of alms.

He who hoards what is left over until the morrow through ignorance shall give these things up to the poor. But if [he does this] through contempt of those who censure him, he shall be cured by alms and fasting according to the judgment of a priest. If, indeed, he persists in his avarice he shall be sent away.[26]

Finally, the power of almsgiving is explicitly stated in *An Old Irish Penitential*:

The Apostle Paul says: Let him who has lived by robbery and theft cease therefrom, and let him labor with his hands, so that he may have what he can give . . . in alms to the poor and needy. For as water quenches fire, so almsgiving quenches sins. Christ says: Anyone who has much wealth or substance should distribute half of it to the poor and needy. As for him who desires to reach the pitch of perfectness, he distributes all he has to the poor and needy and goes on a pilgrimage or lives in destitution in a communal church till he goes to Heaven.[27]

It certainly seems to be the case that by the early medieval period almsgiving had become a way of atoning for individual sins. Receding into the background was the early church's doctrine of giving centered in care for the poor. Furthermore, as the above shows, any call for a more radical commitment to poverty was squarely centered in the counsels of perfection, that is, commitments which go beyond the path of regular discipleship.

Therefore in the main, Christian thinking accommodated itself to wealth throughout the Middle Ages. The deep suspicion of riches was lost except for a few notable exceptions. A commitment to a life of poverty was left to a few spiritual heroes like Francis of Assisi and the order that followed him. But no longer was there the common expectation that all Christians should sacrificially give to the poor.[28]

R. H. Tawney argues that the reason for that is the church itself had its own reasons for maintaining the feudal system:

> Practically, the Church was an immense vested interest, implicated to the hilt in the economic fabric, especially on the side of agriculture and land tenure. . . . The persecution of the Spiritual Franciscans, who dared in defiance of the bull of John XXII, to maintain St. Francis' rule as to evangelical poverty, suggests that doctrines impugning the sanctity of wealth resembled too closely the teaching of Christ to be acceptable to the princes of the Christian Church.[29]

But a changing economy also caused the church itself to prosper in new ways unimaginable to the early Christians. Ancient canon laws against usury began to be relaxed. Certain beliefs were much easier to sustain for agrarian societies than for the increasingly urban and mercantile ones that were emerging during the late Middle Ages. Economically, little had changed from the Old Testament writers up until the late medieval period. Thus, a rapidly changing economy forced many Christians to rethink the ancient prohibitions against lending with interest as well as the natural law beliefs upon which they were partially based.

An entirely new approach to money was coming. In economic terms, the modern era was emerging. Tawney summarizes well the primary distinction between medieval and modern economic thought. It consists

> in the fact that, whereas the latter normally refers to economic expediency, however it may be interpreted, for the justification of any particular action, policy, or system of organization, the former starts from the position that there is a moral authority to which considerations of economic expediency must be subordinated.[30]

Therefore, the chief cultural change beginning at this time was the movement away from an

> insistence that society is a spiritual organism, not an economic machine, and that economic activity, which is one subordinate element within a vast and complex unity, requires to be controlled and repressed by reference to the moral ends for which it supplies the material means.[31]

Onto this cultural stage, the sixteenth-century Reformation entered.

THE REFORMATION

Martin Luther has not been universally praised for his economic thinking. Tawney is notable in his critique, viewing Luther as actually less helpful than the scholastic tradition regarding the use of money.[32] He states:

> Luther's utterances on social morality are the occasional explosions of a capricious volcano, with only a rare flash of light amid the torrent of smoke and flame, and it is idle to scan them for a coherent and consistent doctrine.[33]

But this is hardly a fair assessment. More thoughtful in his response to Luther's economic thinking is Walther I. Brandt:

> It is important to remember in evaluating Luther's statements . . . that his concern was religious in the first instance and only secondarily economic. His primary purpose was to instruct the Christian conscience, though the observations on and suggestions for the business procedures of his time are—if only a by product—among the most significant that remain from that period. . . . Though his formulations may appear largely medieval and reactionary to the superficial observer, his faith certainly shattered the bonds of the past, freeing the economy from the false ideal of sanctimonious poverty, the state from the bondage of ecclesiastically prescribed laws, and the church from a soul-stultifying preoccupation with legalistic casuistry.[34]

Turning to his commentary on the Sermon on the Mount, we see that Luther moved considerably away from much of the patristic speculation regarding money themes. Watchful care is prescribed for the poor, but there is no expectation of universal poverty:

> But you say: "What? Must all Christians, then, be poor? Dare none of them have money, property, popularity, power, and the like. . . . Must they surrender all their property and honor, or buy the kingdom of heaven from the poor, as some have taught?" Answer: No. It does not say that whoever wants to have the kingdom of heaven must buy it from the poor, but that he must be poor himself and be found among the poor.[35]

Luther is explicit in stating that Christ's saying refers to *spiritual* poverty and that "physical poverty is not the answer."[36] Instead, the key to the proper use of money is stewardship:

> All this is intended to say that while we live here, we should use all temporal goods and physical necessities, the way a guest does in a strange place, where he stays overnight and leaves in the morning. He

needs no more than bed and board and dare not say: "This is mine, here I will stay."[37]

The Christian is to remember the proper use and place of money. It should be used to alleviate the sufferings of the poor, but Luther is very careful to observe that physical poverty has no extra blessing before God. But all, the rich and poor alike, are called to the spiritual poverty of which Christ speaks in his sermon.

Kathryn D'Arcy Blanchard offers the following summary of Luther's beliefs regarding money:

> First, what Christians do with their money is indicative of what they believe about God. . . . Second, God's economy is one of grace rather than reciprocity. Jesus did not counsel his followers to give only to the "worthy" poor, but to all who ask for help. . . . Third, not all wealth is the same. God created material goods for the benefit of humankind, but wealth is not to be pursued for its own sake. Wealth is a blessing (not to be confused with a reward) only when it is received as a gift from God, not when it is obtained unethically through "scratching and scraping." . . . Lastly, Luther emphasized that fallen humans are masters of self-deception. Although Christians have "Moses and the prophets" (as well as Jesus) to tell us to live justly and to share what we have, we still easily manage to justify virtually any economic decision we make in the name of prudence.[38]

To gain a more modern insight into the use of money, one must turn to the other great sixteenth-century reformer, John Calvin. Calvin makes provision both for sharing with one's neighbor and enjoying God's good creation. For Calvin the key is to find the middle ground between a "mistaken strictness" and a "mistaken laxity":

> For if we are to live, we have also to use those helps necessary for living. And we also cannot avoid those things which seem to serve delight more than necessity. Therefore we must hold to a measure so as to use them with a clear conscience whether for necessity or for delight. . . . If we must simply pass through this world, there is no doubt we ought to use its good things in so far as they help rather than hinder our course.[39]

Calvin does not believe that there are precise rules for governing the use of money or the things which it can buy. Instead, he believes

> that consciences neither ought to nor can be bound here to definite and precise legal formulas; but insomuch as Scripture gives general rules for lawful use, we ought surely to limit our use in accordance with them. Let this be our principle: that the use of God's gifts is not

wrongly directed when it is referred to that end to which the Author himself created and destined them for us, since he created them for our good, not for our ruin . . . to provide for necessity but also for delight and good cheer.[40]

Here one may rightly discover a modern understanding of Christian steward-ship. Calvin has distanced himself from both the patristic tendency toward an excessive asceticism[41] and the medieval economic prohibitions that neither did justice to the biblical witness nor could make sense of the contemporary mer-cantile-based and growing economy.

Instead of a strict teaching to cover all use of things, Calvin offers four guid-ing principles:

> [First,] to indulge oneself as little as possible; but, on the contrary, with unflagging effort of mind to insist upon cutting off all show of super-fluous wealth, not to mention licentiousness, and diligently to guard against turning helps into hindrances. [Second,] they who have nar-row and slender resources should know how to go without things patiently, lest they be troubled by an immoderate desire for them. [Third,] all those things were so given to us by the kindness of God, and so destined for our benefit, that they are, as it were, entrusted to us, and we must one day render account of them. [Fourth,] the Lord bids each one of us in all life's actions to look to his calling.[42]

Furthermore, Calvin's principles illustrate well the basis for his rethinking of the permissibility of interest lending. An expanding economy still did not allow for forgetting the patristic era's primary teaching on money: the impor-tance of relief for the poor. Still, one will look in vain for hard rules regarding the proper charging of interest. L. F. Schulze summarizes Calvin's perspective:

> Calvin is well aware of the difficulties that surround the question of a fair interest. He knows of the many ways in which interest can be mis-used. Therefore, according to his advice to his friend Claude de Sachin, the fairness of the agreement finally depends on the persons involved; whether they are acting in Christian responsibility and whether both creditor and debtor are prepared to obey the will of Christ. In this way, the personal responsibility of the believer is accentuated.[43]

Rather than hard rules, Calvin employs biblical principles regarding the charging of interest. Chief of these is the ongoing mandate of care for the poor, as noted by W. Stanford Reid:

> The lender must follow the Golden Rule at all times, so that "usury is not now unlawful, except in so far as it contravenes equity and broth-erly union." On the other hand, one should lend to the poor and needy

without expecting to receive any return on the money. One should not, moreover, take any pledge for a loan which is necessary for the support of life by the poor.[44]

Therefore, we would argue that the primary change which occurs in the church's teaching during this time is an economic rather than a theological one. For the first time, it becomes increasingly understood that the poor can be aided not only through almsgiving but also by means of sharing in the increase of capital.

THE MODERN PERIOD

We next turn to the Puritans in order to show the appropriation of Calvin's thought as well as to move the discussion to the American context. Deeply influenced by Calvin in both their theology of vocation and the Christian's relationship to material goods, the Puritans were of great importance for modernizing a Christian approach to wealth and possessions. They understood the Christian goal as neither a call to wealth nor poverty but rather faithfulness in whatever station of life one may find oneself. Wealth was understood as a gift from God, but poverty was not a curse. The recommended path was hard work and accepting whatever advantages may come one's way as faithful stewardship. To do less was considered unfaithful service. Richard Baxter wrote:

> If God shows you a way in which you may lawfully get more than in another way (without wrong to your soul, or to any other), if you refuse this and choose the less gainful way, you cross one of the ends of your calling, and you refuse to be God's steward.[45]

Here one sees both Calvin's views on faithful service to God and lawful uses. One may say that it is an act of impiety not to strive for more. But such strivings must always be checked by love for God and neighbor.

The Puritans are perhaps most helpful in their understanding of the purpose of money. Working with an economic understanding much more coherent to contemporary times, the Puritans still echo the ancient Christian beliefs, as this quotation from William Perkins demonstrates:

> We must so use and possess the goods we have, that the use and possession of them may tend to God's glory, and the salvation of our souls.
> . . . Our riches must be employed to necessary uses. These are first, the maintenance of our own good estate and condition. Secondly, the good of others, specially those that are of our family or kindred. . . .
> Thirdly, the relief of the poor. . . . Fourthly, the maintenance of the

Church of God, and true religion. . . . Fifth, the maintenance of the Commonwealth.[46]

Neither socialists nor consumerists, the Puritans offer a way forward for the proper Christian use of money. Although making allowance for individual gifts and differences, the ultimate vision of a proper use of money is a social one. Christians should neither strive for wealth nor poverty. They should faithfully labor and always keep the greater social good in mind. But there exists an obvious tension in this approach. As Leland Ryken notes:

> On the one hand, the Puritans held attitudes conducive to the amassing of wealth and property: the view that money and property are good in principle, disbelief that poverty is meritorious in itself, and a conviction that a disciplined and hardworking lifestyle is virtuous. On the other hand, to curb the potential for self-indulgence that followed in the wake of their lifestyle, the Puritans had an even longer list of cautions: an awareness that God sends poverty as well as riches, an obsession with the dangers of wealth, the ideal of moderation, a doctrine of stewardship in which God is viewed as the ultimate owner of goods, and a view of money as a social good.[47]

The Puritans offered a useful way to deal faithfully with money while at the same time curbing its power. Many contemporary Christians still willingly follow parts of the Puritans' advice that regard earning, while completely ignoring the counterbalance of faithful spending.

Before turning to the more modern American church, we think it is worthwhile to reference one other important Christian leader. Although deeply influenced by the Puritans, he founded another Christian movement deeply influential in the history of the American church. John Wesley (1703–1792), founder of the Methodist movement, had much advice regarding the proper use of money. Perhaps best known for his guidance "to earn all you can, save all you can, and give all you can,"[48] Wesley took the proper use of money to be of grave importance for faithful Christian living. Before briefly exploring his thoughts on money, two observations are important. First, the earliest Methodists with few exceptions came from the lower end of the eighteenth-century British economy. Many suffered in almost unimaginable poverty. Wesley gave most of his life to working with these people. Second, Wesley practiced what he preached regarding the proper use of money. Albert Outler states:

> Tyerman . . . observes that Wesley was the "proprietor of a large publishing and book concern from which he derived considerable profits . . . but of these he literally spent none upon himself except for an occasional suit of clothes." . . . Wesley was "perhaps the most charitable man in England. His liberality to the poor knew no bounds. He gave

away, not merely a certain part of his income, but all he had. We are persuaded, upon a moderate calculation, he gave away in about fifty years, twenty or thirty thousand pounds."[49]

But Outler also observes that due to Wesley's liberal charity, the Methodist Book Concern was in financial shambles most of the time. Very few of the profits were held back to ensure efficient business practices.[50]

As the Puritans discovered, honest and frugal money disciplines tend to promote a growing affluence. This was certainly the case for the early Methodists and was profoundly troubling to the movement's founder. Toward the end of his life, Wesley dedicated a number of sermons to the question of riches and the proper use of money. Written in 1780, Wesley's sermon "The Danger of Riches" reveals well his thinking with regard to money. He begins by noting how few sermons are preached on the topic:

> Who preaches this? Great is the company of preachers at this day, regular and irregular. But who of them all openly and explicitly preaches this strange doctrine? . . . I do not remember that in threescore years I have heard one sermon preached upon this subject.[51]

Wesley is confident that the Methodists have followed two-thirds of his advice. They have faithfully been earning and saving all that they can. However, they have failed in their giving. They are guilty of surplus accumulation and have ignored Father Wesley's admonishments:

> Having "gained" (in a right sense) "all you can," and "saved all you can"; in spite of nature and custom and worldly prudence, "give all you can," I do not say, "Be a good Jew," giving a tenth of all you possess. I do not say, "Be a good Pharisee," giving a fifth of all your substance. I dare not advise you to give half of what you have; no, nor three-quarters—but all! Lift up your hearts and you will see clearly in what sense this is to be done.[52]

Here we see Wesley at his most radical. Following the Puritan admonitions to secure enough for oneself and family, Wesley then follows a very austere doctrine of giving. It is sinful to keep anything beyond that which is necessary for basic needs.

It is clear from this sermon that Wesley makes a strong connection between the Methodists' failure to give adequately and their cooling commitment to the main practices of the movement. Speaking of the accumulation of wealth, he continues:

> Have they not hurt you already, have they not wounded you in the tenderest part, by slackening, if not utterly destroying your "hunger and

thirst after righteousness"? Have you now the same longing that you had once for the whole image of God? Have you the same vehement desire as you formerly had of "going on unto perfection"?[53]

The early Methodists no longer care for God or neighbor like they once did because, as Wesley tells them, "Gold hath steeled your hearts."[54]

Wesley's final sermons indicate that it has become increasingly clear to him that the Methodists are paying no attention to his teaching about money. This is clearest in his last published sermon, "The Danger of Increasing Riches."[55] However, it must be asked, was Wesley expecting too much of the early Methodists? Was it reasonable to expect them to adopt his austere lifestyle? Did he set a standard too high? It seems to be true. Wesley went beyond the Puritans in explicitly determining the difference between luxuries and necessities, with most extra goods defined as luxuries. He seems to have left very little middle ground for a faithful Christian response that was not a rather severe asceticism. No doubt, increasing wealth played a role in the cooling ardor of early Methodists. But one must also wonder as to whether or not Wesley's own lack of moderation hampered the movement. David Hempton has observed that throughout the early days of Methodism in the United States (1780–1830), it

> was racked by serious financial problems, which both reflected and exacerbated deep-seated structural deficiencies in the Methodist organization. Religious movements as with big businesses, can, up to a point, thrive on deficit finance in periods of expansion, but in religious organizations the great disadvantage is that there is generally no access to liquid capital beyond that which is voluntarily granted by their members or raised by their supporters.[56]

Had Wesley been able to expound and model a more moderate paradigm of faithful stewardship, what financial problems might the early Methodists have avoided? As is so often the case, when the choice lies between a totally austere approach to money and a rather nontheological one, the Methodists (as other Christians) have consistently chosen the latter.

THE AMERICAN CONTEXT

The American Methodists were not alone in their ambiguous positions regarding the Christian use of money. To close this historical overview, we think it appropriate to examine two nineteenth-century Baptist ministers and their radically different conclusions about money. Russell Conwell and Walter Rauschenbusch illustrate the wide scope of Protestant positions regarding the purpose and use of money. Furthermore, they are excellent examples of what Mark Noll has described as the primary relationship for American Protestants regarding faith and money:

> Protestants regularly, consistently, and without sense of contradiction both enunciated traditional Christian exhortations about careful financial stewardship and simply took for granted the workings of an expanding commercial society.[57]

Russell Conwell (1843–1925) is best known as the founder of Temple University and for his lecture "Acres of Diamonds," which he delivered over six thousand times. "Acres of Diamonds" reveals Conwell's primary understanding of one's relationship to money: God desires to prosper his children in order that they might help others. There are unlimited opportunities to grow rich if one will open one's eyes to see them. Conwell was very optimistic regarding the potential of wealth. His primary message was of God's desire to help Christians become wealthy so that they might do good in the world. More often than not, the human unwillingness or inability to see the possibilities in one's midst was the principle reason for poverty.

Another Baptist minister, Walter Rauschenbusch (1861–1918), took a somewhat different approach. Building his theology around his experiences as a pastor in the "Hell's Kitchen" area of New York City, Rauschenbusch became convinced that contemporary American capitalism was the enemy of authentic Christianity. His economic vision was far less optimistic than Conwell's. He offered a fourfold critique of capitalism, as described by Daniel B. McGee:

> He criticized its promotion of competition . . . as primitive and savage. Second, he faulted capitalism as "the last entrenchment of autocracy." . . . Third, he said that the capitalist system promoted dishonesty in business practices because it lacked the crucial sense of solidarity of all people. Finally, while acknowledging that profits were legitimate as just rewards for able work, he claimed that when profits result from the monopoly of power, it was "a form of legalized graft."[58]

Unlike Conwell, Rauschenbusch believed in the necessity of a redistribution of wealth. Much greater intervention was necessary in order to faithfully provide for the needs of the poor. It is our belief that the influence of these two ministers continues on as representative of the two primary Protestant approaches to wealth. Although Conwell would have had significant issues with current formulations, his thought is echoed in the current gospel of prosperity. Since God desires wealth for God's children, those who go without are primarily responsible for their own poverty. On the other hand, Rauschenbusch's influence lives on in a welfare-state approach. External factors are principally responsible for poverty; thus, the state must intervene. The Christian witness is contained in advocating to the state on behalf of the poor.

Both Conwell and Rauschenbusch reflect what Noll describes as a commitment to Christian stewardship and the "workings of an expanding commercial society." The expanding commercial society seems to have been the primary shaper of the vision of most American Protestants. Both views mix together a Christian commitment to alleviating poverty and a secular economic vision. As polar opposites, they reflect the majority of Protestant positions that still hold true today. Neither Conwell's laissez-faire vision, which includes economic deprivation that can be overcome through hard work, nor Rauschenbusch's equally naive belief in economic redistribution does justice to the larger Christian tradition. We would argue that neither position adequately has done justice to the biblical vision or offers a faithful and useful way forward for a theology of money. We will attempt to formulate another way in the next chapter.

DISCUSSION QUESTIONS

1. What would you say are the main teachings of the church concerning money throughout its history?
2. Were you surprised at how negative some Christians have been in describing a Christian's relationship with money?
3. With which of the historical figures discussed here do you most identify?

4

Developing a Theology of Money

We have now seen through our review of the Bible and church history that the Christian tradition has had much to say about money and the things it can buy. We have seen that it offers promise when used in obedience to God but also how it brings great danger when misused. The purpose of this chapter is to develop a theology of money for use in congregations. To do this is to attempt to think coherently about money and its use in the light of the triune God.

JACQUES ELLUL: NAMING MONEY'S POWER

One of the most important theologians of the twentieth century was the social critic and philosopher Jacques Ellul (1912–1994). Ellul is best known for his work on technology's effect upon society, but he is also one of the few serious theologians to attempt to write an extended work on money. This work is a jarring exposé of the role of money in Western culture and particularly within the church. In it, Ellul makes several very important insights. He begins with the common observation that most Western Christians have been raised with two basic ways in which to think about money: the economic theories of Marxism or capitalism.

Unlike most thinkers, Ellul refuses to answer the question as to which one is better or truer to the biblical witness. Instead, he makes a very important assertion: no system can account for the level of influence money possesses. To think first in terms of economic or philosophical systems is to fail to deal adequately in Christian terms with money, for the true quandary does not lie in the adoption of one system over another. Both Marxism and capitalism have points to recommend them as well as points to critique them. Instead, the real problem of money resides in human nature:

> This is the error of all committed economists and others who think they can solve the problem without considering human nature. . . . But it is more than an error: it is also hypocrisy and cowardice. For then I ultimately ask no more than to believe the system-builder. It is so convenient. . . . All I have to do is campaign for socialism or conservatism, and as soon as society's problems are solved, I will be just and virtuous—effortlessly. My money problem will take care of itself.[1]

At this point, it is most important to recognize that Ellul is not arguing for a simplified, individualistic approach—that is, one in which it is up to each person to work out his or her own approach to money. Nothing could be farther from his intention. He is well aware that our radical Western individualism is one of the consequences of our lack of Christian reflection regarding money. One of the primary results of that is our powerful consumer society, which tends to individualize each person into a discrete spending unit. We shall say more about this below.

To speak of money in explicitly Christian terms is to move beyond a simple individualism. The power of money influences communities as well as individuals, and therefore there truly is a systemic problem associated with money. Indeed, the sum of all greediness or covetousness is greater than its parts. Ellul demands that each person examine his or her own relationship to money. The problem cannot be merely objectified and thus solved by a system or in some pain-free way by asking others to sacrifice. The subjective dimension of money is extremely powerful. All individuals participate in the worldly power of money, and thus all are corrupted by it by default. Thus, the problem is not an external one but is located in the heart of each person. Furthermore, for Christians this means that there is ultimately no mediating structure (for example, an economic theory or political party allegiance) between themselves, their money, and God. (We will return to this topic in greater detail in chapter 10.)

Ellul maintains that there are two common ways in which Christians (and particularly Protestants) have historically spoken of money. The first of these we have already considered: money is a blessing. There can be no doubt that the Old Testament links material blessing with faithfulness. But as we have seen, there was never a simple and direct relationship between faithfulness and blessing. Throughout the Old Testament, blessing is always a secondary benefit and never guaranteed. Most importantly, the New Testament radically departs from any emphasis or even reference to material blessings as a result of belief in Christ. Throughout the New Testament, faithfulness is as liable to and even more likely to produce poverty and martyrdom as any material benefit. Ellul writes:

> Christians have turned this blessing into a proof. They have turned it into a mathematical equation: money = blessing. No longer does a person receive money—more than is needed, superfluous abundance given by God—as a result of being blessed. Money becomes in itself a spiritual value.[2]

There is an essential problem with the mathematical certainty connecting the two. If money equals blessing, then why not the reverse: blessing equals money? With this type of certainty it becomes unavoidable to conclude that the wealthy are closer to God. Even though perhaps there are many who think so, this thought runs contrary to much New Testament teaching wherein it is the poor who are explicitly considered the blessed ones: "Then he looked up at his disciples and said: 'Blessed are you who are poor, for yours is the kingdom of God'" (Luke 6:20). The very ones singled out for acknowledgment by Christ are once again ignored and disparaged by this idea of a connection between blessing and wealth.

There is a second problem associated with the idea: the way in which blessing becomes a Christian's primary mode of assurance of God's love. Blessing becomes the subtle impetus to work harder in order to earn more, in order that one can be confident of God's grace, as Ellul observes:

> It is therefore imperative that we make money. And this is where we end up because it is so important to us to be assured of blessing. "Get rich," says a proponent of this doctrine to young Christians who ask him what they should be doing. All activity is then directed toward acquiring money, evidence of the spiritual victory which automatically accompanies it.[3]

Slowly (or perhaps not so slowly) one's relationship with God recedes into the background. Whatever initial association there was between blessing and money has now been completely eclipsed by the money itself. It becomes the core spiritual value. It is sufficient for this life. Finally the question must be asked, "Who really needs anything more from God?"

One need not completely subscribe to Max Weber's thesis regarding the emergence of capitalism to see how this idea of blessing has influenced the rise of secularism in the West.[4] There does appear to be at least a chronological relationship between capitalism, which arose in the Christian West, and a diminishment of the perceived importance of God for one's life. The relationship calls to mind Flannery O'Connor's wonderful character Hazel Motes and his remarkable observation: "Nobody with a good car needs to be justified."[5]

Too close an affinity between money and blessing always seems to lead to Motes's "Church without Christ," "where the blind don't see and the lame don't walk and what's dead stays that way."[6]

Ellul points out that the second way in which Protestants discuss money is under the category of stewardship. This is certainly superior to limiting the conversation to blessing but may in itself create problems. There certainly can be no doubt that stewardship is a major theme of the biblical narrative from Genesis through many of the parables of Jesus. Thus, the problem is not stewardship per se. Rather, it is how the category is used. Ellul fears that stewardship can become a way of setting limits on Christian discipleship:

> The idea of stewardship is a useful reminder that we do not own our belongings and that we will have an account to give, but it becomes downright vicious when we use it to justify ourselves, when it permits us to fix in concrete what God wants us to submit to the Holy Spirit. . . . But the theme of Scripture is exactly the opposite—it concerns a movement. What Scripture shows has the strength and speed of a rushing torrent.[7]

Often at their best, Christians think of stewardship as "one for me" and "one for God" (or perhaps "nine for me" and "one for God"). That is, some formula is used to derive a proportional divvying up of the loot. This must be contrasted with what Ellul refers to as the "torrent" of biblical teaching which teaches that to accept Christ's lordship is to lose final proprietary claim on anything one possesses.

The question can no longer be "What would God have me do with my money?" but must now be restated as, "How will I deal with that part of God's money over which I've been given secondary control?" As long as stewardship is understood as duty or a way of appeasing God, the radical nature of discipleship is lost. This should also include conversations around tithing (which will be taken up in chapter 10).

For our purposes, Ellul's most important contribution to a theology of money is to understand it as one of the New Testament powers and principalities.[8] For Ellul the definitive text for a Christian understanding of money is Matthew 6:24: "No one can serve two masters. Either he will hate the one and love the other, or he will be devoted to the one and despise the other. You cannot serve both God and Money" (NIV).[9] Ellul says:

> This personification of money, this affirmation that we are talking about something that claims divinity . . . , reveals something exceptional about money, for Jesus did not usually use deifications and personifications. What Jesus is revealing is that money is a power.[10]

NEW TESTAMENT POWERS AND MONEY

Before we pursue further Ellul's thinking here, we need to summarize briefly
what the New Testament teaches on this important topic. The language of
powers and principalities is important for this discussion in two primary ways:
First, it is one aspect of the "already and not yet" reality of Christ's authority.
Second, it is a key feature of the cosmic dimension of Christ's victory on the
cross. The primary discussion occurs in Ephesians and Colossians.

As applied to money, there are three main features of the powers and principalities that are of importance. First, the powers are not intrinsically evil.
Created in and through the power of Christ, the powers and principalities also
participated in the original goodness of creation. Colossians 1:15–17 makes
the important point that in some Christian discussions, money appears to be
completely corrupt—not worthy of theological discussion. Instead, this text
reminds us that money, like any other power, has been created through Christ
and therefore is subject to him.[11]

The second feature is that even though the powers are created good, they
also participate in creation's fallen nature. They are no longer the natural
friends of God, nor are they neutral. They now stand opposed to God's
redemptive activity. Concerning Ephesians 2:1–3, Daniel Reid observes:

> The necessity for peace to be made, along with the later assertion of
> Christ's victory over the powers at the cross (Col 2:15) implies that
> something had gone wrong and the powers had turned hostile to God
> and his purposes. . . . Some interpreters have maintained that from
> Paul's perspective the problem with the powers is that they had been
> wrongly regarded by the Colossians as rival to Christ (Col 2:8, 20).[12]

Insofar as money is a power, it no longer is a natural servant of Christ. It abides
as a potential rival, seeking its own way and its own servants. It demands the
loyalty of all who would serve it.

But with the third feature, we come to an all-important turning point.
Through the decisive victory of the cross, the authority of the powers and
principalities is broken. Colossians 2:15–20 tells us that Christians are now
called to live their lives in the light of Christ's victory. The powers continue to
oppose God's good ways, but those in Christ no longer need be subject to
them. These forces will eventually yield completely to the totality of God's victory in Christ, as is made evident in Ephesians 1:20–23. Christians are therefore called to live new lives that are "between the times." Even though the
authority of the powers and principalities is broken, they are still able to work
a malicious influence until the final consummation of Christ's victory. Stephen
F. Noll offers this summary:

> The palace revolution in the heavens has already taken place. Author-
> ity is now vested in Christ as head of all things. But the news has not
> reached the countryside, where the officials of the deposed regime
> continue to function as if nothing has happened. Paul makes the fol-
> lowing points about the principalities that help explain this gap
> between heavenly reality and historical experience. . . . According to
> Paul's distinctive thought, principalities and powers stand for a world-
> wide web of human affairs grounded in a spiritual hierarchy. The spir-
> itual dimension of the world was not originally evil but has been so
> corrupted by sin and Satan that it is experienced more as domination
> than as dominion (that is, right rule). The sphere of the principalities
> overlaps with that of revealed law and natural order.[13]

Christians (those united to Christ and his victory) are called to participate in
this disarming. Through proclamation of this triumph, through new practices
and attitudes, believers show a new way of living that is not bound by those
forces opposed to God. The powers are still actively opposed to God and his
children but cannot come between them, as so gloriously stated by Paul in
Romans 8:38–39. In terms of money, Christians share the gospel truth that people need not be bound by money's influence. By joyful giving, they practice and
live out this new relationship. By attitudes of gratitude and nonanxious living,
they show a new relationship to money. It now may be restored to its proper
place of servant and no longer be master of those who are in Christ.

Returning to Ellul, we see that his presentation of money as a power fits
well the New Testament paradigm. He notes that it has three characteristics:

> [First,] power is something that acts by itself, is capable of moving
> other things, is autonomous (or claims to be), is a law unto itself, and
> presents itself as an active agent. [Second,] power has a spiritual value.
> It is not only of the material world, although this is where it acts. . . .
> Power is never neutral. It is oriented; it also orients people. [Third,]
> power is more or less personal. . . . Money is not a power because man
> uses it, because it is the means of wealth or because accumulating
> money makes things possible. It is a power before all that.[14]

For Ellul, money is not simply an object, but, as a power, is an "active agent."
As we have seen in the New Testament material, its active agency in the fallen
cosmos is oriented against God's agency. It does not naturally serve the purposes of God. It is a position of great naiveté to believe that one may have an
easy and complete freedom regarding money. Its power is great and perhaps
most particularly so in those places dominated by Western culture.

For those who find it difficult to attribute the New Testament category of
fallen powers to money, Ellul maintains that many people actually maintain a
reverential attitude toward it:

> We attribute sacred characteristics to our money. . . . Money affairs
> are, as we well know, serious business for modern man. Everything
> else—love and justice, wisdom and life—is only words. Therefore we
> avoid speaking of money. We speak of business, but when in someone's
> living room, a person brings up the topic of money, he is committing
> a social error, and the resulting embarrassment is really expressing the
> sense of the sacred."[15]

In other words, the hesitation to openly discuss money in the West is actually
a type of piety. For Ellul, what underlies the "social error" is not a lack of man-
ners but actually a display of impious speech. To speak openly of money is to
make common the holy. When in the presence of one's god, proper deference
and silence should be maintained.

In this way, the power of money reveals itself as the object of improper
worship. It desires its followers to acknowledge its power in divine terms. And
there can be no doubt: this false god has many adherents both in and outside
the church. But how can that be? How exactly does money exert its power,
bring so many under its influence? What is the particular control that it holds
over so many human beings, regardless of how much or how little money they
possess?

MONEY'S POWER: GRANTING VALUE

To better understand the particular way that money exerts its power in contemporary society, we turn to the work of theologian Craig Gay. As we have
seen, Ellul maintains that simply adhering to the tenets of any system, be it
political or economic, is not an adequate position for Christians to take
regarding money. No economic theory adequately understands the power of
money in the lives of individuals and communities. Still, one need not demo-
nize economic systems. Craig Gay seeks to understand both the promise and
peril of the Western capitalist system.

To begin, it is important to remember that the Western capitalistic system
is both a product of the Christian West and a significant factor in its increasing secularization. Capitalist systems have done much good in the world. Gay
notes:

> Industrial capitalism has generated and continues to generate the
> highest material standards of living for large masses of people in
> human history. . . . Most of us would simply not be here were it not
> for the market economy's remarkable productivity, and the material
> quality of our lives going forward depends in very large part upon the
> system's continued generation of wealth. Small wonder then, that

many today would argue that the moral legitimacy of free market capitalism is established by its sheer facticity.[16]

There really can be no doubt: modern capitalism has significantly increased
the standard of living for millions of people in the last two hundred years. Particularly in the last fifty years throughout Asia and Africa, standards of living
have improved dramatically as a result of free markets. But not for everyone—
there are still areas of dire poverty. But even here, one can reasonably argue
that often the worst poverty exists where capitalism has been unable to gain a
foothold in the local culture.

But such improvements have not been without significant costs. There are
two primary ways in which capitalism has negatively impacted the world. The
first way is much in the news. The economic growth generated by free markets has created significant environmental problems. We have known for years
the impact on communities of the air, water, and land pollution that accompa-
nies industrialization. And now the conversation has moved to the worldwide
impact of global warming. This is an ongoing conversation of great importance, even though final conclusions for action have not been reached.

For our immediate purposes, however, there is a second by-product of capitalism that has negatively impacted all of us. It is much more subtle but no
less universal in its influence. Ellul describes it this way:

> The particular costs associated with capitalist development that I
> would like to discuss here are not environmental or material but rather
> cultural, psychological, and ultimately, spiritual. Such costs are per-
> haps best summarized under the heading of capitalism's depletion of
> meaning.[17]

Ironically, the very way in which capitalism has conquered the world has also
been the way that it has undermined human flourishing: through the creation
of capital. And this is the primary way in which money exerts its power in our
world: through the monetization of value.

Because of its amazing success in impacting the world, says Ellul, money
has become one of the most important ways in which we measure or determine value in the contemporary world:

> The "monetization" of value, a procedure that the market economy
> puts to very good use, entails a remarkable degree of imposition. After
> all, the "nominal" values we attach to things by means of the abstrac-
> tion we call money do not necessarily reflect—and may actually
> obscure—their real or intrinsic value. Furthermore, when our impo-
> sition of money values upon things is combined with modern science's
> "objectification" of nature, we are actually tempted to doubt that there
> is such a thing as intrinsic value.[18]

This monetization of value accounts for much of the power of money; it brings a level of rationality to the modern age. The immediate problem, of course, is that not all goods in our experience are capable of full monetization. We state this with the common adage "Money can't buy everything." But the reality is that it can buy *almost* everything and thus has the additional power of obscuring the true value of those things it cannot purchase. As Gay points out, this can lead to the common problem of our culture: a skepticism regarding intrinsic value.

In this way, value finally becomes disconnected from things themselves and becomes an extrinsic quality that is imposed by money. How much is a thing worth? Much of contemporary society first thinks of the financial cost. This is the primary danger of money in Western society: its power to assign value. In spite of its many goods (e.g., raising the quality of life for millions of people), it can at the same time become the principal carrier of secularization. Money's power tends to foster a practical atheism. That is, money displaces God as the One who alone may rightly say, "It is good."[19]

Another way to say the above is that when assigning value, money heightens the worth of external goods (power, prestige, and status) while diminishing internal goods such as virtue. The achievement of internal goods tends to benefit others as well as the self. This in part is what is meant by the adage "Virtue is its own reward." It has to be, because money is unable to assess it. Ultimately, this reevaluation of all values is turned toward humans themselves. Peter Berger has written:

> Money with its great power of abstraction can convert all socially relevant phenomena (goods, services, statuses, even identities) into units of specific monetary worth. The individual too can be converted. The American phrase, "What is he worth?" illustrates this monetary conversion very graphically. . . . To assess a man's "worth" in terms of the money he possesses ipso facto puts in brackets whatever "worth" he may have by way of congenital and collective ascription: Nobody chooses his parents, but anyone, in principle, can accumulate capital.[20]

Berger wishes us to understand money's role in the democratization process. Its power to assign worth has done much to help people overcome value based on ethnicity or gender. The question to be asked is "At what cost?" As we have noted, money is a jealous power. It seeks to displace all other forms of valuation.

Ultimately, one of the results of the monetization of value is the ever growing anxiety that many people experience, even in the midst of their prosperity. According to its logic, those with the most money and the things that money can buy ought to have the greatest sense of worth. But the reverse is often the case. Even as people become more and more materially comfortable, there is often an increasing sense of restlessness. This in turn magnifies the need for further purchases or distractions, promoting an endless acquisition of things and experiences. At the same time, the monetization of value discourages other ways of answering the restlessness. The things less easily monetized, such as religious questing (how does money quantify that?), are ignored. In other words, when the power of money dominates, the things money cannot buy slowly (or perhaps not so slowly) are perceived to be of less and less value. Furthermore, even though people repeatedly do not find satisfaction in the acquisition of more things, they are increasingly unable to imagine the value of other categories of meaning.

How then do we respond to the power of money? Ought money to be renounced? This has been one solution practiced by some throughout church history. Some of the greatest saints have repudiated material comforts. But this cannot be a universal response insofar as those courageous saints have been enabled to live their powerful lives of witness through the gifts and resources of those with money. There must be other faithful paths to living the Christian life free of the mastery of money.

Gay maintains that those who desire to not completely capitulate to money's power tend to cope in one of two ways. First, they stop seeking to find meaning in the system as a whole. Christians and others should look to smaller societal units to supply value for living. The "nuclear" family, churches, and other nonprofit organizations are often seen as havens from the cruelty of the "dog eat dog" market. There are, however, two problems with this popular solution. First, as we have already noted, families, churches, and philanthropic organizations are not finally themselves free of money's domination. These "havens" have all been heavily infiltrated by the more subtle aspects of money's power. But there is a more important and theological reason that exposes this classic solution: Even though Christ's lordship is not yet complete, it makes no allowance for half measures. Christ's triumph over the powers is a total one. Its fullness will only be known in the eschaton. However, there is no provision for "havens" or a shared reign with the powers. Christ has not ceded authority over the market or the economy to any other powers.[21] As Abraham Kuyper famously said, "No single piece of our mental world is to be hermetically sealed off from the rest, and there is not a square inch in the whole domain of our human existence over which Christ, who is Sovereign over *all*, does not cry: 'Mine!'"[22]

The second solution is what Ellul describes as the attempt to "reassert the full range of human meanings and purposes and to liberate them from their subjection to economic growth and 'progress.'"[23] In other words, this solution is an attempt to restrict economic expansion on behalf of other societal goods. The environmental movement has been a key worker in this area. Governmental regulations are put in place in order promote certain other goods (such

as cleaner water or air) that at least in the short run raise costs and limit prof-
itability. But Gay rightly asks who will decide which other "human meanings
and purposes" should be promoted. In essence, the American political process
is the ongoing battle to determine who shall decide which other goods beyond
free markets are most important. The problem here, of course, is that politics
also is dominated by money. Such a solution never truly challenges money's
real power of determining value. Both the "havens" answer and the "limita-
tion" response are actually more coping strategies than solutions.

It should be no surprise to us that in Christian terms the only way to deny
money its illegitimate power is through grace. Money as mammon really
becomes a cruel master. One works harder and harder to attain less and less.
In the process, says Ellul, life is drained of what makes it sacred:

> Surrendering to anxiety and fear and choosing to serve mammon, while
> perhaps resulting in a measure of material security, further blinds us to
> the goodness of God, rendering us all the more incapable of placing
> faith in him. . . . Service to money insidiously empties the world of
> grace. . . . It declines our hearts into cynicism and indifference.[24]

Surrender is not an option for those who are in Christ—who have the promise of Christ's liberating power. At the same time, as important as we believe
it is to acknowledge money as a New Testament power, we are not arguing for
what some Christians would refer to as a "spiritual warfare" solution. We find
it rather ironic that the charismatic tradition has both expressed the most
interest in binding the powers and principalities so that God's kingdom may
go forth, and at the same time done much to promote the gospel of prosperity. This is perhaps most instructive for the ongoing need of the contextual-
ization of theology. Forces opposed to God's good reign need not take on any
more overt presence (e.g., paranormal phenomena) when money's cultural
domination is so little resisted within or outside the church. Perhaps this is the
most widespread example of Baudelaire's often-quoted line, "My dear
brethren, do not ever forget, when you hear the progress of lights praised, that
the loveliest trick of the Devil is to persuade you that he does not exist."[25] A
church already dominated by the power of money needs little further interfer-
ence from those forces that continue to fight against Christ's victory.

COUNTERING THE POWER OF MONEY

We will argue in the remainder of this book that money can be brought to
serve God's purposes in the church and the world. This is done in two ways.
First, clergy and other Christian leaders need to have a better understanding

of the way that money works in a church. This knowledge must be both financial and theological. Clergy are often unable to provide leadership in the
money aspects of ministry because of a fundamental lack of knowledge of
budgeting, taxes, and basic accounting practices. A working knowledge of such
things allows clergy and other Christian leaders a better place to stand both to
recognize and to contend with money where it would hold illegitimate power.

Second, we believe that the power of money is best countered by our participation in Christ's victory over all principalities and powers. This is done in
a threefold way. This chapter has been an attempt at the first way—that is, a
recognition of the power of money in theological and biblical terms. But that
first way is only completed through the proclamation of the gospel: Christ has
authority over money, and we need not be bound by money. The second aspect
of this way is through our actions. This is most vividly demonstrated in joyful
giving. We shall take up this topic in chapter 10.

The third aspect of this way is demonstrated in our attitudes. As Richard
John Neuhaus explains, this is primarily lived in an anxious-free life that
refuses to take money and financial matters as the most important force in life:

> The point is that wealth—having it or producing it—really does not
> matter that much. This point is missed both by the avaricious, who
> become captive to their possessions, and by religiously driven ideo-
> logues promoting designs for a just economic order. Both are in dan-
> ger of attributing an ultimacy to something that is, at best,
> pre-penultimate. Both take wealth altogether too seriously. A theolog-
> ically informed appreciation of economic life and the production of
> wealth should be marked by a sense of whimsy and wonder in the face
> of the fortuitous, contingent, chancy and unpredictable realities of
> economic behavior.[26]

Such an attitude is promoted by accepting the sheer giftedness of life. Christians are called to live as if the Adamic curse (Gen. 3:17–18) has been reversed,
because we believe just that. The new Adam (Rom. 5:12–21) has done that. A
free gift gives believers the ability to live life differently. It is a reminder that
the most important goods have not come to us by the "sweat of our faces" but
by God's mercy. This new perspective reminds us that the greatest goods are
not acquired through our work. Ultimately, the prophet Habakkuk teaches,
we live through faith in God's work and not our own:

> Then the Lord answered me and said: Write the vision; make it plain
> on tablets, so that a runner may read it. For there is still a vision for
> the appointed time; it speaks of the end, and does not lie. If it seems
> to tarry, wait for it; it will surely come, it will not delay. Look at the
> proud! Their spirit is not right in them, but the righteous live by their

faith. Moreover, wealth is treacherous; the arrogant do not endure. They open their throats wide as Sheol; like Death they never have enough. They gather all nations for themselves, and collect all peoples as their own. (Hab. 2:2–5)

It is no coincidence that the biblical text which gave rise to the Reformation cry "The just shall live by faith!" also involves a reference to money. There really are two different ways to live. Christians through their participation in Christ's work can pursue a path of freedom. At the same time, their labors may serve greater ends and are not limited to the acquisition of money. It should be noted that there is a symbiotic relationship between giving and the anxiety-free attitude. They reinforce and lead back to one another. The giver is saved from the anxiety of service to money. The anxious-free person is able to give more freely. We believe that Christians are called and empowered to live such a life.

DISCUSSION QUESTIONS

1. Do you agree that money's power can be described in terms of the New Testament categories of powers and principalities?
2. How do you experience money's power to monetize value?
3. Where in your life do you need more freedom from money's power?

PART 2

Applying a Theology of Money

5

Church Finance 101:
Understanding the Basics
of Church Accounting

Too often we hear clergy make comments like this:

> "I just don't understand the financial matters of my church. I'm pretty happy to leave all the money stuff to the businesspeople in my congregation," or

> "I look after the spiritual needs of my congregation and let the church treasurer worry about the money."

We believe that truly effective pastors are pastors who take responsibility for leading their congregations in financial as well as nonfinancial areas. While the daily details of church collections and disbursements are the duties of the church bookkeeper, treasurer, and others appointed by the congregation in this capacity, ultimately the responsibility for *leading* in the area of money rests with the minister. Since money is ultimately a spiritual matter, to abdicate leadership in financial areas is to be less than the full leader God intends the pastor to be.

To take responsibility for leading a congregation financially, the minister needs a basic understanding of the issues surrounding church accounting. She needs to be able to intelligently read and interpret her church's financial statements and reports. The pastor should insist on financial transparency within those financial reports. She must be knowledgeable enough to ask good questions about financial matters.

The good news is that clergy do not need to pursue a degree in accounting! There are gifted laypeople in most congregations who work in the community as bookkeepers, financial managers, bankers, and CFOs. Many of these individuals feel called by God to use their financial skills as lay leaders. Praise God for these individuals, and put them to work! The objective of this chapter is to equip the minister with some of the skills needed to embrace the role of financial leader of the congregation. To be anything less is not what God intends.

CHURCH ACCOUNTING: AN OVERVIEW

In the business world, accounting is commonly referred to as the "language of business." For the church, accounting can be considered the "yardstick of stewardship."[1] The purpose of accounting within the church is to provide a system to accurately capture and record financial transactions, to meaningfully measure progress toward financial goals, and to clearly report the results in a way that is transparent, honest, and helpful in making decisions. To be the "yardstick of stewardship" for the church, the accounting system must result in financial reports that are transparent. Transparent reports are those that accurately reflect the financial position of the church, are readily available to anyone who wants to see them, and do not attempt to conceal, distort, or mislead.

It is not essential for the minister to understand debits and credits. The church bookkeeper or treasurer should be fluent with double-entry bookkeeping, the system invented in Italy in the thirteenth century that is used by virtually all accounting systems today. Double-entry bookkeeping requires that every transaction be recorded simultaneously in at least two accounts and that the total of the debit values equals the total of the credit values. This method guarantees that the accounts overall stay in balance.

So what then does a clergyperson need to know about church finances? In this chapter, we will address six basic things all clergy should know about accounting in the church:

1. The five types of accounts used by all churches, and the basic accounting equation.
2. The purpose of the year-end closing.
3. The difference between the *pure cash basis*, the *modified cash basis*, and the *accrual basis* of accounting.
4. The purpose of funds and how they work.
5. The difference between *unrestricted donations*, *temporarily restricted donations*, *permanently restricted donations*, and *designated donations*.
6. The importance of a gift-acceptance policy.

In chapter 6 we will provide specific strategies about understanding and interpreting financial statements and reports within the church.

FIVE BASIC TYPES OF ACCOUNTS

As a starting point, it is important that the pastor understand the five types of accounts used in a basic accounting system. Every financial transaction that occurs in the church is recorded simultaneously in at least two accounts.

Assets

Assets are "probable future economic benefits obtained or controlled by a particular entity as a result of past transactions or events."[2] More simply put, assets are things that the church owns as well as things the church has a right to take possession of in the future. A church might have cash, investments, buildings, equipment, and prepaid insurance, to name just a few asset accounts.

Management Tip

Most churches own buildings, equipment, vehicles, and other fixed assets. While all for-profit businesses (and most nonprofit organizations) show these long-lived assets on their balance sheet under "property and equipment" as fixed (or capitalized) assets, many churches do not. While it is not incorrect for a church to omit capitalized assets from its financial statements (unless required to do so by the judicatory), it is important to know that such financial statements are not prepared in accordance with generally accepted accounting principles.[3] Later in this chapter, we present financial statement examples for churches that omit capitalized assets as well as for those that include fixed assets.

Liabilities

Liabilities are technically defined as "probable future sacrifices of economic benefits arising from present obligations,"[4] and they include a church's obligation to pay amounts that it owes, such as a mortgage or its unpaid bills. Examples of common liability accounts include accounts payable, wages payable, mortgages, and other loans. A liability may also exist if the church is obligated to provide a service to someone.

Practical Example

Let us say that the church rents out a portion of its facility to a preschool. On December 1, the preschool decides to prepay six months of rent, covering its use of the facility for December through May. On December 31, the church has an *obligation* to provide the facility to the preschool for the months of January through May since it has already received the cash payment. If the church chooses not to provide the facility, it must return the cash. This obligation is represented on the financial reports of the church at December 31 as a liability called "unearned rent revenue."

Net Assets

The difference between the assets and the liabilities of the church is called net assets. In for-profit accounting, this difference is called owners' (or stockholders') equity, which represents the ownership share or net worth of a firm. Since a church does not have owners or shareholders, net assets represent the accumulated surpluses and deficits in the church over time.

Generally accepted accounting principles require that net assets be classified as one of the following:

> Unrestricted net assets, which can be used for any purpose,
>
> Temporarily restricted net assets, which are limited by the donor either as to *when* they may be used or as to the *purpose* for which they may be used, or
>
> Permanently restricted net assets, which are permanently restricted by the donor to be held in perpetuity as an endowment.

At the end of the year, the church's financial position is reflected in what the church owns (assets) minus what the church owes (liabilities). The difference between these two amounts is the net assets of the church. This is commonly referred to as "the accounting equation":

$$\text{Assets} = \text{Liabilities} + \text{Net Assets}$$

For a business, net worth is a cumulative measure of the success of the organization. For the church, however, net assets are not a measure of success. Churches are not meant to accumulate wealth, but to accomplish mission.

Revenues

For a church, revenue consists mostly of tithes and offerings. Revenue may also include interest income, donated goods and services, as well as fee-for-service activities such as rental revenue. Additionally, churches often generate small amounts of revenue from fund-raising activities.

Expenses

Expenses are "outflows or other using up of assets" that result from the carrying out of the church's central operation and mission.[5] In a church, expenses include utilities, wages, office supplies, and anything else necessary to keep the church functioning.

Practice Exercise 5.1

Listed below are common accounts that most churches use as a part of their accounting systems. Identify each account as one of the following five types: asset, liability, net asset, revenue, or expense.

  a. payroll tax withholding
  b. property insurance
  c. income from pledges
  d. cash in savings account
  e. interest income
  f. interest expense

THE PURPOSE OF THE YEAR-END CLOSING: PERMANENT AND TEMPORARY ACCOUNTS

Asset, liability, and net asset accounts are permanent accounts. The balances in these accounts carry over from year to year. For instance, the balance in the church's cash account on the last day of the year is the same as on the first day of the new year.

Revenue and expense accounts are called temporary accounts because they are closed out at the end of each year. The balance in the church's utility expense account at the end of the year is *not* the same as on the first day of the new year. On the first day of the new year, the balance in utilities expense is zero. The temporary accounts (revenue and expense) are closed to net assets at the end of the year. This is what is meant by the term "year-end closing." All accounting systems, whether manual or computerized, have a year-end closing, at which time the temporary accounts are zeroed out.

By closing out the temporary revenue and expense accounts, the church can compare the amount of current year revenue and expense with prior years. This provides information that is useful to those making decisions on behalf of the congregation. If the revenue and expense accounts were not zeroed out at the end of each year, the comparison would be impossible to make, since the revenue account would show all of the contributions collected by the church since its first day in existence.

PURE CASH BASIS, MODIFIED CASH BASIS, AND ACCRUAL BASIS OF ACCOUNTING

Again, the purpose of financial reports in a church is to produce information that is useful in making decisions.[6] To be useful, financial statements should be as transparent and easy to interpret as possible. They should also clearly and accurately reflect the financial position of the church. At the same time, the cost of preparing such statements should not outweigh their benefit. Many churches, especially smaller ones, use the pure cash basis to account for transactions and prepare their financial reports. These churches find the cash basis simple and less costly to use. Many large churches use the accrual basis, since they believe that financial statements prepared on this basis more accurately reflect their financial position. These churches have found that the benefit of presenting accrual basis financial statements outweighs any additional expense.

In this section, we will compare the three common bases of accounting and point out the differences between them. We also will examine the financial statements normally prepared by churches under each of the three methods. The minister should become familiar with all three methods, particularly the one used by his church. In chapter 6, we will discuss how to interpret these financial statements.

Pure Cash Basis

Many churches keep their books on the cash basis, which means that contributions are recorded only when the cash has actually been received and expenses logged only when the cash has been paid. Under this method, all disbursements are expenses, so purchases of equipment, property, and even investments are not capitalized as assets. Churches using the pure cash basis should prepare just one financial statement entitled "Statement of Cash Receipts and Disbursements."[7] All the revenue and expense accounts, as well as the cash accounts, should be presented on this statement. Churches using the pure cash basis would not have need for any liability accounts.

While the cash basis is simple to use and may fit the needs of many small churches, care should be exercised when using this method. Most accounting professionals agree that the modified cash method or the accrual method produce financial information that is more accurate. Using the pure cash method results in financial statements that do not conform to generally accepted accounting principles, which are the standards followed by most businesses.[8]

Practical Example

Valley Church is a small, rural church with a simple financial structure that uses the cash method to prepare its financial reports. The church owns a parsonage, currently valued at $65,000, an organ and piano valued at $25,000, and a computer purchased in 2007 for $1,200. During the current year, the church purchased a riding lawn mower for $1,300. At the end of the year, the church owed $45 of payroll taxes and a 403(b) contribution of $400 that it had withheld but had not yet remitted on behalf of its employees. For the year, the church treasurer prepared the report shown in chart 5.1.

Under the cash method, Valley Church does not report the purchase of the riding lawn mower (or the computer in 2007) as a fixed asset but instead shows these as expenses. Likewise, the $65,000 parsonage and the $25,000 of musical instruments, both assets owed by the church, are not presented on any statement under the cash method.

Chart 5.1

Valley Church
Statement of Cash Receipts and Cash Disbursements
Years ended December 31, 2008 and 2007

	2008	2007
Cash receipts		
Contributions	$60,500	$59,400
Interest income	500	400
	61,000	59,800
Cash disbursements		
Salaries, wages, and benefits	32,000	30,500
Utilities—church and parsonage	15,000	14,500
Insurance—church and parsonage	3,800	3,800
Maintenance—church and parsonage	3,500	4,200
Mission support	2,000	2,000
Purchase of lawn mower	1,300	–
Travel reimbursement	1,200	1,400
Purchase of computer	–	1,200
Office and printing	800	700
Christian education	750	800
	60,350	59,100
Increase in cash	650	700
Beginning cash	7,500	6,800
Ending cash	$8,150	$7,500

Modified Cash Basis

The modified cash basis alters the pure cash method in order to present more accurate financial statements. Some common modifications used by churches might include the capitalization of property and equipment as fixed assets, the depreciation of fixed assets over their useful lives, the recognition of investments in marketable securities as assets, and the recognition of certain liabilities.

Churches using the modified cash basis normally prepare two financial statements. The "Statement of Assets, Liabilities, and Net Assets—Modified

Cash Basis" presents all of the permanent accounts used by the church (assets, liabilities, and net assets). Businesses refer to this statement as the "balance sheet," so named because this is the statement that demonstrates that the accounting equation (assets = liabilities + net assets) is in balance. This statement presents a snapshot of the financial position of the church at the end of the period.

The "Statement of Revenue, Expenses, and Other Changes in Net Assets—Modified Cash Basis" presents all of the temporary accounts used by the church (revenue and expenses). It is similar to an income statement.

Practical Example

Valley Church presents its financial information using the modified cash basis. Using the same facts provided in the practice example above, the church prepares two financial statements. The Statement of Assets, Liabilities, and Net Assets—Modified Cash Basis (chart 5.1) includes the parsonage, organ and piano, computer, and riding lawn mower. It also reflects the fact that the church owes payroll tax and retirement contributions at the end of the year. The net assets of the church reflect the value of its cash and fixed assets as of the end of the year.

The Statement of Revenue, Expenses, and Other Changes in Net Assets—Modified Cash Basis (chart 5.2) presents information that is quite similar to that presented on the Statement of Cash Receipts and Disbursements using the pure cash basis. However, the lawn mower and computer are not included as expenses since they have been capitalized as assets. Additionally, an amount appears for depreciation that reflects the "using up" of the fixed assets.

This statement presents the activity of the church for a period of time, such as six months or one year. A church with a December 31 year end that is preparing its Statement of Revenue, Expenses, and Other Changes in Net Assets as of March 31 would add to the title "for the three months ended March 31, 20xx." Some churches choose to group their expenses into functional classifications, such as program expenses, general supporting expenses, and fund-raising expenses.

Chart 5.2

Valley Church
Statement of Assets, Liabilities, and Net Assets
Modified Cash Basis
December 31, 2008 and 2007

	2008	2007
Assets		
Current assets		
Cash and cash equivalents	$8,150	$7,500
Noncurrent assets		
Property and equipment		
Parsonage	65,000	65,000
Musical instruments	25,000	25,000
Computers and office equipment	1,200	1,200
Maintenance equipment	1,300	–
Less: accumulated depreciation	(23,500)	(18,000)
Property and equipment, net	69,000	73,200
Total assets	$77,150	$80,700
Liabilities and net assets		
Current liabilities		
Withheld payroll taxes and retirement		
contributions	$445	$385
Total liabilities	445	385
Unrestricted net assets		
Unrestricted	7,705	7,115
Represented by property and equipment	69,000	73,200
Total unrestriced net assets	76,705	80,315
Total liabilities and net assets	$77,150	$80,700

Chart 5.3

Valley Church
Statement of Revenue, Expenses,
and Other Changes in Net Assets—Modified Cash Basis
for the years ended December 31, 2008 and 2007

	2008	2007
Unrestricted net assets		
Revenues		
Contributions	$60,500	$59,400
Interest income	500	400
Total unrestricted support	61,000	59,800
Expenses		
Salaries, wages, and benefits	32,060	30,500
Utilities—church and parsonage	15,000	14,500
Depreciation	5,500	4,000
Insurance—church and parsonage	3,800	3,800
Maintenance—church and parsonage	3,500	4,200
Mission support	2,000	2,000
Purchase of lawn mower	-	-
Travel reimbursement	1,200	1,400
Purchase of computer	-	-
Office and printing	800	700
Christian education	750	800
Total expenses	64,610	61,900
Increase (decrease) in unrestricted net assets	(3,610)	(2,100)
Net assets, beginning of year	80,315	82,415
Net assets, end of year	$76,705	$80,315

Practice Exercise 5.2

Examine the financial statements presented in charts 5.2 and 5.3 that were pre-pared under the modified cash basis and answer the following questions:

a. Which statement presents the permanent accounts? Which presents the temporary accounts? Describe the difference between permanent and temporary accounts.

b. How do the two statements connect? Find the number that is present on both statements and describe how it links the two statements together.

c. Compare these two statements with the statement presented in chart 5.1 using the pure cash basis (the Statement of Cash Receipts and Dis-bursements). What major differences do you see? Which method, pure cash or modified cash, provides statements that are more useful? Dis-cuss the value of using the modified cash basis in your church.

The Accrual Basis

The accrual basis is required under generally accepted accounting principles because it presents the most accurate picture of the financial condition of the entity. This is the method used by nearly all businesses, most large nonprofit entities, and many large churches. Very few smaller churches use the accrual basis. Churches using the accrual basis capitalize fixed assets and record depre-ciation expense, as noted in the modified cash basis method above. Further, churches using the accrual basis record income when earned rather than when the cash is received, and expenses when incurred rather than when the bill is paid. A bill for electricity used in June, for instance, would be recorded in June, not in July, when the bill is finally paid. Since the accrual basis requires that expenses be recorded when the resource is used rather than when the cash is paid, a liability account called "accounts payable" is used to hold the amount due until the cash is actually paid.

Practical Example

On January 6, a church receives a heating bill of $1,280 for heating service cov-ering the period December 1–31. Before closing out the year, the church records the $1,280 as an increase to heating expense. At the same time, the church increases accounts payable by $1,280 since, as of December 31, the church has an obligation to pay this bill. On January 24, the church pays the heating bill. The church does *not* record heating expense at this point, since it has already been recorded in December of the prior year. Instead, the church reduces the liability accounts payable and also decreases cash.

Under the accrual basis, churches normally prepare three financial statements: the "Statement of Financial Position," the "Statement of Activities," and the "Statement of Cash Flows." All of the asset, liability, and net asset accounts of a church (the permanent accounts) are presented on the Statement of Financial Position. It is very similar to the modified cash method's Statement of Assets, Liabilities, and Net Assets—Modified Cash Basis, but it includes additional assets and liabilities due to the use of the accrual method. An example of a Statement of Financial Position can be seen in chart 6.8 in Chapter 6.

The Statement of Activities is very similar to the Statement of Revenue, Expenses, and Other Changes in Net Assets—Modified Cash Basis prepared by modified cash method churches. All revenue and expense accounts (the temporary accounts) are included on the statement, and the statement presents the activity of the church for a period of time, such as six months or one year. An example of a Statement of Activities is presented in chart 6.9 in chapter 6.

Churches that follow the accrual basis have financial statements that reflect more clearly their actual financial condition. However, since cash is extremely important in managing any entity, churches on the accrual basis should prepare a third financial statement, the Statement of Cash Flows. The purpose of the Statement of Cash Flows is to provide an analysis of the sources of cash during the period as well as how cash was used. An example of a Statement of Cash Flows is presented in chart 6.10 in chapter 6.

USING FUNDS IN CHURCH ACCOUNTING

Not all contributions made to a church are the same. Some contributions are earmarked by the donor for a specific use, while others are not. When a contribution is made, it is important that the church handle it in the way in which the donor intended.

The easiest way for this to be accomplished is by the use of a fund. A fund is merely a way to designate certain contributions, related expenses, and even assets as separate from other contributions, expenses, and assets of the church. It is *not* necessary to set up a separate checking account to accomplish this. Most churches can exist with just one checking account.

Practical Example

Perhaps a church decides to send a group of members on a mission trip to India in eighteen months. A fund is set up and labeled "India Mission Trip Fund." Extensive efforts are undertaken to educate the congregation about the needs in India, and as contributions are received, they are deposited into the church's one and only checking account. In the accounting records, these deposits are coded to a revenue account that is linked to the India Mission Trip Fund. The church can create as many revenue accounts as it needs for the India Mission Trip Fund.

As the year progresses, the church makes a down payment on the trip to the travel agent. A check, drawn on the church's only checking account, is cut for the payment. In the accounting records, the check is coded to a travel expense account that is linked to the India Mission Trip Fund. The church can create as many expense accounts as it needs for the India Mission Trip Fund.

At the end of the year, total contributions of $12,000 have been recorded in the revenue accounts linked to the India Mission Trip Fund. The payment to the travel agent totaling $5,000 has been recorded in the expense accounts linked to the India Mission Trip Fund. When the year is closed, both the revenue account and the travel expense account are zeroed out to net assets. The India Mission Trip Fund (a permanent net asset account) would have a balance after this closing of $7,000, which would be available for the new year.

As the new year begins, the church would continue fund-raising and paying expenses for the trip. At the conclusion of the trip all funds should have been spent, and the fund can be closed.

Funds provide a very simple way to track contributions to ensure that they are used as the donor intended. Churches can and should have as many funds as needed to keep restricted contributions separate from unrestricted contributions. The church should be careful to select software that is either designed for nonprofit accounting or that can be easily adapted for use by a nonprofit entity.

Most contributions made to the church are unrestricted. This includes most of what is dropped in the offering plate on a Sunday morning. Unrestricted contributions are normally coded to an operating fund and can be used to pay the general operating expenses of the church. Unrestricted contributions are almost always preferred to restricted contributions, since the church can put the unrestricted funds to whatever use it wants.

Restricted donations are contributions made by a donor for a specific purpose. The donated funds can be either temporarily restricted or permanently restricted. Temporarily restricted donations must be set aside by the church to be used for the specific project or purpose for which they were contributed. For example, money contributed to a building fund or to finance the beginning of a music ministry within the church are considered temporarily restricted. When the building is started or the music ministry commences, the funds can be spent.

When a donor makes a permanently restricted donation, the church is permanently constrained in its use of the gift. The income resulting from the investment of such a donation can be either unrestricted or can also be restricted by the donor. We know of a church, for instance, that had a sizable permanently restricted donation. The income from that donation was restricted by the donor to be used only to support the airing of a daily radio message in the community.

Occasionally, the operating fund runs low while the restricted building fund or the restricted organ fund has money just sitting there waiting until it accumulates enough to build the building or buy the organ. Inevitably, someone will suggest taking money from the building fund to use for operations and to "tide us over through this dry spell."

The restriction on a donation can only be changed by the donor. The minister should counsel church leaders to resist the urge to borrow from a restricted fund. While it is not illegal to do so, it is often a quick fix that masks the underlying problem of spending beyond the church's means. Borrowing presents a short-term solution but often leads to a long-term nightmare, since the borrowed funds must eventually be paid back in order to honor the intent of the original donors. Furthermore, donors can sue a church or other nonprofit for spending their restricted contributions for a purpose other than what was intended.[9]

We know of one church that began to innocently borrow from its building fund to support operations. Several years of doing so left the church tens of thousands of dollars in debt to its own building fund. At that point the church leadership decided to take out a bank loan to restore the borrowed money to the building fund. The church would have been far better off had it disciplined itself to spend within its means rather than to have turned to the easy solution of borrowing from a restricted fund.

DESIGNATED FUNDS

Occasionally the church board will choose to designate, or set aside, funds for a specific purpose. For example, if the church is considering construction of an addition to the building and is also in the enviable position of having excess money in the operating fund, church leaders may decide to designate some of that excess to be used for construction. Remember that general contributions can be used in any way that the church sees fit, so to designate general contributions for the church addition is entirely appropriate.

Unlike restricted donations, which can only be changed by the donor, designated funds are a part of unrestricted contributions and can be undesignated at any time by the church board. In contrast, contributions made as a part of a capital campaign for the new addition are restricted and may only be used for the building. In this case, both restricted and designated funds will exist for the construction of the addition.

Management Tip

The minister should advise lay leaders to keep a clear record of these two different types of funds. In the event that the capital campaign is highly successful, the designated funds may not be needed to support construction. Since these monies are only designated and not restricted, they can be returned to the operating fund for another use. But what can be done with the restricted funds if more than enough money is raised? We will address that question in the following section.[10]

Practice Exercise 5.3

During the month of March, the following activity occurred at First Church:

a. Received a total of $28,765 in general tithes and offerings.
b. Received a special one-time gift of $45,000 from an estate of a parishioner to be held in perpetuity. The interest from the gift is to be used to support the music program of the church.
c. Received a total of $12,876 paid on pledges for the building fund.
d. The board designated $32,000 toward construction of the new building.

Match each activity above with one of the following categories:
    unrestricted
    temporarily restricted
    permanently restricted
    designated

GIFT ACCEPTANCE POLICY

If no gift acceptance policy exists, the pastor should request that the board institute one. The purpose of such a policy is to protect the church and the minister in several ways. First, the policy should state who has the right to accept a noncash gift or a restricted cash gift on behalf of the church. The board or a gift committee should have this responsibility rather than any single individual, including the pastor.

Additionally, it is possible that a donor may want to make a noncash contribution to the church that is not in the best interest of the church to accept. When put on the spot by the donor, the minister might agree to accept such a gift—which later turns out to be disastrous for the church. A gift acceptance policy and procedure can protect the minister and the church by clearly outlining a process for the consideration and acceptance of a noncash gift or a restricted cash gift.

One important part of a gift acceptance policy is a statement declaring the church's right to remove a restriction placed on a contribution by the donor if it is deemed by the board to be in the best interest of the church. This inclusion protects the church in the event that a fund-raising campaign is successful beyond what is required to fund the project. For instance, if the capital campaign for the addition to the building raises more money than needed to fund the addition, the church can redirect the contributions to other needs. This policy should be clearly stated in the fund-raising materials provided to donors so that they are aware of the policy in advance of making a gift.

Practical Example

The following true story provides an incentive to adopt a gift acceptance policy:

> A well-known Midwestern charity received a gift of not one, but two, paint factories in the early 1980s. These gifts soon matured into Environmental Protection Agency Superfund sites. It cost the charity roughly $1 million over the value of the property to settle the joint and several liabilities imposed by CERCLA (Comprehensive Environmental Response, Compensation, and Liability Act) to extricate itself from the first gift, and somewhat more than that to settle the second gift.[11]

To draft a gift acceptance policy, the church should consult with an attorney. Additional resources, such as gift acceptance guidelines, are available at

the Evangelical Council for Financial Accountability's Web site: http://www
.ecfa.org.

Management Tip

Some churches have restricted funds that contain several thousand dollars but
will never reach the amount needed to achieve the purpose for which they
were given. We know of one church, for instance, that had a stained-glass window fund of $2,000. The money was given by the family of a longtime mem-
ber who always wanted the church to install stained-glass windows. Since no
one in the church shared this member's desire for stained-glass windows, and
since installation of windows would cost far more than $2,000, the $2,000 sat
in the fund year after year. To clean up funds like this, the gift committee or
representatives of the board should approach the donor and explain the situation. They should respectfully suggest several other uses for the donation. If
the donor is unwilling to redirect the contribution, the church can offer to
return the donation. Returning a donation most likely has tax consequences
to the donor, so this step should not be taken without explaining the effect of
the refund to the donor.

CONCLUSION

Even a basic understanding of financial matters can equip the pastor to be a
more effective leader. Clergy who grasp the difference between unrestricted,
temporarily restricted, and permanently restricted donations can lead their
governing boards in setting wise capital campaign and gift acceptance policies.
Ministers who are familiar with fund accounting and its purpose can ask intel-
ligent questions, which can guide the finance committee to make responsible
decisions about spending and borrowing. In the next chapter, we will dig even
deeper into the complex area of church finances, with the intention of providing clergy with a set of tools that can be used to interpret key church financial
reports and statements.

DISCUSSION QUESTIONS

1. What is the purpose of the year-end closing in an accounting system?
2. What is the primary difference between the pure cash basis, the modified
   cash basis, and the accrual basis? Which method does your church use?

3. Why do most churches use funds in accounting for their transactions?
4. What are the primary differences between unrestricted donations, temporarily restricted donations, permanently restricted donations, and designated funds? Does your church have any permanently restricted funds?
5. What is the purpose of a gift acceptance policy? Does your church have one?

ANSWERS TO PRACTICE EXERCISES

Practice Exercise 5.1
a. liability; b. expense; c. revenue; d. asset; e. revenue; f. expense

Practice Exercise 5.2
a. The Statement of Assets, Liabilities, and Net Assets—Modified Cash Basis presents the permanent accounts. The Statement of Revenue, Expenses, and Other Changes in Net Assets—Modified Cash Basis presents the temporary accounts. Permanent accounts are not closed at the end of the year and include assets, liabilities, and net assets. Temporary accounts are closed at the end of the year and include revenues and expenses.
b. "Net assets, end of year" of $76,705 is on the bottom of the Statement of Revenue, Expenses and Other Changes in Net Assets. "Total unrestricted net assets" of $76,705 is also included on the Statement of Assets, Liabilities, and Net Assets near the bottom. This number is the "link" between the two statements, since the difference between revenues and expenses (the temporary accounts) is closed out at the end of the year to net assets.
c. The modified cash basis statements present information about the church's fixed assets and certain liabilities. Because of this, they present a more complete financial picture of the church.

Practice Exercise 5.3
a. unrestricted
b. permanently restricted
c. temporarily restricted
d. designated

RECOMMENDED FOR FURTHER READING:

Busby, Dan. *Donor-Restricted Gifts.* Winchester, VA: Evangelical Council for Financial Accountability, 2006.

Evangelical Joint Accounting Committee. *Accounting and Financial Reporting Guide for Christian Ministries.* Norwalk, CT: Evangelical Joint Accounting Committee, 2001.

Guinn, James E., Robert D. Smith, Elizabeth A. DiTommaso, Brenda A. Cline, Stephen B. Eason, Carole A. Burgess, Janice Burns, and Laura A Billingsley. *PPC's Guide to Religious Organizations.* Fort Worth, TX: Thomson Tax & Accounting, 2007.

6

Church Finance 201: Understanding Church Financial Reports

Each month, the minister sits in finance and board meetings where money is discussed. The conversation focuses on the financial reports of the church. Those in the room who understand these reports have an advantage over those who do not. When the chairpersons of the finance committee and the board comprehend the financial reports but the minister does not, the minister's ability to lead the church to accomplish mission may be diminished. In this vaccum, the power of money can exert control.

In order to lead the congregation in embracing the mission God has ordained, it is crucial for the minister to be a full participant in meetings where money is discussed. To do so, the pastor must develop a basic understanding of how to read and interpret the financial reports and statements of the church.

Developing into a leader in this area takes work. Just as learning to exegete Scripture requires study, so exegeting a church's financial statements demands effort. In this chapter, we maintain that any minister who is willing to (1) *learn the basics* about the monthly financial reports and statements, (2) *prepare ahead* by interpreting the reports and analyzing the trends *before* entering the meeting, and (3) *identify key indicators* of the church's financial success and *focus* on those key indicators can become an effective participant in the financial leadership of the congregation.

In this chapter, we will first provide an overview of church financial reports and statements. Then using this three-step approach, we will turn our attention to some specific monthly reports and then to the church financial statements.

AN OVERVIEW OF CHURCH FINANCIAL REPORTS
AND STATEMENTS

Most churches prepare financial statements and reports each month to be used internally by the finance committee or board to manage the church and to make decisions. Since this *managerial accounting information* is intended for internal use, there are no rules to follow in its presentation. Often these statements and reports can be generated quickly and easily from the church software by the bookkeeper.

At year's end, most churches produce an annual financial report that is made available to the congregation and to outside parties. This *financial accounting information* should be prepared in accordance with certain rules, which when followed make the financial statements of one church comparable to the financial statements of other churches. Additional care should be taken in preparing these year-end financial statements in accordance with generally accepted accounting principles or another comprehensive basis of accounting, such as the cash basis or modified cash basis, as discussed in chapter 5. The job of preparing these statements should be left to the church treasurer if that individual is knowledgeable about accounting principles. If the treasurer is not, the board should consider either hiring an accountant or finding a qualified volunteer to compile the financial statements on behalf of the church. Further, if an audit is required by the judicatory or another outside party, the board should hire an independent accounting firm to conduct an audit or a review.

There are a variety of reports and financial statements that a church board or finance committee may look at on a monthly basis. Unfortunately, no two churches format their reports or statements in quite the same way or even prepare the exact same reports. Some of this variation occurs because of the accounting method chosen by the church. As discussed in chapter 5, churches using the cash method generally prepare only one financial statement, while churches using the accrual method prepare three statements. The good news here is that the clergyperson need not master the financial statements for all three accounting methods, just the method chosen by his or her church.

In addition to financial statements, many churches produce other reports that are used to manage the church on a monthly basis. These frequently go by a variety of names, but generally most churches prepare some type of cash summary (such as a bank reconciliation or a listing of checks written), a fund activity report (sometimes called a treasurer's report), and a trial balance report, (or even a general ledger).

DEVELOPING INTO THE FINANCIAL LEADER OF THE CHURCH: A THREE-STEP PROCESS

Becoming the leader of your church in this area of money requires study and hard work, just as was required of you to become the spiritual leader. Using our three-step approach, we will first turn our attention to some common monthly reports and then to the church financial statements.

Common Monthly Reports

On a monthly basis, most church boards or finance committees discuss several reports, commonly a cash activity summary (or bank reconciliation), a fund activity report, and/or a trial balance report. If your church uses a report at its monthly meeting that is not included here, compare that report to the examples provided in this chapter to see if there are similarities. It is possible that the report in question is similar to one presented here but goes by a different name. Unfortunately, there is little in the way of standardized church reports.

Management Tip

The minister (and other committee members) should always be given all monthly reports (and financial statements) in advance of the meeting. If this is not the practice in your congregation, gently ask the treasurer to begin providing you the reports in advance. This will enable you to prepare to ask questions and intelligently engage in the discussion. Remember that step two of our three-step process requires you to prepare ahead of time.

Common Monthly Report Number One: The Summary of Cash Activity or the Bank Reconciliation

Step One: Learn the Basics

Since most of the financial activity of a church flows through its checking account, many finance committees review some type of analysis of the checking account on a monthly basis. These two reports provide summary information about the activity in the cash account. The purpose of the "Bank Reconciliation" (chart 6.1) is to tie the cash balance according to the bank with the amount of cash reflected on the church's records. This report is similar in basic form to what you should be preparing each month for your own personal checking account.

The Bank Reconciliation normally begins with the amount of cash that the bank shows in the church's account. This amount comes directly from the bank statement. Checks that have not yet cleared the bank must be subtracted from the balance, shown by the bank, since they have already been deducted from the church's record of cash. Deposits that have not yet cleared the bank must be added to the balance, shown by the bank, since they have already been included in the church's record of cash.

Chart 6.1

First Church
Bank Reconciliation
June 30, 2008

Balance per the bank statement at June 30, 2008		$11,092.33
Less: outstanding checks		
check #1928	$18.74	
check #1929	2,976.13	
check #1930	596.00	
check #1931	7.29	
check #1932	33.39	
Total outstanding checks		3,631.55
Add: deposits in transit at the end of the month		
June 29, 2008	298.63	
June 30, 2008	1,718.58	
Total deposits in transit		2,017.21
Adjusted bank balance		$9,477.99
Balance per the church's checkbook at June 30, 2008		$9,477.99 [A]

The "Summary of Cash Activity" (chart 6.2) generally provides a summary of the major categories of cash receipts and disbursements. It answers the questions "Where did our cash come from this month, and what did we spend it on?" The ending cash balance on this report should agree with the balance of cash in the church's other reports.

Chart 6.2

First Church
Summary of Cash Activity
for the month ended June 30, 2008

Cash balance at May 31, 2008		$8,630.65[B]
Add transactions from		
Contributions	$29,885.09	
Interest income	21.58	
Rental income	200.00	
Transfers	-	
Adjusting entries	-	
Total additions		$30,106.67[C]
Less transactions from:		
Expenses	28,764.33	
Automatic withdrawals	495.00	
Transfers		
Adjusting entries		
Total subtractions		29,259.33[D]
Cash balance at June 30, 2008		$9,477.99[A]

Step Two: Prepare Ahead

Perform the following steps using either the Bank Reconciliation or the Summary of Cash Activity, depending on which your church uses:

1. Check to see if the beginning cash on this month's Summary of Cash Activity agrees with the ending cash on last month's report (see B on chart 6.2). If it does, this means that the report is complete and includes all transactions that have run through the cash account since last month. If it does not, then it is likely that some cash transaction has not been included in the report. You should then ask for an explanation at the meeting.

(Cash is inherently risky. In many smaller churches, no one scrutinizes cash on a monthly basis. It is entirely appropriate to ask questions about cash, especially if any of the steps outlined here raise uncertainties in your mind.)

2. If the church has only one cash account, then the ending cash on either the Bank Reconciliation or the Summary of Cash Activity should be the same as the ending cash on all other reports and financial statements. Trace ending cash (see A on chart 6.1 or chart 6.2) from the Summary of Cash Activity or Bank Reconciliation to any of the following reports or financial statements:

> Trial Balance Report (chart 6.4)
>
> Statement of Cash Receipts and Disbursements (chart 6.5)
>
> Statement of Assets, Liabilities, and Net Assets—Modified Cash Basis (chart 6.6)

Note that while our examples in this chapter do not allow for it, ending cash from the Summary of Cash Activity or Bank Reconciliation would also tie to the cash account on the "Statement of Financial Position" (chart 6.8) and "Statement of Cash Flows" (chart 6.10).

3. Frequently churches will have a checking account plus a savings account and perhaps several investment accounts. If that is the case, then the treasurer should provide a Summary of Cash Activity or a Bank Reconciliation for all cash accounts, and the sum of all of these ending balances should agree with the cash balance reported on the other reports and financial statements detailed in step 2.

4. Rather than just focusing on cash at the end of this month, compare the cash balance to prior months. Is there a trend that you can identify? If cash is trending up month after month, ask why. Perhaps there are new parishioners who are giving or current members who are giving more than planned. The finance committee may need to consider transferring cash into some type of investment account rather than simply leaving an excess of cash in the checking account, where it earns little or no interest.

5. If cash is trending down month after month, ask why. Have regular contributors moved away or left the church? The finance committee may need to consider reducing future spending or arranging for short-term borrowing.

Step Three: Identify Key Indicators

Your key indicator for these reports is simple: ending cash. You should always be aware of the church's cash balance. In for-profit businesses, cash is often referred to as "king" since even profitable businesses that neglect to manage cash can fail. Bills are paid with cash, not profits.

The same is true for churches; cash flow is critical. If the church has prepared a cash budget (chapter 7), compare the actual ending cash for the month with the budgeted ending cash for the month. Given the actual ending cash this month, will there be adequate cash available to cover all the cash requirements identified in the cash budget? If not, the finance committee needs to act now to reduce discretionary spending in the coming month, or to arrange an alternate source of cash.

Practice Exercise 6.1

In preparing for the May meeting of the finance committee, you notice the following trend in the cash balance: January—$6,580, February—$5,202, March—$5,585, April—$3,850. Your cash budget indicates that the cash balance should have been around $6,000 each month except for March, when it was anticipated to rise to $7,000 because of special Easter collections. In May, the church is planning to purchase office equipment for $3,700.

    a. Discuss some possible explanations for the decline in cash.
    b. What actions should the finance committee consider at the meeting?
    c. Consider the coming months. Is there any additional reason for concern?

Common Monthly Report Number Two: The Fund Activity Report

Step One: Learn the Basics

The purpose of the "Fund Activity Report" (sometimes referred to as the "Treasurer's Report") is to provide detailed information about the activity within each fund in the church. Typically, this type of report provides the beginning balance in the fund, the amount of receipts and disbursements in the fund, and any transfers that were made between funds. The report can show just the activity for the month or can present year-to-date activity.

Chart 6.3

First Church
Fund Activity Report
for the month ended June 30, 2008

	Beginning balance at May 31, 2008	June receipts	June disburse-ments	June trans-fers	Ending balance at June 30, 2008
Operating fund	$2,638.80	$25,442.67	$(24,497.73)	-	$3,583.74
Missions fund	1,398.65	3,228.00	(4,076.00)	-	550.65
Youth fund	895.00	450.00	(500.00)	-	845.00
Building maintenance fund	1,698.20	986.00	(185.60)	-	2,498.60
Music fund	2,000.00	-	-	-	2,000.00
Total	8,630.65	30,106.67	(29,259.33)	-	9,477.99
	B	C	D		A

In the example presented in chart 6.3, First Church has only one bank account, which it uses for all the activity of the church. As we have seen, there is no need to have a separate bank account for each fund. Since First Church also uses the cash basis of accounting, the total of all funds equals the cash balance. If First Church had more than one bank account, it would be necessary to add the ending balances in the cash accounts together to agree with the total of all funds. If First Church used the modified-cash or accrual basis, then the total of all funds would not equal cash but would equal all assets minus liabilities.

Step Two: Prepare Ahead

Perform the following analytical steps using the Fund Activity Report:

1. If your church uses the cash basis and has just one bank account, trace the ending fund balance to the ending cash balance on either the Bank Reconciliation/Summary of Cash Activity (chart 6.1 and 6.2) or the "Trial Balance Report" (chart 6.4). In chart 6.3, letter A can be traced to chart 6.1 and 6.2. If your church uses the cash basis and has more than one bank account, add the ending cash balances together and trace them to the ending fund balance.

2. Trace the beginning balances in each fund to the ending balances in each fund from the prior month. There should never be a difference between ending and beginning balances.

3. Examine the Fund Activity Report for the receipts and disbursements. These amounts should agree with receipt and disbursement totals reported on other statements, such as the Summary of Cash Activity (chart 6.2) or the Statement of Cash Receipts and Cash Disbursements (chart 6.5). In chart 6.3, letters C and D can be traced to chart 6.2.

4. Check the Fund Activity Report for transfers between funds. If transfers occured, were they authorized by the finance committee? Normally, there should be no transfers between funds unless directed by the finance committee.

5. Check the Fund Activity Report for disbursements out of restricted funds. If so, have those disbursements been authorized by the finance committee? Generally, the finance committee should be aware of any disbursements from a restricted fund. For instance, a disbursement out of a building fund when there is no building project underway may indicate an irregularity.

6. Examine the Fund Activity Report for funds with negative balances. A fund with a negative balance has essentially "borrowed" from another fund. While this is not necessarily a problem, it could be an indication that restricted funds have been used for a purpose other than that for which the funds were originally contributed. The matter should be identified and discussed at the monthly meeting.

7. Compare the Fund Activity Report from this month to prior months to identify trends. Are certain funds continuously disbursing more than they are receiving?

Step Three: Identify Key Indicators

Watch for funds that consistently spend more than they receive and funds with negative balances. A trend of consistently negative balances in a fund may indicate that the fund is overspending and is being subsidized by other funds that could hold restricted contributions.

Practice Exercise 6.2

In preparing for the monthly meeting of the finance committee, you observe that total cash available at the end of the month on the Summary of Cash Activity is a healthy balance of $36,500. However, when you look at the Fund Activity Report, you also notice that once again, disbursements out of the general fund have exceeded receipts by a significant amount, leaving a negative ending balance in the general fund of $5,500. As you check this report from prior months, you can see that this is the sixth straight month in which this has occurred, and each month the deficit has grown. The building fund balance has remained unchanged for months at $42,000.

1. What exactly has happened here? How can the cash balance be $36,500 while the ending balance in the general fund is a deficit of $5,500?
2. Is there reason for concern?
3. What should you do?

Common Monthly Report Number Three: The Trial Balance Report

Step One: Learn the Basics

The Trial Balance Report is simply a listing of all the accounts used by the church and their balance at the time when the report was run. Each account has either a debit or a credit balance. The total of all of the debits must equal the total of all of the credits on the Trial Balance Report. The normal balance in an asset and expense account is a debit, while the normal balance in a liability, net asset, and income account is a credit.

Chart 6.4 provides a Trial Balance Report for First Church. Note that the balances in the asset, liability, and net asset accounts represent a snapshot of that account as of the date of the report, since these are permanent accounts. The balances in the revenue and expense accounts are cumulative, presenting the amount of income recorded to the account since the start of the year. For instance, the balance in "Pastor salary" represents the amounts paid to the pastor for the months of January–June. That amount will grow until the end of the year, when "Pastor salary," along with all the revenue and expense accounts (the temporary accounts) are closed to net assets.

The "Year-to-date surplus/deficit" reflects the extent to which year-to-date revenue has exceeded year-to-date expenses (surplus) or to which year-to-date expenses have exceeded year-to-date revenue (deficit). First Church's contributions have exceeded their expenses by $1,753.23 for the six months ended June 30, 2008. An amount in the debit column indicates a surplus; an amount in the credit column indicates a deficit.

Chart 6.4

First Church—Trial Balance Report
June 30, 2008

Account Number	Account Name	Debit	Credit
101	Cash—checking	9,477.99[A]	
201	Payroll witholding—federal		-
202	Payroll witholding—state		-
203	Payroll withholding—city		-
301	Operating fund		3,583.74
302	Missions fund		550.65

Account Number	Account Name	Debit	Credit
303	Youth fund		845.00
304	Building maintenance fund		2,498.60
305	Music fund		2,000.00
401	Contributions—operating fund		122,580.00
402	Contributions—missions fund		13,296.00
403	Contributions—youth fund		2,694.00
404	Contributions—bldg maint fund		5,670.00
405	Contributions—music fund		-
406	Interest income		129.48
505	Pastor salary	16,000.00	
510	Pastor housing allowance	9,000.00	
515	Pastor health insurance	3,500.00	
520	Pastor retirement contributions	800.00	
525	Youth pastor salary	12,500.00	
530	Youth pastor housing allowance	6,000.00	
535	Youth pastor health insurance	3,500.00	
540	Youth pastor retirement contrib	625.00	
545	Music wages	1,250.00	
550	Admin wages	9,250.00	
555	Staff payroll taxes	803.25	
560	Staff benefits	845.00	
565	Office expense	1,289.00	
570	Purchase of office equipment	10,640.00	
575	Bulletins	405.00	
580	Worship supplies	553.00	
585	Postage	189.00	
590	Newsletter supplies	62.00	
595	Sunday school supplies	933.00	
600	VBS supplies	1,359.00	
605	Youth group supplies	4,110.00	
610	Mission spending	25,380.00	
615	Music supplies	1,282.00	
620	Telephone	1,420.00	
625	Gas	2,334.00	
630	Electric	3,492.00	
635	Janitorial service	12,500.00	
640	Insurance		2,520.00
645	Maintenance—church roof	15,115.00	
900	Year-to-date surplus/deficit	1,753.23	
	Total	156,367.47	156,367.47

Step Two: Prepare Ahead

Examine the Trial Balance Report and do the following:

1. Check to see if the Trial Balance Report balances—in other words, total debits equal total credits. If it does not balance, all the other reports and statements are also likely to be incorrect and should be considered unreliable. The finance committee must determine the cause of the problem before doing anything else.
2. Look for accounts with incorrect balances. Since asset and expense accounts should have debit balances, look for asset and expense accounts with significant credit balances. At the meeting, ask why the account has a credit balance. Similarly, since liability, revenue, and net asset accounts should have credit balances, check to see if any have debit balances and ask about them. Generally, asset accounts are listed first on the Trial Balance Report, followed by liability accounts, net asset accounts, revenue accounts, and finally expense accounts.
3. Check to see if the following balances on the Trial Balance Report agree with other reports:

   a. Cash account agrees to cash on the Bank Reconciliation/Summary of Cash Activity.
   b. Fund balances all agree with the ending balances on the Fund Activity Report.
   c. "Year-to-date surplus/deficit" traces through to the financial statements prepared using the modified cash basis or accrual basis (as illustrated below).

Step Three: Identify Key Indicators

Look for a trial balance that balances (debits equal credits).

Practice Exercise 6.3

Using the Trial Balance Report in chart 6.4, perform the following:

1. Identify each account as an asset, liability, net asset, revenue, or expense.
2. Examine the Trial Balance Report. Is there anything that you would question about the report using the items listed in the Step Two: Prepare Ahead section?
3. Trace the fund balances from the Fund Activity Report (chart 6.3) to the Trial Balance Report.

Financial Statements

In addition to the monthly reports described above, many church boards or finance committees discuss the church's financial statements each month. At a minimum, the church prepares financial statements annually to be included in its year-end reports. The number and types of financial statements prepared by the church should be determined by the accounting method used. (The three major accounting methods—cash, modified cash, and accrual—were described in detail in chapter 5.) The good news is that you do not need to master all of these financial statements, just the ones that are used by your congregation based on its accounting method. If your church uses a financial statement at its monthly meeting that is not included here, compare that statement to the examples provided to see if there are similarities. It is possible that the statement in question is similar but that it goes by a different name.

We will again use the three-step approach to becoming an informed user of financial statements. Again, the minister (and other committee members) should always be given all financial statements and reports in advance of the meeting in order to prepare adequately to ask questions and engage intelligently in the discussion.

Accounting Method: Pure Cash Basis

Financial statement commonly prepared:
  Statement of Cash Receipts and Cash Disbursements

Step One: Learn the Basics

If your church uses the pure cash basis of accounting, this section is important for you to master. As detailed in chapter 5, the Statement of Cash Receipts and Cash Disbursements is normally the only financial statement prepared by churches using the pure cash basis. It may be labeled "Income Statement" or "Statement of Revenue and Expenses." Accounting professionals agree that it is best to use the title "Statement of Cash Receipts and Cash Disbursements," particularly at year's end, when the statement is made widely available.

Generally, the statement should list cash received by the church followed by cash disbursed. It is entirely appropriate to group the disbursements by functional classification, such as program expenses, general supporting expenses, and fund-raising expenses. If this is done, however, it is helpful to also have a more detailed listing of expenses to use at monthly meetings. Generally, this statement provides the beginning and ending balances in the cash account. It is common and very helpful to provide comparative prior year or budget information on the statement.

Chart 6.5

First Church
Statement of Cash Receipts and Cash Disbursements
for the one month and six months ended June 30, 2008

		Current month actual	Year-to-date actual	Year-to-date budget
Cash receipts				
Contributions		$30,085.09	$144,240.00	$142,500.00
Interest income		21.58	129.48	100.00
	C	30,106.67	144,369.48	142,600.00
Cash disbursements				
Salaries, wages, and benefits		17,148.41	64,073.25	64,000.00
Utilities—church and				
parsonage		4,899.55	7,246.00	8,000.00
Program, youth, office		2,949.77	20,822.00	20,500.00
Maintenance		185.60	25,095.00	25,000.00
Mission support		4,076.00	25,380.00	24,500.00
	D	29,259.33	142,616.25	142,000.00
Increase in cash		847.34	1,753.23	$ 600.00
Cash—beginning of the				
period	B	8,630.65	7,724.76	
Cash—end of the period	A $	9,477.99	$ 9,477.99	

Step Two: Prepare Ahead

Examine the Statement of Cash Receipts and Cash Disbursements for the following:

1. Ending cash (A) should agree to the Bank Reconciliation/Summary of Cash Activity (chart 6.1 or 6.2) and the Trial Balance Report (chart 6.4). You can also trace beginning cash (B) to the Summary of Cash Activity.
2. The total receipts (C) and total disbursements (D) for the period should tie to the Fund Activity Report (chart 6.3).
3. If year-to-date information is provided, compare the current month

amount with the year-to-date amount. Does the amount for this month seem reasonable in relationship with the year-to-date amount?

4. If the statement has been prepared using prior month and year data for comparison, compare the current month with the same month in the prior year. The amounts should be similar.

5. If the Statement of Cash Receipts and Cash Disbursements has been prepared using budgeted data for comparison, compare the year-to-date with the annual budget. How close is the church to being on budget?

Step Three: Identify Key Indicators

Clearly, a key indicator is that cash receipts exceed cash disbursements. If budgeted information has been provided, also focus on large variances from the amount budgeted.

Accounting Method: Modified Cash Basis

Financial statements commonly prepared:

> Statement of Assets, Liabilities, and Net Assets—Modified Cash Basis
>
> Statement of Revenues, Expenses, and Other Changes in Net Assets—Modified Cash Basis

Step One: Learn the Basics

If your church uses the modified cash basis of accounting, this section discusses the financial statements with which you no doubt will be dealing. Churches on the modified cash basis, as described in chapter 5, may refer to the Statement of Assets, Liabilities, and Net Assets—Modified Cash Basis as a "Balance Sheet" or to the Statement of Revenues, Expenses, and Other Changes in Net Assets—Modified Cash Basis as an "Income Statement." Most accounting professionals agree that at year's end, when the statements are made more widely available, it is best to use titles that comply with the most recent accounting guidance available for religious organizations using the modified cash basis method.

The Statement of Assets, Liabilities, and Net Assets—Modified Cash Basis should include all assets, liabilities, and net assets of the church (the permanent accounts). As discussed in chapter 5, this method modifies the cash basis to include property, plant and equipment, accumulated depreciation, and certain liabilities. Chart 6.6 provides a Statement of Assets, Liabilities, and Net Assets—Modified Cash Basis for First Church. This statement provides a snapshot of the financial position of the church as of a particular date. Total assets on the statement must equal the sum of total liabilities and net assets. Often, prior year information is provided to allow for comparison.

Chart 6.6

First Church
Statement of Assets, Liabilities, and Net Assets—Modified Cash Basis
June 30, 2008

	2008	
Assets		
Current assets		
Cash and cash equivalents	$9,477.99	A
Noncurrent assets		
Property and equipment		
Parsonage	105,000.00	
Furniture and equipment	33,640.00	
Less: accumulated depreciation	(32,500.00)	
Property and equipment, net	106,140.00	
Total assets	$115,617.99	
Liabilities and net assets		
Current liabilities		
Withheld payroll taxes and retirement contributions	$445.00	
Total liabilities	445.00	
Net assets		
Unrestricted net assets:		
Unrestricted	9,032.99	
Represented by equipment	106,140.00	
Total net assets	115,172.99	E
Total liabilities and net assets	$115,617.99	

The Statement of Revenues, Expenses, and Other Changes in Net Assets—Modified Cash Basis includes all revenue and expense accounts of the church (the temporary accounts). This method modifies the cash basis to include depreciation and certain accrued expenses. Chart 6.7 presents such a statement for First Church. (This statement provides an increase/decrease in net assets rather than an increase/decrease in cash, as reported on the cash basis Statement of Cash Receipts and Disbursements).

Since the Trial Balance Report for First Church in chart 6.4 reflects the cash basis, it does not include the parsonage of $105,000, the furniture and equipment of $33,640, or the depreciation expense. Further, the purchase of office equipment for $10,640 recorded on the cash Trial Balance Report as an expense in account 570 would be recorded as a fixed asset rather than as an expense under the modified cash method. Therefore, year-to-date expenses under the modified cash method are less than under the cash method, because this purchase is recorded as a capitalized asset. Additionally, depreciation expense is included as an expense under the modified cash method but not under the cash method.

If First Church had "temporarily restricted net assets" and/or "permanently restricted net assets," it would provide information about the changes in these categories of net assets on this statement. See the accrual basis "Statement of Activities" (chart 6.9) for an example of such a presentation.

Chart 6.7

First Church
Statement of Revenues, Expenses,
and Other Changes in Net Assets—Modified Cash Basis
for the one month and six months ended June 30, 2008

	Current month actual	Year-to-date actual	Year-to-date budget
Unrestricted net assets			
Revenues			
Contributions	$30,085.09	$144,240.00	$145,000.00
Interest income	21.58	129.48	100.00
Total unrestricted support	30,106.67	144,369.48	145,100.00
Expenses			
Salaries, wages, and benefits	17,148.41	64,073.25	64,000.00
Utilities—church and parsonage	4,899.55	7,246.00	7,400.00
Program, youth, and office expenses	2,949.77	10,182.00	11,000.00
Maintenance—church and parsonage	185.60	25,095.00	25,000.00
Mission support	4,076.00	25,380.00	24,500.00
Depreciation expense	1,200.00	7,100.00	7,300.00
Total expenses	30,459.33	139,076.25	139,200.00
Increase (decrease) in unrestricted net assets	(352.66)	5,293.23	$ 5,900.00
Net assets, beginning of period	115,525.65	109,879.76	
Net assets, end of period	$115,172.99	$115,172.99	E

It is entirely appropriate, even preferred, to group the disbursements by functional classification, such as program expenses, general supporting expenses, and fund-raising expenses. However, if this is done, it is helpful also to have a more detailed listing of expenses on a supplemental schedule, particularly if the statements are being used by the church leadership at monthly meetings. It is common and very helpful to provide comparative prior year or budget information on this statement.

Step Two: Prepare Ahead

Analyze the following:

1. Be sure that cash on the Statement of Assets, Liabilities, and Net Assets—Modified Cash Basis (chart 6.6) agrees to the ending cash as presented on the Bank Reconciliation/Summary of Cash Activity.
2. Check to see that "total assets" equal "total liabilities and net assets" on the Statement of Assets, Liabilities, and Net Assets—Modified Cash Basis.
3. Tie "net assets" (E) on the Statement of Assets, Liabilities, and Net Assets—Modified Cash Basis (chart 6.6) to "net assets, end of period" (E) on the Statement of Revenues, Expenses, and Other Changes in Net Assets—Modified Cash Basis (chart 6.7).
4. Compare the current month with the current year-to-date on the Statement of Revenues, Expenses, and Other Changes in Net Assets—Modified Cash Basis. Does the amount for this month seem reasonable in relationship with the year-to-date amount?
5. If the Statement of Revenues, Expenses, and Other Changes in Net Assets—Modified Cash Basis has been prepared using budgeted data for comparison, compare the year-to-date with the annual budget.

Step Three: Identify Key Indicators

The modified cash basis is not as comprehensive as the accrual basis in recognizing all of the financial realities of the church. However, it provides a much more complete view than does the cash basis. Rather than recognizing cash as the only asset of the church, the fixed assets available for use by the church are shown at the amount that was paid for them, less depreciation, on the Statement of Assets, Liabilities, and Net Assets—Modified Cash Basis. If the church has financed any purchases with bank loans, those amounts would be present here too.

A key indicator that should be watched is the level of debt used by the church. In watching this number, it is sometimes helpful to look at the amount of debt in relationship to total assets. This is referred to as the "debt-to-asset ratio." Basically, it tells the user the portion of assets of the church that were financed by debt.

Debt-to-asset ratio =   Total liabilities
                        Total assets

Example: if the church has cash and fixed assets totaling $500,000 and lia-
bilities of $200,000, its debt-to-asset ratio would be 40 percent. This indicates
that roughly 40 percent of the church's assets were paid for by using borrowed
money. A lower ratio is generally considered better than a higher ratio,
because it indicates less reliance on debt.

Another key indicator is to compare "actual" to "budgeted" and "current
year" to "prior year" on the Statement of Revenues, Expenses, and Other
Changes in Net Assets—Modified Cash Basis. A quick analysis of these variances can provide an indication of problem areas that may exist.

Accounting Method: Accrual Basis

Financial statements commonly prepared:

> Statement of Financial Position
> Statement of Activities
> Statement of Cash Flows

Step One: Learn the Basics

The accrual basis is primarily used by large churches and by churches that
need to provide financial statements in accordance with generally accepted
accounting principles. It recognizes all expenses when incurred, rather than
when the cash is paid, and all revenue when earned, rather than when the cash
is received. Unlike the cash basis, the accrual-basis church capitalizes as an
asset all amounts spent on property and equipment and investments.

Churches on the accrual basis might refer to the Statement of Financial
Position as a "Balance Sheet" or to the Statement of Activities as an "Income
Statement." Most accounting professionals agree that, particularly at year's
end, when the statements are widely available, it is best to use titles that are
generally accepted for accrual-basis religious organizations.

The Statement of Financial Position should include all assets, liabilities,
and net assets of the church (the permanent accounts). This statement provides a snapshot of the financial position of the church as of a particular date.
Total assets on the statement must equal the sum of total liabilities and net
assets. Frequently, prior year information is provided to allow for comparison
(see chart 6.8).

Chart 6.8

Community Church
Statement of Financial Position
December 31, 2008

Assets
    Cash and cash equivalents $371,875 G
    Other assets   2,500
    Property and equipment   1,487,500
Total assets $1,861,875

Liabilities
    Accounts payable $30,937
    Accrued expenses   34,625
    Loans payable   19,625
Total liabilities   85,187

Net assets
    Unrestricted   1,418,188
    Temporarily restricted   338,750
    Permanently restricted   19,750
Total net assets   1,776,688 F
Total liabilities and net assets $1,861,875

The Statement of Activities (chart 6.9) includes all the revenue and expense accounts (the temporary accounts) of the church. It presents the activity for a period of time, such as one month, six months, or a year. Activity is presented for each category of net assets: unrestricted, temporarily restricted, and permanently restricted. Expenses are grouped by functional classification, such as program expenses, general supporting expenses, and fund-raising expenses. Frequently, churches also provide a supplementary schedule of expenses, which provides more detail. It is common and very helpful to provide comparative prior year or budget information on this statement.

Chart 6.9

Community Church
Statement of Activities
for the year ended December 31, 2008

	Unrestricted	Temporarily Restricted	Permanently Restricted	Total
Contributions and other income				
Regular contributions	$800,000			$800,000
Parsonage renovation fund		$81,250		81,250
Interest income	625	22,500	$1,000	24,125
Total support	800,625	103,750	1,000	905,375
Net assets released from restriction				
For programs	15,000	(15,000)		–
Expenses				
Program	482,625			482,625
Administrative support	312,500			312,500
Fund-raising	12,500			12,500
Total expenses	807,625			807,625
Increase (decrease) in net assets	8,000	88,750	1,000	97,750
Net assets, beginning of year	1,410,188	250,000	18,750	1,678,938
Net assets, end of year	$1,418,188	$338,750	$19,750	$1,776,688

F

The Statement of Cash Flows (chart 6.10) provides an analysis of the sources of cash during the period as well as how cash was used. Cash basis and modified cash basis churches do not prepare a statement of cash flows, since these churches already report information about how their cash was generated and spent on their Statement of Cash Receipts and Cash Disbursements (cash basis) and the Statement of Revenues, Expenses, and Other Changes in Net Assets—Modified Cash Basis. Accrual basis churches, however, need to provide clear information to users about cash flows, since this information is critical in conducting a thorough evaluation.

Chart 6.10

Statement of Cash Flows
for the year ended December 31, 2008

Cash from operating activities	
Increase in net assets	$97,750
Adjustments to reconcile changes in net	
assets to cash from operating activities	
Depreciation	59,500
Decrease in prepaid assets	3,813
Increase in accounts payable	1,562
Decrease in accrued expenses	(12,750)
Net cash provided by operating activities	149,875
Cash used for investing activities	
Purchase of equipment	(31,250)
Cash used for financing activities	
Payments on notes payable	(25,000)
Increase in cash and cash equivalents	93,625
Cash and cash equivalents—beginning of year	278,250
Cash and cash equivalents—end of year	$371,875 G

The Statement of Cash Flows groups cash flows into three categories:

> Cash provided by/used for operating activities
> Cash provided by/used for investing activities
> Cash provided by/used for financing activities

For a church, "operating activities" include the cash received in contributions and the cash spent to operate the church. It is very important for this number to be positive, signifying cash flowing into the church, because that indicates that the church received more cash than it spent on operations.

Among other things, "cash provided by/used for investing activities" most commonly includes cash that was spent on property, plant, and equipment (fixed assets). Usually this number is negative, indicating cash flowing out of the church, since the church has spent money on capital investments. If it is positive, it most likely means that the church has sold a fixed asset and that cash is flowing into the church as a result of the sale.

"Cash provided by/used for financing activities" generally includes cash flowing into the church from borrowing and cash flowing out of the church for repayments on loans. In a year when the church finances a purchase, this number will be positive, since cash has flown into the church from the loan. In the years when the church repays debt, the number will be negative, since cash is flowing out of the church to pay down the loan.

Step Two: Prepare Ahead

Examine the following:

For the Statement of Financial Position (chart 6.8):

1. Be sure that "cash" agrees to the ending cash as presented on the Bank Reconciliation/Summary of Cash Activity.
2. Check to see that "total assets" equal "total liabilities and net assets."
3. Tie "total net assets" (F) to "total net assets, end of year" on the Statement of Activities (chart 6.9).

For the Statement of Activities (chart 6.9):

4. Compare the current month with the current year-to-date. Does the amount for this month seem reasonable in relationship to the year-to-date amount?
5. If the Statement of Activities has been prepared using budgeted data for comparison, compare the year-to-date with the annual budget. Are the current year's expenses of the church in line with the amounts budgeted?

For the Statement of Cash Flows (chart 6.10):

6. Compare "cash" (G) on the Statement of Financial Position with "cash at the end of year" on the Statement of Cash Flows. These two amounts must agree.
7. Examine "cash from operating activities." This number should be positive, indicating that the cash flowing into the church related to contributions has exceeded the cash flowing out related to general operations for the period. If the number is negative, check to see if prior periods have also reported a negative number. If a trend of negative cash from operating activities appears to exist, this is cause for great concern.
8. Examine "cash provided by/used for investing activities." If this number is consistently negative, it indicates that the church is growing, since cash is flowing out of the church for the purchase of equipment, vehicles, building projects, or property. If the number is frequently positive over time,

this could indicate that the church is selling off property and equipment to provide cash to continue operating. This is generally a sign of an unhealthy church.

9. Examine "cash provided by/used for financing activities." Ideally, the church has no debt and this number is zero. Generally, it is better for this number to be negative, indicating that the church is repaying its loans. If there has been a trend of positive cash from financing, this could indicate that the church is borrowing consistently to provide cash to continue operating. This is generally a sign of an unhealthy church.

Step Three: Identify Key Indicators

A key indicator that can be easily determined by studying the Statement of Financial Position is a measure of liquidity. Liquidity is an indicator of the church's ability to pay obligations that will soon be coming due.

$$\text{Current ratio} = \frac{\text{Current Assets}}{\text{Current Liabilities}}$$

A current ratio of 2 indicates that the church has twice as much current assets (cash and accounts receivable) as it does current liabilities (accounts payable and the portion of loans that are currently due). The current ratio for Community Church is computed as follows: current assets of $371,875 divided by current liabilities of $65,562 ($30,937 + $34,625) equals a current ratio of 5.67. Community Church is highly liquid and in an excellent position to pay its obligations as they come due.

Another important key indicator is the debt-to-asset ratio. This ratio was described in depth on page 91 and is an indicator of the proportion of the church's assets that have been financed using debt. The debt-to-asset ratio for Community Church is total liabilities of $85,187 divided by total assets of $1,861,875, or 4.6 percent. This means that just 4.6 percent of Community Church's assets have been financed by debt, reflecting the financial strength of the church.

Final key indicators are found by examining the Statement of Cash Flows. Most essential is that the "cash flow provided by/used for operating activities" be positive, since this represents the very heart of the church. If this figure is consistently negative, this is a major indicator of issues that must be addressed. If negative "cash from operating activities" is accompanied by consistently positive "cash provided by financing activities" and/or consistently positive "cash provided by investing activities," this may indicate that the church is funding its general operations by selling off property and equipment and/or taking on debt.

Practice Exercise 6.4

On its Statement of Cash Flows, a church reports "cash provided by operating activities" of $20,000, "cash used for investing activities" of $300,000, and "cash provided by financing activities" of $280,000. What can you conclude about this church?

Practice Exercise 6.5

On its Statement of Financial Position, a church reports current assets of $75,000 and current liabilities of $25,000. What is the current ratio for the church? What does this mean?

CONCLUSION

Once the minister develops a confident understanding of the financial reports and statements of the church, he or she can begin to lead with authority in the area of money. By using the key indicators described above to monitor cash, scan for negative fund balances, compare actual results to amounts budgeted, observe the debt-to-asset ratio and the current ratio (for modified cash and accrual basis churches), and watch cash from operating activities (for accrual basis churches), the minister can easily keep a finger on the financial pulse of the church.

Armed with key financial indicators and a clear understanding of the financial reports, the minister can confidently participate in the monthly finance and board meetings. Instead of being sidelined due to a lack of knowledge, the minister can fully participate in the conversation. And rather than passively accepting the old excuse, "Well, Pastor, we could never afford to do that here at First Church," the minister can prayerfully challenge the board to step into new areas of ministry.

DISCUSSION QUESTIONS

1. Which financial statements or reports are most used by your church?
2. Why is cash considered a key indicator? How can an awareness of cash help you better monitor the financial situation of your church?

3. Why are negative fund balances a key indicator? What danger can they pose to the church?
4. Why are the variances between "actual" and "budgeted" key indicators? Are all positive variances (where actual spending is less than the budgeted amount) good?

ANSWERS TO PRACTICE EXERCISES

Practice Exercise 6.1

a. The decline in the cash balance is clearly unanticipated, since the cash budget provides for a steady, healthy cash balance. It might be caused by spending in excess of what was budgeted, or by declining contributions. At the meeting, you should definitely raise the issue, and the finance committee should determine the cause.

b. The finance committee should consider:

1. Delaying the May purchase of office equipment, since this could put the church in an extremely tight cash position. If the equipment is critical, the committee could consider financing the purchase rather than paying cash.
2. Revising the cash budget to reflect more accurate levels of cash.
3. Reducing monthly spending.

c. Summer is coming, when contributions generally decline. Rather than entering the summer months with a strong cash balance, the church could be entering summer in a weakened cash situation. In light of this, the committee should consider what options might exist for generating cash, especially if summer spending cannot be reduced.

Practice Exercise 6.2

1. Overall, the cash position of the church is good. The $36,500 in the bank is accurate. The general fund, however, has been overspent, leaving the fund balance negative. Total fund balances equal $42,000 less $5,500, or $35,500, which is equal to the cash balance.
2. There is reason for concern, especially if the building fund is restricted. The general fund has been unofficially borrowing from the building fund. In effect, the general fund has a balance of zero, and the building fund balance is not $42,000 but $35,500. If the building fund is restricted, this presents an issue. Donors to the restricted building fund expect their contributions, all $42,000 of them, to be used for the building, not for the general operations of the church.

3. Since this has gone on for six months, it needs to be discussed at the finance committee meeting. The overspending of the general fund needs to stop, and the building fund needs to be restored to its balance of $42,000. The committee needs to discuss steps required to make this happen.

Practice Exercise 6.3

1. Asset accounts include only the cash account (account number 101). If your church uses the cash basis of accounting, it will likely have just cash accounts recorded as assets. Churches using the modified cash and accrual basis methods will have property and equipment and perhaps investment accounts listed as assets.

   Liability accounts include all accounts beginning with 200. Cash basis churches have very few liabilities, if any, while modified cash and accrual basis churches have many more.

   Net assets include all accounts beginning with 300.

   All accounts beginning with 400 are revenue accounts.

   All the remaining accounts (500 through 645) are expense accounts.

   The year-to-date surplus/deficit account is what makes the interim Trial Balance Report "balance."

2. The Trial Balance Report is in balance, so this is not of concern. The one question you might have is why account number 640 (insurance) has a credit balance. Expense accounts normally have a debit balance, so this is odd. A possible explanation is that a refund on an insurance premium was received or an insurance claim was paid to the church. There may be a better place to classify such an amount that would allow the amounts of premiums paid by the church for the year to be clearly identified.

3. You should be able to trace the ending fund balances from the Fund Activity Report to the following accounts as listed on the Trial Balance Report:

Fund name	Ending balance	Trial Balance Report account number
Operating fund	$3,583.74	301
Missions fund	$550.65	302
Youth fund	$845.00	303
Building maintenance fund	$2,498.60	304
Music fund	$2,000.00	305

Practice Exercise 6.4

This church is growing but does not have a lot of cash to spare. It is financing its building or equipment purchases with debt. It is currently generating enough cash to cover its operating expenses but should keep a close eye on operating activities during this period of growth.

Practice Exercise 6.5

Current ratio = 75,000/25,000, or 3. This means that the church has three times the current assets it needs to cover its current liabilities.

7

Budgeting in the Church

Each year churches make a statement of faith in which they reveal that which is most important to them. This statement of faith usually is not declared on a Sunday morning, and quite possibly the majority of the church members never see or hear it. Nevertheless, this confession reveals the mission and everything else that the congregation values most. It is not a historic document or creed; this statement of faith is the annual operating budget.

Annual budgets are not usually thought of in such terms. However, we believe they are the clearest statements of what congregations do primarily affirm. In the end, only those things that churches are willing to fund can be said to be of value to them. Congregations may speak of evangelism and social witness on Sundays, but it is their finance committee and administrative board meetings during the week that more truly reveal their deepest commitments. And those midweek commitments often do not match the rhetoric of Sunday mornings.

As an ever increasing percentage of the expenditures of the average church is consumed with paying for staff salaries and benefits as well as maintaining and heating the church building, less and less is available to fund God's work in the world. In the forty years that ended in 2003, benevolent spending has dropped from $0.21 to $0.15 per every dollar collected.[1] This trend in spending has created churches that are increasingly inner-focused, introspective, and self-absorbed.

With no outer vision to unite congregations, the church has become increasingly focused on providing a variety of services to members who often function like consumers, choosing some programs and ignoring others. John and Sylvia Ronsvalle write that, rather than "a community of faith gathered around a common vision or purpose provided by the New Testament," some "congregations might better be described as coalitions of special interest groups that have gathered out of mutual convenience around a single physical plant."[2] As these special interest groups compete for money, which always seems scarce, the power of money grows. The divorce recovery group, the mothers' day out program, the quilting club, the fall bazaar, the Christmas ladies luncheon, and the aerobics group all compete for resources, participants, and especially for funding. Funding ministries becomes a "zero sum" game of winners and losers, and a unified sense of mission is lost in the process.

The power of money can be seen in the ways in which some groups or committees wield control through managing the money of the church. In many congregations, the finance committee holds primary responsibility for approving expenditures. Even though the finance committee only exists to carry out the will of the congregation, it often functions as a separate and powerful entity. The proverbial "tail wags the dog" in many congregations. John and Sylvia Ronsvalle observe:

> A key factor in attempting to understand money dynamics in the congregations of America is the separation that exists between the missions committee and the finance committee. The missions committee appears to have the responsibility to outline the broader vision of the church. However, it is the finance committee that decides how much of that vision is practical for the congregation. The power of the finance committee in the current structure of most congregations must be understood in greater detail if present giving patterns in the church are to change.[3]

The finance committee, which is focused on paying all the bills on time, has power to set the spending priorities of the church.

One of the main tools for disarming the power of money within a church is the budget. When a unified church budget is agreed upon by all members of the church, the special-interest mentality can begin to evaporate. In this way, a budget unmasks the operative power. The power that money had to divide the congregation into factions, each of whom had its own pool of money, is disarmed and replaced by a unified budget that is the product of a process of discernment. When all members can provide input to the budget and are given a copy of the final version of the budget, the dominance and authority of the finance committee begins to diminish. The power that money provided the finance committee to control church spending is neutralized. And when the budget approved by the congregation clearly allocates for example 15 percent of spending to support missions outside of the local church, the introspective mentality of the church begins to fade. The power that money had to hold hostage the missional outreach of the church is broken.

Robert Bacher writes that budgets and balance sheets are "deeply doctrinal documents," since they reflect the core beliefs of a congregation.[4] A church budget that allocates 99 percent of its expenditures to maintaining the operations of the local church reveals a congregation that has placed its belief in its buildings and its staff. While the congregation does not literally sing hymns to its staff or pray to its building on Sunday mornings, the ways in which it spends its money demonstrates that it is fundamentally inner-focused. When a congregation claims to have a mission of care and outreach to those outside its walls and at the same time spends most of its budget on keeping the doors open, a noticeable inconsistency exists. That inconsistency is obvious to everyone who hears the claim and yet sees the reality in the daily operation of the church.

A consistent church is one whose spending reflects its declared purpose. And to walk in faith infers boldly determining purpose before considering budget. In many churches, the budgeting process is simply a matter of taking last year's numbers and adding a fixed percentage (if even that). That budget is offered to the congregation for its approval, along with the annual stewardship letter. There is no effort to reflect upon the appropriateness of last year's expenditures, no pause to consider where God might be leading in the coming year, and never an attempt to connect money to mission.

When God's mission is considered first, however, budgeting can occur within a larger context. Many churches have never stopped to ask the fundamental question "What work is God doing in our community that God would like us to join?" We believe that this is a key area of money leadership for the minister—not to actually crunch the numbers of the budget but to provide the spiritual guidance to challenge the church to think beyond just paying its bills.

We believe that budgeting is only one part of a three-phase process that includes *discerning God's mission*, *planning*, and *budgeting*. The diagram below illustrates the relationship between each phase. The practice of discerning God's mission for the church should both begin and conclude the cycle; in fact, we maintain that the practice of discernment should be ongoing.

Discerning God's Mission for the Church

If your church has never embarked upon a process to discern God's mission for the congregation, consider asking the congregation to do so before any budget setting takes place. We believe that this is the single most important role that the minister plays in the annual budgeting process. No one else in

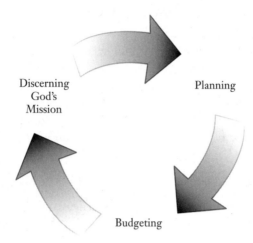

Discerning God's Mission

Planning

Budgeting

the congregation can lead as effectively in this area as the minister, since this is a spiritual, not a fiscal, matter.

Here is one possible timetable. Four to six months before the budget is to be completed, invite the congregation to join you in a period of prayer, asking God to reveal what the church is to be about in the coming year. The minister needs to guide the congregation into understanding that this is not the *church's* mission but *God's* mission; the church is merely seeking to discern how it might participate in God's ongoing work. It is not the church's money but God's money, and God will provide additional support to fund mission. It is not the church's building but God's building to use as God might see fit.

At the conclusion of these weeks, members of the congregation should meet to share what God has laid upon their hearts. With a clear view of God's mission for the church for the coming year, the church can then invite God to enter the planning and budgeting process, where specific details and dollars are determined. This type of budgeting process has the added benefit of allowing the church to understand itself as a unified whole—a "body," to use the apostle Paul's metaphor in 1 Corinthians 12.

Planning to Accomplish God's Mission

With God's mission for the church clearly in focus, the church should next ask for God's guidance in planning to accomplish this mission. What specific steps would God have the congregation take in the coming year to participate in God's ongoing work? Can all of the work be done now, or is some of it better suited to further down the road? How can the church know if it is being effective in the work it is doing? And how can God's resources that are present in the church best be spent to accomplish the work? While the minister's involvement here is important, it is less crucial than in the discernment phase. Much of the activity here is practical rather than spiritual in nature. A member of your congregation may have had experience in using similar planning techniques on the job. If so, put that person to work!

We believe that effectively planning to accomplish God's work generally includes the following steps:

1. Determining the viability of each suggestion. During this step, church members gather information about the requirements and costs associated with each project. The abstract suggestion becomes fairly concrete as the details are determined, and any unviable suggestions are eliminated.
2. Identifying the specific objectives and outcomes of each suggestion. In this stage, the goals of the project must be formalized. Why would the church want to engage in this type of mission? These goals should be as specific and measurable as possible. Additionally, the method for evaluating the progress of the project should be determined. Finally, the means of providing feedback to the congregation about the project should be decided at this point. In our experience, church members are far more likely to continue to support their church's mission if they are informed about how their current contributions are being used.
3. Ranking the projects. Generally, there will be more viable suggestions than there will be resources available. Since this is often the case, the church should prayerfully consider which projects should be given priority for the coming year. In doing this, the objectives of the project should be critically evaluated. How well does the project advance the kingdom of God? The viability of the project must also be examined. Perhaps the project is not feasible this year but could become workable long range. The projects can be ranked in order of priority, and that list can be presented to the congregation. We believe that the church should not eliminate any viable suggestion. Rather, any project that is not developed this year should be kept for next year, when it should reenter the discernment process.
4. Matching resources to mission. A request for mission funding, along with the ranked project list, is presented to the congregation with an appeal for resources. Each project on the list is briefly described to the congregation, along with information about (a) the resources needed to fund it, (b) the specific goals of the project, (c) the method that will be used to evaluate progress that is made on the project, and (d) the way in which the congregation will be provided with feedback about the project and its progress. The congregation can then be challenged to provide resources to fund the mission of the church. We believe that when concrete projects are presented, members become motivated to support and give when they otherwise may not. Care should be taken, however, to present the mission of the church as a unified whole rather than as a collection of discrete projects. The congregation should be invited into the process of funding, and while the number of projects undertaken will be determined

by the level of funding, the congregation should not be asked to pick and
choose which projects to support.

Practical Example

During the *Discerning God's Mission* phase of First Church's annual budgeting
cycle, a suggestion is raised that the church should begin providing a daily
lunch to low-income residents of the neighborhood. At the planning phase,
the following steps are taken with this suggestion:

1. Determining the viability of the suggestion. Questions are asked about the
   resources required for the project. Would the church need to hire someone to cook and manage, or are volunteers willing to provide these functions? How much would it cost to provide food for each meal? Would the
   cost of cleaning the church rise as a result of this suggestion? Would there
   be an effect on insurance? Are there state health regulations that need to
   be investigated? Would any equipment need to be purchased? As answers
   are found, they are incorporated into a formal proposal.
2. Identifying the specific objectives and outcomes of this suggestion. The
   church needs to determine what specifically it hopes to accomplish with
   this program. Perhaps it is determined that the goal of the lunch program
   is not only to serve a hot lunch to low-income individuals but also to meaningfully impact the lives of these individuals with the good news of the
   gospel. If that is the case, how will the church determine if it is reaching
   that goal? And how will progress on the project be communicated with the
   congregation?
3. Ranking the projects. First Church has numerous suggestions for mission
   outreach for the coming year. In evaluating which projects should be supported, the objectives of the free-lunch program are critically evaluated.
   How well do these goals reflect the purpose of First Church? Additionally,
   the viability of the project should be assessed. Perhaps the program would
   require volunteer resources as well as financial resources that cannot be
   quickly mobilized. If so, the church can include the free-lunch program in
   its long-range planning.
4. Matching resources to mission. If the free-lunch program is included in
   the annual mission budget of the church, then full information about it
   should be submitted to the congregation.

Budgeting

A church budget is simply a plan for allocating the resources of the congregation. The budget attempts to state the church's plan for the year in terms of
the money required to make it happen. It also provides a road map that mea-

sures where the church has been and where it is heading in terms of accomplishing its plan. Since it has been agreed upon by the church before the year even begins, this road map constantly guides committees throughout the year by settling disputes as to the use of resources and focusing committee members on meeting their objectives. Some churches unwisely try to operate without a budget, often with disastrous results. Most of those disasters are of a chronic rather than critical nature. The greatest disaster of all is the slow death of congregational inattention to God's purposes.

Richard Vargo provides ten excellent reasons why every church, no matter how small, needs a budget. A budget:

1. Formalizes planning, which enhances the church's ability to achieve its goals.
2. Reduces emotion-charged discussions as to the use of funds in the church.
3. Is a basis for performance evaluation, since it allows for the comparison of actual results to expected results.
4. Is a basis for control, since expenditures that vary from what was budgeted can be easily investigated.
5. Assists in communication and coordination between groups and committees of the church.
6. Gets members involved, which increases commitment to the success of the program.
7. Increases the commitment to giving, since people who participate in the formulation of the budget are more likely to support it financially.
8. Generates confidence in the church's leadership.
9. Allows for continued operation when cash receipts and disbursements are mismatched, which is discussed in this chapter in the section entitled "The Cash Budget".
10. Allows time to lend or borrow prudently, which is also discussed under "The Cash Budget."[5]

Many budgeted items are routine, ordinary, and necessary expenses of operating a church, including staff salaries, building utilities and upkeep, office supplies and postage, and insurance, to name a few. When correctly done, the process of preparing a budget can force the congregation to take a close look at where money has been spent in the past; this often leads to creative ideas of how to conserve resources for the year to come. And every dollar conserved on expenses inside the church is a dollar that can be sent outside the church to fund mission.

Mechanically, the preparation of the budget need not be difficult. Some church management software products have tools to help with the preparation of an annual budget. Spreadsheet software can also do an excellent job in providing a basic budget. While crunching the numbers is pretty straightforward, the process of arriving at a unified budget is far from simple due to the human ele-ment. Church members often have much to say about how their money is spent.

The rules of your denomination may dictate who sets the budget within your church. In this chapter, we will refer to the *budget committee* as the group that actually meets to determine the budget. Generally, it is wise not to restrict budgeting to the budget committee but rather to involve as many church members in providing input to the budgeting process as possible. A budget that is determined in a participatory style with a high level of involvement by members of the congregation is more likely to be supported by the congrega-tion. Involving more people in budgeting also helps disarm the power of money that certain committees, usually finance-related committees, hold over the church. Top-down budgets, which are prepared by a small group with no outside involvement, tend to be less well received by the congregation. They are perceived as secretive and exclusive. Budgets prepared in this way preserve the perception that certain groups within the church have power because of their access to money.

While the actual number crunching can be rather mechanical, the method chosen to prepare the church budget can greatly increase the complexity of the budget and the time required to develop the budget. For some churches, a more complex budget is necessary; for others it is not. Generally, we believe it is wise to choose the simplest type of budget possible.

Most churches prepare their budget using one of three basic approaches, or a variation thereof: (1) incremental budgeting, (2) zero-based budgeting, and (3) program budgeting. While the incremental approach is fairly simple, both the zero-based and the program approaches are decidedly more complex to implement. They each provide certain benefits, however, that should be con-sidered by the church.

Incremental Budgeting

This approach is the method most widely used by the budget committee of most churches because it is relatively easy to implement and understand. The committee starts with the amount budgeted and actually spent during the prior year and simply adjusts each line by the amount it is expected to change. While some budget items are simply increased incrementally by a flat amount, such as 5 percent, time must be spent in considering how cer-tain other expenses might behave in the coming year. How much will the heating bill increase? Will health insurance for the staff hold steady for the coming year?

Practical Example

First Church uses an incremental budgeting approach in preparing its annual budget. Presented below is the section of the budget that deals with the church building. Most of these line items are anticipated to rise slightly due to basic inflation, determined by the budget committee to be 3 percent for the coming year. Two items require more discussion, and the committee concludes the following: First, heating oil prices are expected to rise significantly in the coming year. Reliable estimates show that an increase of $300 would not be unreasonable. Second, the janitor has been granted a 5 percent raise.

Chart 7.1

First Church

	Current year actual expense	Budgeted for coming year
Electric	$1,262	$1,300
Water	587	605
Telephone	500	515
Heating	2,030	2,330
Building insurance	1,801	1,855
Janitor wages	5,000	5,250
Building maintenance	485	500

In this example, all line items are increased by a flat 3 percent, except for "heating" and "janitor wages."

The problem with incremental budgeting is that established expenditures are rarely questioned. If $800 was budgeted and spent for choir music last year, then $800, or perhaps $810, should be budgeted this year. No one questions if $800 is an appropriate amount to spend for choir music; even worse, no one asks if incrementally more should be spent in the future. The choir director knows she must spend all $800 or risk losing it the next year when someone notices that the budgeted amount was not spent. Robert Welch writes that in churches which use an incremental budgeting approach, "review and evaluation tends to cease. Dead or dying programs are often sustained when the funds could be better used in other ministries."[6] Another problem might occur if the church is facing a budget shortfall and chooses to reduce all lines of the budget incrementally. Without considering the impact of this reduction to certain line items, essential ministries or key church programs might be damaged beyond repair.

Zero-Based Budgeting

Unlike the incremental budgeting approach, the budget committee of a church using this method must build the budget from zero each year. Since each budgeted expense must be justified annually, this approach can be an excellent way to reduce expenditures that have no real value but that have been present in the church budget for years. The $800 that was budgeted for choir music last year would need to be reviewed and critically evaluated.

Since zero-based budgeting is very time consuming, it is not widely used on an annual basis. It may be helpful for the church to undertake the zero-based budgeting process occasionally, or to decide to review certain programs by using this method. For instance, when a new music minister is hired, that may be a good time to implement a zero-based budgeting process for expenditures related to the music program of the church. At this point, the $800 budgeted for choir music would require analysis and justification.

Program Budgeting

This method divides the church budget into many smaller budgets, one for each program of the church. Each church program must have its own purpose and its own budget, and all of these budgets combined together are the church's master budget. This budgeting approach provides the best picture of how much the various programs of the church actually cost. To use this method correctly, the shared costs of the church must be allocated between the various program budgets. This allocation of shared costs can make the method complex to implement.

For instance, the music program of the church would have its own budget. The $800 budgeted for choir music described above would clearly appear on the music budget, since it can be directly traced to the music program. But indirect costs, such as the church's utilities and insurance, the pastor's salary, the secretary's salary, the janitor's wages, postage, computer, and copier expenses, to name a few, would also need to appear. These shared expenses must be allocated to the music budget based on an estimate of usage. Making these allocations to each of the program budgets can be tricky and time consuming. The results, however, can be truly helpful to the church in making important funding decisions.

Chart 7.2

First Church
Music Ministry Budget

Part-time music minister	$6,000
Senior pastor—2%	600
Pianist—60%	1,200
Church secretary—5%	900
Music	800
Robe cleaning	250
Instrument repairs and tuning	350
Building utilities—3%	120
Building insurance—3%	55
Postage and photocopying—5%	50
Janitor—3%	150
Total	$10,475

While it may be helpful to First Church to see that the music program costs $10,475 to operate, users of this information need to exercise caution. Since this program budget includes shared costs, users need to be aware that if they choose to eliminate the entire music program, they will not save $10,475. Costs that are shared, like the senior pastor's compensation, would need to be reallocated to another program budget. Only the direct costs would be eliminated if the music program was ended.

Finalizing the Operating Budget

Whichever budgeting method is adopted, most budget committees begin the budgeting process by forecasting the amount of giving they expect for the coming year based on past experience and on membership or attendance trends. By examining a history of giving, it is possible to predict a preliminary amount of income that will result from both pledges and cash collections. Churches should also forecast other income amounts, such as income from renting out the facility and interest income. It is usually wise to be conservative in preparing estimates of income. Next, expenses should be entered, using one of the methods described above. The result is the operating budget of the church.

Frequently in churches, it seems that expenses exceed income. Since most churches do not have a savings account to which they can turn to make up the difference, they must either reduce expenses or increase income in order to balance the budget. If the church has faithfully sought to discern God's direction for the coming year and has prayerfully attempted to reduce nonmissional spending to as low a level as possible, the budget committee should challenge the congregation to fund this budget. If the congregation is unable to provide the needed support, difficult choices must be made. Programs that appear to be critical may need to be reevaluated, and cuts will need to be made. James Berkley writes, "You thought each expense was a priority or you would not have included it in the budget. But if there is no income to pay for a portion of the expenses, God must have a different idea."[7]

The Cash Budget

The operating budget described above normally is prepared on an annual basis. It presents the projected income of the church for the year and the estimated expenses for the year. But most contributions to the church are not made annually, in full on January 1. Nor are most expenses of the church paid in full on January 1. Contributions flow into the church throughout the year, just as bills are paid by the church throughout the year. The annual operating budget, with its single set of numbers, is not adequate for managing the cash flows of the church.

As part of the annual budgeting process, the budget committee should prepare a monthly cash budget. Once the operating budget is complete, the monthly cash budget is relatively easy to compute. Generally, giving patterns need to be examined to see if certain months provide more or less cash contributions than other months. Usually, giving is down in most churches during the summer and up at Easter and at the end of the year. Expenses should also be analyzed to determine if they occur evenly throughout the year. The church may have a large cash outflow periodically for a nonroutine expense such as insurance.

Once this analysis is complete, a monthly cash budget can be easily prepared by using spreadsheet software. The cash budget begins with the amount of cash expected to be available on January 1. To that, the cash projected to be collected in January is added and the cash anticipated to be spent paying bills in January is subtracted. The ending balance will be either positive, indicating adequate cash, or negative, indicating a shortage of cash. This ending balance becomes the beginning cash balance for February.

Chart 7.3

The Village Church
Monthly Cash Budget

	Jan	Feb	Mar
Beginning cash	$1,200	$785	($830)
Plus: cash receipts			
Pledges	4,500	4,200	4,500
Nonpledged contributions	800	600	800
Special offerings	0	0	1,300
Interest income	10	10	10
Rental income	150	150	150
Total cash receipts	5,460	4,960	6,760
Cash to fund disbursements	6,660	5,745	5,930
Cash disbursements			
Clergy salary and housing	1,750	1,750	1,750
Clergy benefits	375	375	375
Secretarial help	750	750	750
Organist	300	300	300
Utilities and building upkeep	1,200	1,200	1,200
Office expenses and mailings	200	200	200
Property insurance	0	700	0
Denominational assessment	300	300	300
Youth ministry	125	125	125
Sunday school	125	125	125
Missions	750	750	750
Total cash disbursements	5,875	6,575	5,875
Surplus (deficit) of cash	$785	$(830)	$55

With a monthly cash budget in hand, the church can easily plan in advance for handling a shortage of cash that is projected for any month throughout the year. It may be necessary to delay a planned cash outflow that falls in a month when a cash shortage exists. For example, the budget committee can inform the worship team that its request for a new keyboard has been approved but that the actual purchase cannot take place until May. Sometimes it may be necessary for the church to develop a plan for financing the shortage. For instance, the budget committee may realize that the insurance payment due in February in the sample cash budget above cannot be delayed. A short-term loan or line of credit can be arranged with a bank to provide the necessary cash to cover the payment. Interest payments and the actual repayment of this loan should be included as a cash outflow in following months.

Planning for the Future

The conclusion of the annual budgeting process is the perfect time to begin planning for the future! Jack Henry wisely counsels that it is at this point in the year that "you will probably find that you have a list of ministries and projects that you really want to do but cannot afford in your budget for this year. Do not throw your list away. Save it and develop a long-term plan for accomplishing those ministries and projects too."[8] Long-range planning can be a wonderful way to raise a congregation's vision from the immediate needs and programs and to challenge it to look toward the future.

The long-range plan can be as simple or as complex as needed. Some churches use their annual operating budget and prepare a future projection that looks forward one, two, three, or even five years. Using the same assumptions upon which they built the current year's budget, they forecast forward several years to create a long-range plan that can guide them into the future.

We believe a better approach might be to complete this process of budgeting by returning to the starting point, that is, the discernment process. At the beginning of this chapter, we observed that the starting place of any budget must be a process of discernment in which the church seeks to know God's plan. If God has laid six separate needs on the heart of the congregation but money is available to fund only three of those needs, it is wrong for the church to assume that the unfunded needs are unimportant.

Those needs should be prayed for, discussed, and kept before the congregation throughout the year. Perhaps there are ways in which members of the congregation can continue to develop the project idea without the church providing funding. For instance, the church decides it is unable to contribute $15,000 toward the construction of a medical clinic in Central America; instead, several members volunteer to go and work on the building project. By keeping the idea alive, the process of discernment can continue. Would God have the church participate in funding this clinic in the future? When it is time for the annual budgeting process to begin again, the congregation will have been engaged in an ongoing, yearlong practice of discernment on this matter.

Another important way in which the church should consider planning for the future is by building a reserve fund to draw upon if there is an unexpected expense. This type of fund can also be used as an internal line of credit that the church can use during months when cash outflows exceed inflows. In order to successfully build a reserve fund, the church must budget for it. Bear in mind that transfers to a contingency fund are not expenses but simply movement of cash from one fund to another. The size of the contingency fund should be determined by the amount of risk that exists for the church. For instance, if the church has a building that is in need of many repairs, risk is high that the roof may need work or that the heating system may need to be replaced. Such a church should build a reserve fund adequate to provide funding if such an emergency arises.

Using the Budget to Manage

And so the New Year begins. The annual budgeting nightmare is over, and the operating budget, cash budget, and long-range plan are all locked safely away in a file cabinet somewhere until next year, right? We maintain instead that these documents become valuable tools that can be used by the minister to disarm the power of money. The very process of budgeting outlined in this chapter can begin to diminish money's place of power in the church. The practice of *discerning God's mission* says, "God, it's your church, your money, your plan, not ours." The work of *planning* demands communication between members, some of whom may formerly have been more comfortable in their own special interest group. And the process of *budgeting* should be an act of discipleship that reflects the faithful and communal response of a particular part of the body of Christ.

In the Lord's Prayer, Christians pray, "Thy kingdom come." To what kingdom do our budgets point? We also pray, "Give us this day our daily bread." Our budgets reveal who we include in that prayer for sustenance. Church budgets are always confessional statements for individual congregations. To what God do they actually witness?

DISCUSSION QUESTIONS

1. Discuss the method of budgeting you have most often seen used within the church: incremental, zero-based, or program.
2. In this chapter, we describe a three-phase process for budgeting. In which of the three phases is your church strong? In which is it weak?
3. Is your church's budget consistent with its mission statement and/or the doctrinal beliefs of your denomination?

8

Financial Transparency
in the Church

Secrecy provides a place for the power of money to grow and take root. As head-lines earlier in the decade about Enron, Tyco, and WorldCom have illustrated, business organizations that conceal their actions from their stakeholders gen-erally do so because they are hiding operational inefficiencies, related-party transactions, and financial improprieties. Likewise, churches that operate under a cloak of secrecy may be concealing from their members expenditures that are excessive or unauthorized. Church leaders may not want it widely known that certain vendors, suppliers, or contractors have been chosen to do business with the church because of a relationship with someone in the church. The treasurer or bookkeeper may prepare vague or even false financial reports because he is covering up the fact that he has embezzled money from the church. In all cases, secrecy provides the environment in which money can be misused, controlled, and misappropriated. When financial transparency is absent, secrecy reigns.

Perhaps the most powerful example of this comes from the connection found between the clergy sexual abuse scandal and the lack of financial trans-parency in the Catholic Church by researchers Charles Zech and Robert West:

> As the scandal unfolded, parishioners learned that in some dioceses, payments related to the scandal had been taking place for years. Some of the payments went to victims in the form of settlements or to pay for counseling; some went to pay for the "rehabilitation" of priests accused of sexual abuse; and some funds were paid out in lawyers fees. The vast majority of Catholics was unaware of these payments, and therefore surprised by the magnitude of the scandal. A number of

parishioners pointed out that if the Church had been more open in its finances, the expenses associated with clergy sexual abuse, and hence the nature and magnitude of the problem, would have been uncovered much sooner than it was. This might have caused church leaders to take action earlier and prevent some of the abusive behavior, especially that by repeat offenders.[1]

One Catholic lay leader, in commenting on the Archdiocese of Boston, stated that "the archdiocese, under the old leadership, had followed practices that can best be described as secretive. That's not an uncommon word when you talk about Church matters."[2] Had transparent financial reporting been in place, the secrecy surrounding these payments might have been shattered.

There is no place for secrecy within the church. Yet the World Christian Database estimated that in 2000, a staggering $16 billion of church funds were embezzled worldwide by leaders of churches and religious organizations. In the United States alone, the amount reached nearly $7 billion.[3] In their recent survey within the Catholic Church, researchers West and Zech found that 85 percent of respondents reported that embezzlement had occurred within their dioceses in the last five years.[4] Recent stories of financial impropriety within the church have made headlines in most major news publications.

In response to what has been described as a crisis resulting from a lack of financial transparency within the church and the resulting increase in public and governmental scrutiny, programs have recently been established at Villanova University, Boston College, and Seton Hall University Law School aimed at helping primarily Catholic parishes and church-related nonprofits, as well as clergy and lay leaders, to become better managers.[5] Within evangelical Protestant circles, the Evangelical Council for Financial Accountability (ECFA), "an accreditation agency dedicated to helping Christian ministries earn the public's trust," has been providing over two thousand ministries with guidance focused on board governance and financial transparency for nearly thirty years.[6] In 2007 the ECFA created a new division focused on providing the same type of assistance to churches, particularly to smaller congregations.

FINANCIAL TRANSPARENCY

So what exactly is transparency? We believe that financially transparent churches are churches that

conduct an annual audit of their financial statements,
share complete, clear, audited financial information openly with the congregation,

have a comprehensive system of internal control in place,

actively engage in preventing fraud, and

purposefully foster an internal culture of openness.

Financial transparency is a way of disarming the power of money, while secrecy places money in a position of power.

The Annual Audit

Denominations vary as to their requirements regarding an annual audit. Some recommend but do not require it. Others do not make it clear who should conduct the audit, leaving open the possibility that someone connected to the financial operations of the church might be qualified. Still other denominations are silent on the matter. Clergypersons should be familiar with the requirements of their respective denominations but should articulate to their congregations the goal of financial transparency rather than simple compliance with judicatory standards.

If your church has never had an audit, or if there is reason to suspect some financial irregularity, we highly recommend that the church engage an independent CPA firm to conduct a full financial audit. Since this type of audit can be costly, the congregation might consider conducting this type of audit only every three years. In the intervening years, the church can hire a CPA firm to perform a review, which is substantially less costly and less comprehensive than an audit. Another option is for the church to engage knowledgeable church members to perform an internal audit in these intervening years. Since church members are not independent of the church, their audit is considered "internal" in nature rather than "independent."

An internal audit by members who are familiar with accounting terms, concepts, and practices can be highly effective. The church treasurer, bookkeeper, or financial secretary should not serve as a member of the audit committee, nor should anyone who counts the offering or is involved in any way with the financial operations of the church. The minister should not serve on the audit committee or even be involved in the selection of members of the committee. The audit committee should be given full access to all accounting reports and information. Guidelines for conducting the internal audit should be available from the CPA firm who has performed a full independent audit or from denominational headquarters. Several fine resources are available from the following sources:

United Methodist Church General Council on Finance and Administration:
http://www.gcfa.org/PDFs/Local_Church_Audit_Guide.pdf

Massachusetts Conference United Church of Christ: http://www.macucc
.org/stewardship/audit.pdf

Sharing Complete, Clear, Audited Financial Information
Openly with the Congregation

Often in churches, the fact that individual giving records are kept confiden-
tial fosters the misconception that all financial information is secret. The
minister should clearly communicate to the church leaders that, while giving information is protected, the financial reports of the church are open to
all. The church should not engage in any financial transaction that it is
unwilling to share openly with the congregation. If it needs to be hidden, it
shouldn't be done.

Churches that are financially transparent make their audited financial
information readily available to the congregation and other interested parties
on a timely basis. Additionally, transparent financial information is clear, easy
to understand, and provides enough detail for the user to get a correct picture
of the situation. Salary information is an area where transparency is crucial. If
the minister's salary is combined with the salary and benefits for the entire
staff, that number does not provide enough clear detail to be helpful. This is
an area where the clergyperson can lead by example. He can demonstrate disarming of the power of money by insisting that clear, forthright salary information about his compensation package be presented in the financial
statements.

A Comprehensive System of Internal Control

Churches, like all organizations, have the responsibility and the obligation
to effectively manage and use their resources to accomplish their mission.
Internal control refers to the systems, activities, and procedures in place that
ensure the safeguarding as well as the efficient management and use of
church resources. However, research into the internal control structure of
churches has revealed a frightening lack of basic controls, particularly in
small churches.[7]

Ultimately, the minister is the one responsible for ensuring that a system of
internal control is functioning in the church. One study found that, in spite of
a lack of training in business and accounting, ministers have a reasonably good
understanding of what is necessary for a sound internal control environment.
Yet in many cases, internal controls do not exist in the church. The study concludes that "pastors choose to trust church employees and members rather

than to implement basic internal control procedures in their churches."[8] Some clergy believe that if they require implementation of a system of internal control in their church, it will be viewed as unloving, uncaring, and ultimately unchristian. In our opinion, nothing could be further from the truth.

There is perhaps no administrative activity more loving and caring in which the minister can engage than that of implementing a comprehensive system of internal control for the church. Establishing financial controls is an act of leadership that demonstrates gratitude and respect for the stewardship and hard work of church employees, members, volunteers, and contributors. Controls in the church can provide a buffer that helps protect church employees and volunteers from the temptation to steal cash or misuse church assets. Controls supply a shield against false accusations of fraud or misappropriation. Secrecy is abolished when controls are present, so controls create the environment of openness in which transparency can grow. Controls protect donors by ensuring that their gifts are kept safe and used for the mission of the church.

Generally, the internal control system should (1) help safeguard the church's assets against theft or accidental loss, (2) promote the efficient use of the church's assets, and (3) help provide sound financial information to be incorporated into the church reports and financial statements. Many specific procedures can be used to accomplish these objectives, some of which might be unique to a specific church given its situation. Broadly speaking, however, most of these procedures fall into one of the following six categories of what are considered pervasive control activities:

> Physical controls to safeguard assets
> Segregation of duties
> Authorization procedures
> Documented transaction trails
> Reconciliation controls
> Competent, trustworthy employees[9]

Physical Controls to Safeguard Assets

In addition to keeping cash in a secure location, other church assets, such as computers and data files, financial records, and blank checks must be kept secure as well. Some general procedures that can be implemented to help safeguard church assets include

1. Keeping the church offering, and all other cash, securely locked at all times and deposited as quickly as possible.
2. Restrictively endorsing all checks as soon as possible.

3. Counting the offering in a secure location using two or more counters at all times.

4. Depositing the entire offering intact. It often appears convenient to pay small church expenses out of the offering. For instance, the youth leaders may need to be reimbursed for pizza purchased for the youth group on Sunday evening. This reimbursement should not be made out of the Sunday morning collection, but by a check.

5. Keeping the church computer system in a secure location.

6. Restricting access to software programs via passwords.

7. Keeping blank checks locked in a secure location.

8. Backing up data files regularly and storing backups in a secure, off-site location.

9. Keeping historical church financial records, bank statements, and payroll records in a secure location at the church, rather than in the home of the church treasurer or bookkeeper.

10. Carefully monitoring the distribution of keys to the church and church office.

Practical Example

First Church prides itself on its procedure for depositing its Sunday collection promptly and safely. After the morning offering, two ushers take the plates to the locked church office, where they are left on the secretary's desk until after the service. After the service, the offering is bagged and locked in the safe until Monday, when it is counted and deposited at the bank.

This system appears to be sound. However, nearly everyone at First Church has a key to the church office. The offering is far from secure during the Sunday morning service.

Segregation of Duties

A key category of internal control activities involves procedures that are designed to prevent one person from committing a fraudulent act and covering it up. In order for segregation of duty controls to work, different people must be responsible for

authorizing the financial transaction,

having custody of the asset, and

recording the transaction in the accounting records.

Separation of duties can be extremely challenging in a small church. With limited staff and volunteers, it may seem impossible to divide a financial task in the way described here. A carefully designed system that creatively uses board members and other nonfinancial volunteers to do just one task in the process, however, can effectively create the separation needed.

Whether the church is large or small, the minister should have absolutely no role in any of the regular financial transactions. He should not authorize payments, sign checks, record contributions, count the offering, take it to the bank, make withdrawals, transfer funds, handle payroll, write reimbursement checks, reconcile the bank statement, or anything else of a financial nature. The best possible advice for the clergyperson is to stay as far away from cash and all financial transactions as possible.

Specific procedures for the separation of duties within the church include

1. Two or more unrelated counters count the offering and take it to the bank. Counters should be rotated regularly.
2. Someone other than the counters records the receipt of cash into the accounting records.
3. The bank statements are reconciled by someone other than the person writing checks and recording transactions into the accounting records.
4. Cash disbursements and payroll are authorized by someone other than the individual who prepares the checks.
5. Checks are signed by someone other than the individual who prepares the checks. The check signer examines the supporting invoice or documents for approval and appropriateness before signing the check.
6. All employees are required to take an annual vacation of at least one week, and preferably two weeks, in length. It is important for this to be a mandatory policy and that the days off not be scattered throughout the year but taken in a block. Since fraud generally requires the perpetrator to be present and continuously attentive to the scheme, a mandatory vacation policy can help reduce the risk of embezzlement.
7. All volunteer financial positions are rotated every two or three years.

Practical Example

After the Sunday service at First Church, the treasurer takes the offering from the secretary's desk, bags it, and places it in the safe. On Monday morning, he counts the offering, records it in the computer, and takes the offering to the bank.

The problem here is that the treasurer is acting alone to count the offering, to keep custody of the offering both at the church and on the way to the bank, and to record the cash receipt into the accounting records. There are numerous opportunities for him to make errors or misappropriate cash. By separating the duties of authorization (counting), custody, and record keeping, errors will be detected and theft prevented.

Authorization Procedures

Another area of basic control procedures within the church is that of authorization. Only authorized purchases should be made, only authorized payroll checks should be written, and only authorized individuals should access the offering, the computer, and other church assets. Authorization is a key part of the segregation of duties. Church leaders should develop a clear policy identifying the authorization procedure for each of the following transactions:

> payroll
> expense reimbursements
> routine cash disbursements
> major cash disbursements
> signing checks
> transfers of cash between accounts
> investment activity
> changes to computer programs

Practical Example

The volunteer church treasurer receives time sheets from the janitor and the secretary twice a month and prepares their paychecks. A member of the board is authorized to sign checks and carefully compares the time sheets to the paychecks before signing.

Since no one has approved the time sheets, however, there is no way to be sure that the amounts reported on the time sheets were actually worked by the employees. Someone supervising the work of the janitor and the secretary needs to approve their time sheets before payment is made.

Documented Transaction Trail

A key element of a strong internal control system is a trail of documentary evidence that supports each financial transaction. Churches that lack a reliable internal control system provide little documentation to substantiate their financial activities. When an internal audit team or external auditor performs the annual audit of the church, they look at the documentation of transactions that occurred during the year. Computerized accounting systems normally produce a better audit trail than manual systems because controls are incorporated directly into the software. Certain reports are programmed to print automatically to document the steps taken by the system to record a transaction.

Examples of documentation procedures include the following:

1. Count sheets are used by count teams when the Sunday collection or cash from a church dinner or fund-raiser is counted.
2. Preprinted giving envelopes are provided to all contributors. Used envelopes are retained, and the envelope provides an audit trail for cash receipts.
3. All cash disbursements are authorized, and the authorization is clearly documented.
4. Reimbursements made to individuals for church expenses paid for personally are supported by receipts, and the examination of receipts before payment is clearly documented.
5. Prenumbered checks are used, and all voided checks are accounted for.
6. For payroll, hours paid are documented by an approved time card.

Reconciliation Controls

An important area of internal control is activities that reconcile *actual* with *what has been recorded*. The job of checking for agreement should be performed by someone independent of both the physical custody of the asset and the recording of the transaction. Within the church, reconciliation controls are particularly critical in the collection and deposit of the Sunday collection, cash collected at church dinners and fund-raisers, and all other cash received by the church. Examples of reconciliation controls include these procedures:

1. The count sheet is compared to the bank deposit by someone independent of counting and taking the deposit to the bank.
2. The bank reconciliation is prepared by someone independent of counting or recording the collection, and the reconciler compares each deposit to the count sheets.
3. Donors are given quarterly giving statements and informed to direct any inquiries or irregularities to someone independent of the process of recording contributions.
4. Preprinted giving envelopes are provided to all contributors. Counters compare the contents with the amount indicated on the envelope and document any variance.

Practical Example

On Monday morning, the count team arrives at First Church to count the Sunday offering. With calculators clicking, they carefully fill out the count sheet, prepare the deposit slip, and place the offering in a bag that will be dropped off at the bank by one of the counters on her way home. The count sheet is carefully filed away in a file drawer until the end of the year, when it will be boxed up along with other records from the year and taken to the church attic for storage.

This procedure is flawed, however. The purpose in the count sheet is to document the amount of offering collected. The count should be identical to the deposit recorded by the bank. However, if no one ever checks to make sure that the cash counted is the same as the cash deposited, the potential exists for fraud. Under this current system, there is nothing to prevent the individual who carries the cash to the bank from removing money from the bag.

Competent, Trustworthy Employees and Volunteers

Employees and volunteers need to be trained in their jobs and informed about the controls in place. Counters should be taught how to count the offering, and the controls in place in the counting process should be explained to them. Ushers should be instructed not only about how to take the offering but about the importance of the safeguards used to protect the offering from theft. The church should never assume that a volunteer understands how to do a task or realizes the purpose behind the controls that are in place. When people are not aware of the reasons for a safeguard, they can easily justify omitting it.

Written procedures should be developed for the collection and handling of the Sunday collection, the counting and deposit of offering, the processing of payroll, cash disbursements and check writing, monthly bank reconciliations, preparation of monthly reports, transfers of cash between accounts, handling of investments, and purchase of fixed assets. Each written procedure should document the internal controls designed into the system. If updated periodically, these procedures can greatly help in providing training for new volunteers and employees.

In conclusion, implementing the internal control procedures necessary within a specific church can be a daunting task. The suggestions provided above are general in nature, and each church has peculiar circumstances that need to be considered. If no one within the church has expertise in this area, the clergyperson should consider encouraging the leadership to hire a CPA firm to assess and develop a system of internal controls. If volunteers within the church, particularly those involved in the internal audit, feel capable of examining and implementing an internal control system, here are several excellent resources that can help:

The Church Guide to Internal Controls by Richard J. Vargo (Church Law and Tax Report, 1995)

PPC's Guide to Religious Organizations by James E. Guinn et al. (Thomson Tax and Accounting, 2007)

Tips for Preventing and Catching Misuse of Church Funds by the General Council for Finance and Administration, United Methodist Church: http://www.gcfa.org/misuseofChurchFunds.html.

Zondervan 2008 Church and Nonprofit Tax and Financial Guide by Dan Busby (Zondervan, 2008)

Actively Engage in Preventing Fraud

Even financially transparent churches with fully functioning systems of internal controls can be victims of fraud. Employees and volunteers may steal cash or other assets from a church for a variety of reasons. Research indicates that most individuals who commit fraud are not career criminals but average, law-abiding citizens.[10] Most are trusted employees who have worked for their organization for years.[11] So why do these people steal?

The fraud triangle, the most widely accepted model for explaining why otherwise trustworthy people turn to fraud, incorporates three factors that must all be present for fraud to occur: perceived pressure, perceived opportunity, and rationalization.[12]

1. *Perceived pressure* results when an employee or volunteer needs money and feels that she has nowhere to turn. The volunteer church treasurer who faces a personal financial crisis due to a job layoff or unexpected bills may feel trapped. The church secretary with an unexpected pregnancy or a gambling or drug problem may feel unable to confide in anyone about the problem.
2. *Perceived opportunity* exists when the individual has access to cash or other assets of the entity and the ability to cover the crime. The usher who carries the offering plate by herself from the sanctuary to the church office has the opportunity to remove cash from the plate. The bookkeeper who writes and signs checks and also prepares the bank reconciliation has the opportunity to write checks to himself.
3. *Rationalization* is the justification made by the individual for the crime he is committing. In the church, rationalization may sound like this:

   "I'm only borrowing the money this once and will pay it back after I get my next paycheck."

   "This church has too much money anyway."

   "Pastor Sue gives money to needy people who come in off the street all the time. I'm sure she'd give me this money if I asked her."

   "I get paid less since I work at a church. This money is really what they owe me for all the hard work I do."

When pressure, opportunity, and rationalization are all present, fraud can and most likely will occur. If the volunteer treasurer who has lost his full-time job and has bills stacking up at home (pressure) has the ability to transfer cash into his personal checking account because of weak internal controls in the church (opportunity) and feels like the church spends most of its money unwisely on worthless things (rationalization), he most likely will commit fraud. To protect against fraud, the clergyperson should encourage church leaders to address each area of the fraud triangle.

Minimizing Perceived Pressure

Perceived pressure occurs when an employee or volunteer needs money, cannot share that need with anyone, and feels that she has nowhere to turn. To help prevent fraud, church leaders should discuss strategies for helping employees and volunteers handle these types of pressures. A clergy open-door policy can provide employees and members with a place to turn to share financial and personal concerns. Clergy who are approachable, open, and caring offer a safe place for employees and volunteers to unload their concerns and develop strategies for coping with the pressure. Additionally, the board should approve a policy to handle pay advances to employees, and the policy should be communicated to employees. Often, just knowing that an advance on pay is available can defuse the pressure that might otherwise lead to fraud.

A more ambitious but excellent approach is for the church to develop a program to provide personal and financial guidance to volunteers and employees. Similar to the employee assistance programs provided by many corporations, government agencies, and even some denominations to help their employees deal with substance abuse problems, financial concerns, and other personal problems, this type of program is led by lay members with expertise in financial management, counseling, and law. The team of lay leaders can be activated as needed to meet with the employee or parishioner in need and provide the spiritual, financial, and personal guidance necessary to diffuse the perceived pressure. One study of Fortune 500 companies found that 92 percent of respondents believed that "assisting employees with personal financial pressures helped prevent employee fraud."[13] So too can this type of program serve to help inhibit fraud by employees and volunteers within the church. (We discuss the clergy's role in financial mentoring in chapter 11.)

Minimizing the Opportunity for Fraud

The pastor should encourage the board to carefully consider ways in which opportunities to commit fraud in the church can be reduced. The primary way to limit opportunity is through a sound system of internal control. Physically safeguarding assets, particularly cash, can greatly reduce the opportunity for fraud. Segregating duties can eliminate the opportunity for a single person to both steal cash and cover up the act. Having a system in place to actively monitor controls can further minimize the opportunity for fraud to continue undetected.

The opportunity for fraud to occur can also be reduced by adequately supervising and observing employees and volunteers. For instance, the offering count should be conducted in a secure room, and the counters should be visible to other volunteers or employees while conducting the count. The volunteer who drops the deposit at the bank should be accompanied by a second, unrelated volunteer. Perhaps more importantly, the behavior and lifestyle of employees and volunteers should be observed. When an employee has a standard of living that is inconsistent with his income, this could be an indication that fraud may be occurring.

Reducing Rationalization

The third factor of the fraud triangle, rationalization, must also be present for fraud to occur. The minister should lead the board in consideration of ways in which rationalization can be reduced among church employees and volunteers. Robert Simon describes both belief systems and boundary systems as necessary for adequate control of an organization.[14] Belief systems are those statements of purpose, vision, and core values that sum up what the organization stands for. Boundary systems include the code of conduct and the specific expectations required of each employee. It is critical that both belief and boundary systems be clearly communicated throughout the organization.

Belief Systems

Within the church, employees and volunteers must know that honesty, truthfulness, integrity, and openness are core values in the daily operations of the church. More importantly, however, these beliefs must permeate the culture of the church; they must be modeled by church leaders; they must be the very air that is breathed within the church. When employees and volunteers observe a tone of integrity at the top, rationalization is diminished. Statements like "Everyone around here helps themselves once in a while" and "Pastor Tom has plenty of parishioners taking care of him; why shouldn't I get my share occasionally?" are less defensible when a culture of honesty and transparency has been cultivated.

Boundary Systems

Within the church, employees and volunteers must know which behaviors are acceptable and which are not. Boundary systems, such as a code of conduct, make clear the church's expectations of its employees and volunteers, and clear expectations reduce rationalization. Fraud expert Steve Albrecht recommends that employers have their employees read and sign the code of conduct periodically to emphasize to the employees the importance of these standards to the organization: "When employees are required to acknowledge that they understand the organization's expectations, they buy into the idea that fraud hurts everyone, that not everyone is a little dishonest, that the organization won't tolerate dishonest acts, that dishonest behavior is serious, and that unauthorized borrowing is not acceptable."[15]

Purposefully Fostering an Internal Culture of Openness

Nothing does more to disarm the power of money within the church than the purposeful nurturing of a culture of openness. While secrecy creates an atmosphere in which the power of money can thrive, openness helps to neutralize money's power. In business, the responsibility for developing this culture of transparency rests with the CEO. Much has been written lately in business literature about the "tone at the top." The idea is that, no matter how comprehensive the audit or how expert the auditors, no matter how extensive the system of control procedures, no matter how thick the ethics manual, if the person at the top of the organization sets a tone of dishonesty, of secrecy, of bending the rules, that attitude will trickle down and affect the entire entity.

The same is true, we believe, for churches. As the leader of the church, the pastor alone can truly create and foster a culture of honesty and openness. So each time the pastor quietly arranges for a family member to receive the contract to install the new heating system for the church, or has the church bookkeeper discretely pay for repairs to his personally owned home, or waives the fees for camp for his own children, or sidesteps a committee's authority by quietly authorizing an expenditure that should have been approved by the committee, he sets a tone at the top that is observed by the congregation. This disregard for transparency trickles down to all parishioners and sends the message that the power of money is alive and well.

We believe that the pastor should lead in this area by initiating conversations with church leaders aimed at developing a definition of transparency for the church. What will it mean to the congregation to no longer tolerate secrecy in its daily operation or in its financial dealings? Are there areas within the church where money is used to control people, programming, or mission? What detailed financial information will need to be provided to the congregation that was previously concealed? Conversations of this nature can bring healing and freedom to a church that has been bound by the tyranny of money.

There is no place for financial secrecy in the church. In John 8:12 we hear

Jesus say, "I am the light of the world. Whoever follows me will never walk in darkness but will have the light of life." Financial secrecy is a denial of Jesus' power to illuminate all things. Clergy are called to model and encourage an environment in which Christ's light shines in all areas of the church.

DISCUSSION QUESTIONS

1. What is meant by the term "financial transparency"? How might your church begin moving toward greater financial transparency?
2. Examine the procedure currently used by your church to count and deposit the Sunday collection. What weaknesses are evident? What improvements might you suggest?
3. Using the model of the fraud triangle, analyze your church's susceptibility to fraud. What steps could your church implement to reduce perceived pressure, perceived opportunity, and rationalization?

9

Money in the Personal Life
of the Pastor

———————————

Many clergy live in awe of money in their own lives. There is never enough
of it, yet they are not comfortable asking their congregations for more. They
are not sure if they will have enough of it to retire on and worry about the
best place to invest any excess they might have. And even though it feels like
they pay a lot of taxes each year, they've been told that being ordained provides a tremendous tax advantage. We believe that money assumes a place of
power in the lives of many clergy because they do not understand it.

In this chapter we discuss four important areas in the clergyperson's life that
all deal with how he personally handles money: paying tax, structuring the
compensation package, personal spending, and personal giving. We attempt
to provide the newly ordained clergyperson with insights in these areas that
will enable her to begin disarming the power of money in her own life.

Since entire books have been written on clergy tax and financial planning
issues (some of which we will recommend later), this chapter will in no way
equip the new pastor to prepare his own tax return or do his own retirement
planning. Rather, we hope that it serves as a starting place for the student or
newly ordained pastor, as well as those who have served in ministry for years,
to recognize and guard against the potentially powerful place that money can
assume in one's personal life.

PART ONE: PAYING TAXES—DISARMING THE POWER
OF MONEY BY LEARNING THE BASICS

The rules surrounding the computation of clergy income tax are complex,
perhaps one of the more complicated areas of individual income tax law.

New ministers often are confused and overwhelmed, and some that we have known through the years have had literally no idea what is expected of them by the IRS. They are behind before they even begin, because they have never learned the rules. For these individuals, the IRS becomes an irrational enemy, and taxes become a powerful weapon that can threaten their way of life.

Knowledge is the key to disarming the power of taxes. The clergyperson can either learn enough about taxes herself to correctly prepare her returns and pay her tax, or can hire someone to help. Our advice is this: *find a good clergy tax professional and happily pay him for his services—this will be money wisely spent.* Unless you are willing to devote much time and energy to learning about federal and state income taxes in general, and clergy income taxes in particular, you should find a qualified, competent tax preparer.

If you choose to prepare your own returns, there are many wonderful resources to help. We recommend the books and Web sites listed at the conclusion of this chapter as a good starting point. If, as we highly recommend, you choose to hire a professional, it is critical to find someone who specializes in clergy taxes. Many skilled tax preparers and certified public accountants have never prepared a tax return for a minister. Ask other clergy in your area whom they use and if they are satisfied with the service they have received. Talk to someone at your denominational or judicatory headquarters and ask if they have recommendations available. Look online at the growing number of national services that specialize in clergy tax preparation.

Even if you choose to hire a qualified professional to prepare your tax return, you still need to be familiar with the basic issues surrounding clergy income tax. It is important to remember that using a professional preparer does not absolve you of responsibility and liability for the accuracy and completeness of your tax return. In part 1 of this chapter, we provide an introduction to six unique aspects of clergy taxes that make it a particularly challenging subject:

1. Social Security and Medicare taxes versus federal income tax
2. Self-employed status versus employee status
3. The tax treatment of clergy housing: federal income tax versus Social Security and Medicare taxes
4. Opting out of Social Security and Medicare
5. Maximizing the clergy housing benefit
6. Paying your taxes

The material contained in this section is intended only as an overview of these issues and is not adequate to help you prepare your own tax return. Our hope is that awareness of these matters will enable you to communicate better with your tax preparer. We firmly believe that understanding these issues can empower you to make wise decisions about money in your personal life.

Who Is a Minister?

Many of the rules discussed on the following pages only apply to those who are considered ministers by the IRS. A basic definition of a minister is provided in the Internal Revenue Code, but that definition has been interpreted throughout the years by the tax courts, IRS guidelines and publications, and IRS private letter rulings. Most experts agree that a minister is one who is ordained, commissioned, or licensed and does at least some of the following:

1. administers sacraments,
2. leads the church in religious matters,
3. conducts religious services and worship, and
4. manages by taking responsibility in the control, conduct, or maintenance of the church.[1]

If you are unsure as to whether or not you meet this description, you should consult with your denomination or with a qualified tax professional before reaching a determination. Bear in mind that not everyone with the title of "pastor" or "minister" is considered by the IRS to have met the above definition. In this tax section, all the issues discussed apply only to those meeting the IRS designation of a minister.

Social Security and Medicare Tax Versus Federal Income Tax

The Social Security and Medicare tax is levied on nearly all employees and self-employed individuals to fund the Social Security and Medicare programs. Employees are taxed at a rate of 7.65 percent of their wages; employers contribute a matching 7.65 percent. Self-employed individuals must pay both the employee and the employer share of the tax, at a rate of 15.3 percent of their net earnings from self-employment.[2]

Federal income tax is a completely different system, the purpose of which is to provide revenue to operate the federal government. The amount of federal income tax owed by an individual is computed on the annual income tax return, Form 1040. Most employees (but not the clergy, as discussed later) have federal income tax withheld from their pay to cover the amount that they will owe annually.

Self-Employed versus Employee

For Social Security and Medicare tax purposes, clergy are always considered self-employed, because the Internal Revenue Code, in sections 1402(c)(4) and 3121(b)(8), defines them as such.[3] This means that they owe Social Security and Medicare tax at a rate of 15.3 percent on their net earnings from self-employment.

For federal income tax purposes, clergy are not statutorily defined in the Internal Revenue Code as either self-employed or as employees of their churches. A clergyperson who claims to be a self-employed, independent contractor receives a Form 1099-MISC from the church and reports income and expenses on Schedule C of Form 1040. A clergyperson who is an employee receives a Form W-2 from the church and reports wages on line 7 of Form 1040.

Historically, many clergypersons considered themselves self-employed for federal income tax purposes, no doubt because they were considered self-employed for Social Security and Medicare purposes. That trend has reversed in recent years, and now most experts agree that most clergy more closely resemble employees than self-employed. Few ministers can meet the IRS common-law test to qualify as a self-employed independent contractor. Additionally, clergy are generally better off being classified as employees, since employees can receive certain benefits from their employer on a tax-free basis. For instance, health insurance and retirement benefits paid by an employer are not considered taxable benefits to the employee. Since they are not employees, however, self-employed clergy must include health insurance and retirement contributions paid by the church as income. Further, the possibility of an IRS audit is normally much higher for self-employed persons than for employees.[4] For these reasons, most ministers are considered employees of their churches.

Additional income earned by a pastor during the year from weddings, funerals, and other various church-related activities, however, is considered self-employment income. Frequently these payments are made directly to the minister and are not included on the church-prepared Form W-2 at the end of the year. The clergyperson should include these payments on a Schedule C as self-employment income.

To recap, clergy are unique in that they have dual tax status, since most are considered employees for federal income tax purposes, but *all* are self-employed for Social Security and Medicare tax purposes. As a self-employed person, a pastor pays all of the Social Security tax due on her earnings rather than sharing this burden with her employer, as she would if she were considered an employee.

Tax Preparation Tip

Be sure to discuss the dual-status issue with your tax preparer. She should be able to answer your questions and provide additional guidance on this complicated distinction. Additionally, if your church gives you a Form 1099-MISC at the end of the year (the form used to report payments to self-employed independent contractors) rather than a Form W-2 (the form used to report wages paid to employees), discuss this matter with your tax professional. She can determine the best way to handle the issue on your tax return. Since this is a common mistake made by many churches, you may need to help your church understand this important distinction and prepare the correct form in the future.

The Tax Treatment of Clergy Housing—Good News and Bad

Most churches either provide a parsonage or a manse for the minister to live in, or provide a housing allowance that the pastor can use to rent or buy her own home. The good news is that both church-provided housing (a parsonage or a manse) and a housing allowance are income-tax free, within limits described below, to members of the clergy. Section 107 of the Internal Revenue Code states:

> In the case of a minister of the gospel, gross income does not include—
> (1) the rental value of a home furnished to him as part of his compensation; or (2) the rental allowance paid to him as part of his compensation, to the extent used by him to rent or provide a home and to the extent such allowance does not exceed the fair rental value of the home, including furnishings and appurtenances such as a garage, plus the cost of utilities.

This is a great benefit that is available to most ordained clergy, whether they live in a parsonage or are buying or renting their own home.

Practical Examples

Manse or parsonage—Pastor Dan takes a church after seminary that offers him a salary of $28,000 plus the benefit of living for free in the church-owned manse. The manse has a fair rental value of $1,000 per month including utilities, which the church pays. Dan includes only the $28,000 of salary in income for federal income tax purposes.

Housing allowance—Pastor Kelly takes a church after seminary that offers her a salary of $28,000. Since this church does not own a manse, Kelly is offered an additional $1,000 per month for a housing allowance to provide a place to live. Kelly, like Dan, includes only the $28,000 of salary in her income for federal income tax purposes.

Now the Bad News—Social Security Tax

Again, all ministers are considered self-employed for purposes of the Social Security and Medicare tax, which means that they pay this tax at twice the rate of someone who is an employee. The housing benefit described above must be included in net earnings subject to self-employment tax, so housing provided to the pastor, either in a church-owned parsonage or as an allowance to pay for a home if the church does not have a parsonage, is taxed at the rate of 15.3 percent.

Practical Examples, Continued

Manse or parsonage—Pastor Dan must include both his $28,000 salary plus the $12,000 annual fair rental value of the parsonage in computing his Social Security and Medicare tax.

Housing allowance—Pastor Kelly likewise must include the $12,000 paid to her to provide a home in computing her Social Security and Medicare tax.

Both Dan and Kelly must compute tax on $40,000 of self-employment income at a rate of 15.3 percent, which is approximately $5,650.

For this reason, many new clergy pay far more in Social Security and Medicare tax than they do in federal income tax. The Social Security and Medicare tax is regressive, which means that lower-income individuals pay a much higher portion of their income in taxes than do higher income individuals, in part because the wages subject to Social Security tax are capped for higher-income earners. When the newly ordained pastor realizes this fact, it becomes very attractive to consider opting out of Social Security and Medicare. We have one word for that: DON'T.

Opting Out of Social Security and Medicare

Newly ordained clergy who decide early in their ministry that they conscientiously object to public welfare benefits can opt out of Social Security and Medicare by signing IRS Form 4361. As appealing as that sounds for the reason described above (as well as for the numerous gloomy predictions about the future of the Social Security system), this is not a wise choice, nor is it a position that most clergy can honestly take.

The IRS guidance on this issue specifically states that the clergyperson must be "conscientiously opposed to public insurance because of your individual religious considerations (not because of your general conscience)," or "because of the principles of your religious denomination."[5] As the noted clergy tax expert Richard R. Hammar has observed, "Few people, outside of the Amish, could plausibly say that."[6] Yet Hammar's research indicates that three of every ten ministers in America have opted out of Social Security and that "the vast majority of clergy who did opt out of Social Security never replaced it with another retirement scheme."[7]

Designed into most denominational retirement plans is the assumption that clergy will receive Social Security and Medicare benefits upon retirement to supplement denominational coverage. For this reason, most denominations strongly discourage clergy from opting out. Clergy tax expert Dan Busby cautions, "Opting out of Social Security is one of the most abused provisions of the tax law that applies to ministers. Too often, ministers have opted out because they are concerned about long-term safety of the program or they feel they have a better way to invest the funds. These reasons do not provide a basis to sign Form 4361."[8]

Maximizing the Clergy Housing Benefit to Save Federal Income Tax

Everyone who meets the IRS definition of a minister can ask the church to designate a portion of his compensation as a housing allowance. This portion is then excluded from taxable income. The minister still receives the cash, but these payments are excluded from the amount reported to the IRS on Form W-2 by the church at the end of the year. Both those living in a church-owned parsonage and those buying or renting their own residence are entitled to use a housing allowance.

The amount of the annual housing allowance must be formally designated in writing by the church in advance of any payment. (Excellent examples of housing allowance resolutions are contained in the books recommended at the end of the chapter.) Throughout the year, the pastor is responsible for keeping records of all the housing-related expenses she has incurred; there is no need to give those receipts to the church. At the end of the year, the church includes the amount paid to the pastor less the amount of the housing designation in box 1 (wages, tips, and other compensation) of the minister's W-2. For informational purposes, the church can choose to provide the amount of the housing designation in box 14 (other) with a description such as "parsonage" next to the amount.

Those living in a church-owned parsonage should ask the church to designate enough salary (subject to the limits discussed below) to cover everything necessary to provide a home in the parsonage, such as furniture, appliances, interior decorating, any utilities not paid by the church, cable TV, telephone, cleaning supplies, insurance on the contents of the home, improvements or repairs, appliance repairs, and landscaping.[9]

Practical Example, Continued

Pastor Dan lives in a church-owned manse with a fair rental value of $1,000 per month. Since this is a parsonage, this amount of $12,000 per year is *not* officially designated anywhere and does not reduce Dan's salary of $28,000. However, Dan can have the church designate an additional $2,000 of his annual salary to cover out-of-pocket costs that he might incur to provide a home in the church-owned manse. If Dan's church correctly designates this additional $2,000 as described above, then the amount reported on Dan's W-2 at the end of the year drops from $28,000 to $26,000.

Those living in their own home should have enough designated to cover rent or mortgage principal payments, payments for mortgage interest and real estate tax, insurance on the home and contents, home improvements, along with everything necessary to provide a home, such as furniture, appliances, interior decorating, any utilities not paid by the church, cable TV, telephone, cleaning supplies, insurance on the contents of the home, improvements or repairs, appliance repairs, and landscaping, subject to limits described below.[10]

Practical Example, Continued

Pastor Kelly has been offered a salary of $28,000 plus $12,000 more to be used for housing. If Kelly estimates that it will really cost her $13,000 to provide a home rather than $12,000, she can ask for more to be officially designated as housing allowance. The amount reported on her W-2 would be $27,000 rather than $28,000.

A long-debated question deals with how much of a minister's salary can be excluded as a housing allowance. When the constitutionality of the clergy housing benefit came under fire in 2002, Congress acted swiftly and decisively by unanimously passing the Clergy Housing Allowance Clarification Act of 2002.[11] This act states that the minister may exclude the *lesser* of

1. the amount actually used to provide a home;
2. the amount designated as a rental allowance; or
3. the annual fair rental value of the home, including furnishings, utilities, and decorator items.

These three limits are all crucial to understand. The amount actually used to provide a home is quite simply the amount one has spent during the year on housing-related items as described above. The amount designated as a rental allowance refers to the amount officially designated by the congregation in an official meeting. The annual fair rental value of the home (which should be considered fully furnished with utilities) can be determined in several ways:

Ask an unrelated expert, such as a realtor, to provide an estimate of the rental value of the fully furnished home, including utilities.

Determine the fair market value of the home, based on real estate records, and multiply this times the rate of return on investment that would be required by an unrelated landlord if he were renting out the home. In a recent tax case, the Tax Court used 13 percent.[12] For example, if the fair market value of the home is determined to be $100,000, the annual fair rental value of the home could be assumed to be $13,000 by using a required return on investment of 13 percent.

Understanding the limits when designating the housing allowance is critical, as the examples below illustrate.

Practical Example

The church designates $13,000 of Pastor Kelly's compensation as a housing allowance. During the year, Kelly spends only $11,000. The annual fair rental value of the home is determined to be $15,000. How much can Kelly actually exclude on her tax return?

Kelly can exclude just $11,000 because it is the least of the three amounts. Since the church has reduced the amount reported on Kelly's W-2 by $13,000, Kelly will need to add $2,000 of additional income on line 7 of her 1040 for the year. A description should be entered on line 7 describing this $2,000 as "excess clergy housing allowance."

Practical Example

The church designates $13,000 of Pastor Kelly's compensation as a housing allowance. During the year, Kelly spends $16,000. The annual fair rental value of the home is determined to be only $10,000. How much can Kelly actually exclude on her tax return?

Kelly can exclude just $10,000 because it is the least of the three amounts. Since the church reduced the amount it included on Kelly's W-2 by $13,000, Kelly must add $3,000 back into income on line 7 of her 1040 with a description "excess clergy housing allowance."

Practical Example

The church designates $13,000 of Pastor Kelly's compensation as a housing allowance. During the year, Kelly spends $16,000. The annual fair rental value of the home is determined to be $15,000. How much can Kelly actually exclude on her tax return?

Kelly can exclude just $13,000 because it is the least of the three amounts. Kelly does not need to make any adjustment to her tax return, since the church reduced the amount included on her W-2 by $13,000. Kelly would have been able to reduce her taxable income by $15,000, but she is limited because she did not have the church designate enough.

It is unfortunate to be in this situation and limited by the amount that has been designated. To avoid this, it is better to have the church designate too much than not enough, since adding back an amount overdesignated is simple for one's tax preparer to do at the end of the year.

Tax-Planning Tips

Meet with your tax preparer in advance of your church's annual meeting to discuss the amount of your housing allowance for the upcoming year. Your preparer can provide assistance in determining the fair rental value of your parsonage or home.

Set up a system to track all your housing-related expenses. Remember that you do not need to report these expenses to the church. Rather, provide a detailed listing of these expenses to your tax professional when your tax return is prepared for the year.

Exemption from Federal Withholding

Churches are not required to withhold federal income tax from the minister's paycheck. While this may seem like a tax break to some, there is no advantage to being exempt from federal withholding; in fact, it represents an inconvenient disadvantage to most clergy. While churches are not required to withhold federal income tax, ministers are still required to pay it, and to pay the tax as the income is earned. Being unaware of the rules surrounding the timely payment of estimated taxes is not an excuse for failing to pay.

The pastor can ask the church to withhold enough to cover both her federal income tax and her self-employed Social Security and Medicare tax. While we advise that you ask your church to withhold and remit federal taxes on your behalf, be aware that the church is not required to do so, and smaller churches may not be willing. Churches that are already withholding and remitting payroll taxes for other nonclergy employees, however, will often be happy to help the pastor in this way.

The pastor can also make estimated tax payments to the IRS on or around April 15, June 15, September 15, and January 15 of each year. Your tax professional can assist you in determining the amount of tax to pay and can provide you with the necessary forms or set you up for automatic electronic funds withdrawal from your checking or savings account. Payment by credit card is also available but should be used with caution. When making estimated tax payments, it is important to set aside part of each paycheck for taxes so that the cash is available when the payment needs to be made.

Tax-Planning Tip

Each year while preparing your taxes, your tax professional will compute an estimate of the tax that will be due for the coming year. She will provide you with the amount to pay, the date the payment is due, and the forms necessary for paying the tax. Many preparers will even send you a reminder note before each payment is due. Be sure to inform your preparer of any major changes to your tax situation, such as a possible move, the purchase of a new house, a baby on the way, or a child heading off to college.

PART TWO: COMPENSATION PLANNING—
DISARMING THE POWER OF MONEY BY
DISCUSSING COMPENSATION

Money, particularly compensation, determines the value that others place on what we do, and often how much we are paid for what we do also determines our self-worth. What is true for the general population is true for clergy as well; the amount of pay the minister receives is a measure of the value placed on his work by the congregation and often also determines his self-worth.

Yet over the last fifty years, clergy, particularly those serving in mainline churches, have lost significant ground in terms of salary. James Hudnut-Beumler writes:

> In the early 1960s the fully-appointed Methodist minister made—by himself—something just over the median household income for a family of four in the US. Thus, as a sole breadwinner, the Methodist pastor could reasonably expect that his family could be solidly middle-class. But by the mid-1980s and continuing down to our time, a fully appointed United Methodist minister could expect to make only about half of median family income in the United States.[13]

In fact, some maintain that clergy are having a difficult time "retaining a place in the professional middle class."[14] It would seem reasonable to expect that a middle-class church would provide a level of compensation to its minister that would support a middle-class way of life, but in fact, many clergy have fallen behind. Becky McMillan and Matthew Price observe that "the main source of stress for clergy around salary is not so much from a lack of material possessions, but rather from the inability to maintain a lifestyle consistent with middle-class expectations and expenditures."[15]

To make matters worse, many newly ordained clergy are entering the profession with high levels of student debt. A recent study by Auburn Theological Seminary finds a marked increase in both the number of seminary students who graduate with debt and the amounts of debt carried. In 2001, more than 33 percent of seminary graduates reported borrowing $20,000 or more, up from 7 percent just ten years earlier; 21 percent reported borrowing $30,000 or more, up from 1 percent in 1991.[16] While these levels are low when compared to the debt load associated with law school, medical school, or graduate business school, the debt becomes a significant issue when combined with the low starting salaries and future earning potential for seminary graduates. The report concludes:

Many theological school graduates report that their level of debt is affecting their career choices, holding them back from purchasing homes, preventing them from saving for their children's education, limiting their retirement savings, causing them to delay health care needs, and creating stress in their personal and professional lives.[17]

As clergy compensation falls behind and seminary expenses rise, one thing remains as it always has been: the power of money is evident in the way in which compensation determines one's value and self-worth. Most of us are at our worst when we compare our compensation to others. Clergy struggling to maintain a standard of living equitable to those in their congregations can become envious of their parishioners. The pastor serving a rural congregation feels the injustice of receiving significantly less pay than her counterpart who is serving a suburban parish. As Bishop Kenneth Carder has observed:

> Morale among clergy seems to be tied very closely to compensation. Being appointed to a church with a higher salary is interpreted as an affirmation while moving on the same salary level or with less salary is seen as a "demotion." Comparison with colleagues' salaries is almost universal and where one ranks with peers in salary affects that clergy's self-image and confidence.[18]

One way to disarm the power of money, along with the envy and anger that compensation issues can create, is by entering into a frank and open discussion of compensation with church leaders. This conversation should take place before the minister accepts a call from or is appointed to serve a specific church. It should also occur annually in conjunction with the minister's performance evaluation. These dialogues should carefully consider both salary and benefits with a goal of structuring the package in a way that is most advantageous to the minister.

Educational Debt

If you are one of the many new clergy who have begun ministry with student loan debt, consider asking your church for help. The Auburn study provides an estimate of the level of annual income needed to service educational loans by using a common rule of thumb: no more than 8 percent of income should be committed to the repayment of student loans. Using this rule, if your monthly student loan payment is $250, you should be earning $37,500 per year.[19] To compute your required annual salary, multiply your expected monthly loan payment by twelve to annualize the number. Divide the total by 8 percent for your required annual salary.

Practical Example

Pastor Jennifer graduates from seminary with substantial student loan debt that will carry an expected monthly payment of $275. She is considering a call to a church that will pay her $30,000 per year, plus a parsonage.

1. How much salary does Jennifer need to earn to service her student loan debt by using the rule of thumb discussed above? Jennifer needs to earn $41,250. Jennifer's estimated annual loan payment will be $3,300 ($275 times twelve months). That annual figure of $3,300 divided by 8 percent (the rule of thumb) is $41,250.
2. How much of the $30,000 proposed salary will be absorbed by Jennifer's student loan debt? Jennifer will be paying about 11 percent of her $30,000 salary to cover her student loan debt ($3,300 divided by $30,000).
3. Does the parsonage help at all? No. Student loan debt must be paid in cash, so the parsonage is of no help.
4. What should Jennifer do? Ask the church for help!

Jennifer should ask the church to consider funding part of her student loan debt. The Auburn study suggests this:

> One proven way of reducing the burden of student loans is to promote better negotiation of compensation packages. Many churches have been willing to increase the candidate's salary package in considera-tion of the candidate's educational loan repayment. Sometimes the opportunity arises only once, when the candidate is first hired and the salary, housing and other terms of employment are being settled. In other cases, the issue can be raised as part of annual budgeting.[20]

Negotiating an Amount

How much should the clergyperson ask for? First of all, it is important to remember that the church is the beneficiary of your education. It will not, however, be the only church to benefit from it, so it may be excessive to ask your church to cover your entire student loan payment. We believe that it is entirely appropriate to ask the church to cover the difference between the level of student loan debt that the current salary would support and your actual stu-dent loan debt.

Practical Example, Continued

Pastor Jennifer has been offered a salary of $30,000. Using the 8 percent rule of thumb, that salary is enough to service a student loan payment of $200 per month ($30,000 times 8 percent is $2,400, or $200 per month). Jennifer will be paying $275 per month for her student loans. Jennifer should ask the church to increase her salary by $75 per month to cover this difference. Better yet, she should ask for $100 per month, since these payments will be fully taxable to her as additional compensation. This will amount to a $1,200 increase in compensation for Jennifer.

In asking for this increase, the minister should honestly share the details of his student loan obligations with the compensation committee. He should gently educate the board about the 8 percent rule of thumb and point out that the compensation the church has offered does not provide adequate funds for him to make his student loan payments. He should point out that the church is a direct beneficiary of his years of hard work and educational debt. He is asking the church to help him begin repayment of these loans (which normally take ten years to repay fully). By doing so, the church is participating in his seminary education, which likely fits well with the church's mission.

Again, any additional amount approved by the church to help the pastor with an educational loan repayment is additional compensation, fully subject to both income tax and Social Security and Medicare tax. These amounts are not tax-advantaged in any way but are simply an approach to obtaining more equitable compensation.

Strategic Use of Housing

The basics of clergy housing have been described in depth in part 1 of this chapter, with a focus on the tax ramifications of the allowance. Here we would like to reiterate the important strategic aspects of clergy housing rules.

It is almost always better to own your own home than to live in a church-owned residence. By owning her own home, the pastor can (1) build up equity in the house, which can be realized upon sale of the home, and (2) deduct home mortgage interest and real estate taxes on her tax return, which provides the unique tax advantage of taking a deduction for something never included in income.

For some, having a parsonage is a true gift. Our first appointment was to a wealthy suburb of a large city. Having just finished school, we had no cash available for a down payment on a home. Three years after moving there, we were on our way to the next appointment. In this situation, a parsonage provided an ideal solution. We would have been unable to purchase a home in this affluent area even if we had had a down payment, and selling a home within three years would likely have created a loss, rather than equity for us.

For other clergy, however, a parsonage feels like a death sentence. The home is too small for the family, too close to the church, too open to parishioners who (rightly) feel that they own the parsonage, too old, and too in need of major repairs. Some pastors find themselves in a situation where their personal financial condition would permit the purchase of a home, but the church owns a parsonage. These pastors feel keenly that the opportunity to be building equity in a home is slipping away, and they worry about where they will live when they retire.

Homeownership is the largest investment that most Americans make. Most experts agree that buying a home is generally a wise investment, barring economic downturn. When the church owns the home, the church is making the investment and building up the equity. Churches that provide parsonages generally pay lower salaries to their ministers, so it could be said that the church is financing its real estate investment by paying the minister less. Since real estate investment is not part of the mission of most churches, one could argue that this arrangement is completely wrong.

Nationwide, the use of parsonages is declining and the trend is toward clergy owning their own homes, with one study indicating that only 32 percent of pastors live in a parsonage. [21] If it makes financial sense for you to purchase a home but the church owns a parsonage, consider discussing the matter with the church. As a solution, some churches choose to rent the parsonage and use the cash received from renting to provide a housing allowance to the pastor. This presents tax issues for the church, since the church must report and pay tax on the net rental income.

Other churches choose to sell the parsonage and place the proceeds from the sale in an investment account. The income earned on the proceeds can go toward providing a housing allowance to the pastor. With both of these approaches, the cost to the church of providing a housing allowance should be offset, at least partially, by income generated from the existing parsonage.

If it makes no financial sense for you to purchase a home and you are living in the parsonage, there is one final consideration. Since the church is building up the equity if it owns the parsonage, some argue that the church should pay an equity allowance to the clergyperson to replace this lost equity. This type of arrangement costs the church additional money and results in additional taxable income to the pastor, unless placed in a tax-exempt retirement plan. According to tax attorney J. David Epstein, if a tax-exempt retirement plan is used, "the money builds up tax free, and is available to the minister on retirement to buy a home, or for any other purpose, and is taxable when the money is taken out at retirement."[22]

A final strategic consideration in the area of housing is the amount of allowance to designate. As noted in the tax section of this chapter, it is better to have the church designate too much to cover housing than to designate too little. Designating too much merely means that the excess must be added back into income when preparing the tax return. Designating too little will result in income tax being paid unnecessarily.

Health Insurance and Medical Reimbursement Plans

The rising cost of health care is a major challenge of our time. While medical insurance is a key benefit provided by most major denominations in the United States today, many denominations are struggling to determine solutions that will allow for equitable and just, yet affordable coverage. If you are serving a church that does not provide health insurance coverage, you should ask your church to consider providing this benefit. We believe that health insurance premiums for the minister and her family, while costly, should be paid by the church.

Even with health insurance many medical expenses, such as deductibles, copays, and premiums, are frequently paid by the insured. There are various tax-advantaged plans that allow the taxpayer to pay for these types of expenses with before-tax rather than after-tax dollars. Since these are widely used plans that are not unique to clergy, most competent tax professionals or financial planners can provide advice on using them.

The following plans should cost the church little or no additional cash, since they allow funding by salary reduction. Both of these plans are use-or-lose plans, so any amount unspent at the end of the year is lost.

> *Cafeteria plans (Section 125 plans):* These plans allow an employee to reduce her taxable salary and use the amount of the reduction to pay for a variety of benefits, among them medical and dental expenses and dependant care expenses. These plans may not discriminate in favor of highly compensated employees. Normally these types of plans are maintained by larger organizations due to their complexity and cost. The pastor should check with her denomination, since some denominations provide cafeteria plans.
>
> *Flexible spending accounts (FSAs):* These are like cafeteria plans but only allow funding of medical and dental expenses with pre-tax dollars. FSAs require a written plan and have nondiscrimination rules.[23]

Practical Example

Pastor Karen has a salary of $20,000 and a housing allowance of $15,000. She knows that her medical and dental expenses for the coming year will be high, since her son will be getting braces. Her denomination offers an FSA, so

Karen elects to reduce her salary for the year by $3,000. Throughout the year, Karen submits her medical and dental bills to the denomination and is reimbursed. At the end of the year, Karen's W-2 shows $17,000 of taxable wages. Karen has submitted medical and dental bills to the plan of $2,700. Karen will lose the remaining $300.[24]

The following plans may not be funded by salary reduction. Since this is the case, the church must fund these plans for the pastor. An advantage of these plans is that they are not use-or-lose plans, which means that the amount unused at the end of a year may be carried over to the next year.

> *Health savings accounts (HSAs)* were created by Congress in 2003 and are designed to help certain individuals save on a tax-free basis for medical expenses. They are only available to those with a high-deductible health plan (HDHP). [25] Usually such a plan offers a lower premium in exchange for a higher deductible. The HSA is owned by the individual, can be administered by a bank, credit union, insurance company, or other financial company, and stays in place regardless of where the individual is employed. Contributions can be made tax free to the plan by either the individual or the employer, so contributions made by the church on behalf of the minister are not considered compensation. The income earned on the funds is not taxable, and the amounts withdrawn to pay for medical expenses are not taxable.
>
> *Health reimbursement arrangements (HRAs)* are funded by the employer to cover the medical expenses of the employee. A formal plan must be created by the church, and the plan cannot discriminate against any employees of the church. The amounts paid into the plan on behalf of the minister are not considered compensation, and the balance in the account at the end of a year can be carried over to the next year.

Practical Example

Pastor Karen has a salary of $20,000 and a housing allowance of $15,000. She knows that her family's medical and dental expenses for the coming year will be high, since her son will be getting braces. Her denominational medical insurance plan is considered an HDHP, so Karen decides to contribute $2,000 personally to an HSA plan that she has set up at her bank. Additionally, her church agrees to contribute $1,000 to Karen's HSA account. Karen is the church's only employee. Throughout the year, Karen is reimbursed for her uncovered medical and dental expenses out of this account. At the end of the year, Karen's W-2 shows $20,000 of taxable wages. On her 1040, Karen will make an adjustment to her income on line 25 for $2,000, which will reduce her federal and state taxable income (but not earnings subject to Social Security and Medicare tax). Throughout the year, Karen has submitted medical and dental bills to the plan of $2,700. The remaining $300 will be available to Karen the following year.

Retirement Contributions

Nearly all financial advisors will give you the same advice about planning for retirement: start contributing to a retirement fund early, contribute consistently, and contribute as much as you are able. In studying those who have successfully planned for retirement and those who have not, researchers have found that the key difference lies not in how much you know about financial planning or even in how much you earn. "What matters instead is how you handle the all-too-human inclination to undersave and procrastinate."[26] Starting early is vital because of compound interest, by which the interest earned on the original contribution is added to the contribution, so interest is continuously earned on interest.

Practical Example

Pastor Mark began contributing to an IRA at the age of 13 with money that he earned on his paper route. He contributed $1,500 to the IRA each year for five years until he graduated from high school. From that point on Mark never saved another dime, since everything he earned went toward paying for college and seminary. By the time Mark reached the age of 65, those five contributions of $1,500 each had grown to over $382,000 (at a rate of return of 8 percent). However, if Mark had waited until age 30 to begin saving and had put away $1,500 each year through age 35, these contributions would have grown to only $103,285.

Beginning to save early for retirement is crucial. But many pastors just entering the ministry feel unable to reduce the cash in their paycheck by even a small amount. While it is sometimes difficult to do, it is a very wise short- and long-term strategy that can provide tax savings today and security at retirement.

Many major denominations have a formal retirement plan in place to cover clergy. Experts generally agree that these plans offer the best vehicle for clergy retirement savings. Frequently, denominations or churches provide a 403(b) plan, or tax-sheltered annuity plan (TSA). TSAs are commonly funded by salary reduction, so rather than taking all the pay now, the minister chooses to defer a portion (within limits) of the pay until retirement (elective deferral). Additional amounts (within limits) can be contributed by the church to the TSA.

Within the annual limits, both elective deferral amounts and additional contributions made by the church are excluded from income for income tax purposes and are not subject to Social Security and Medicare tax. This means that the minister will save money currently in taxes by contributing to a retirement plan, since the contribution lowers taxable income. Long-term, contributions to a TSA now will grow tax free throughout the years to provide funds needed at retirement. When funds are withdrawn in retirement, they are not subject to Social Security and Medicare tax. Additionally, denominational plans can designate distributions from the plan paid to retired clergy as housing allowance (subject to the rules surrounding the housing allowance described earlier), which can make a portion of the distributions free from income tax as well.

If you have not enrolled in your church's 403(b) plan, stop procrastinating and do so now. Even a small contribution will save you money on taxes today and will make a major difference later on when you are ready to retire. If your church or denominational plan matches your contribution, your failure to contribute carries an additional cost, since you can never recover the lost matching contribution. For instance, let's assume that your church or denomination matches 50 percent of any contribution you make up to 6 percent of your salary. With a salary of $30,000, the church would make a matching contribution of $900 on your contribution of $1,800. By failing to contribute $1,800, you would forfeit forever the $900 match that the church or denomination would have made on your behalf. Additionally, since the $1,800 contribution would reduce your taxable income, you would pay more in income and Social Security and Medicare taxes. And most importantly, that single $1,800 contribution and the $900 match would grow to over $27,000 (assuming an 8 percent annual return) in thirty years. Each year that you fail to contribute, you lose these future retirement benefits.

If your personal budget is particularly tight, consider beginning your contributions when you receive a raise and contributing all or part of your raise to the 403(b). This can make the contribution painless. Since elective deferrals are taken out of your wages before they are paid to you, you will never miss them! Begin thinking about retirement now. A recent study shows that "respondents who report they planned for retirement enter their golden years with higher wealth levels"[27] than those who report that they did not plan. Take advantage of the resources available from your denomination to learn about planning for retirement.

Church-Related Expense Reimbursement

When negotiating a compensation package, many churches discuss the reimbursement of expenses in tandem with clergy compensation. The church often views this as reimbursement of the *pastor's* expenses, and as such, additional compensation (or a benefit) to the clergy. In fact, this is reimbursement to the clergy of amounts that are the *church's* expenses. We believe that this is an important distinction. If the minister is driving to the hospital to visit parishioners who are ill, this is an expense of the church. If the pastor attends a denominational meeting, this is an expense of the church.

This area can be muddied by the fact that some church-related expenses do appear to benefit the clergyperson individually. If a pastor attends a workshop to supplement her preparation for a study she is teaching, she will gain knowledge that she will take with her when she leaves the church. If she has lunch with the head of the administrative board to discuss an upcoming meeting, she benefits personally from the meal. Yet these are church-related expenses, since it is in the church's best interest to have a well-prepared minister and a board that is ready to conduct business.

Personal expenses should be paid for personally by the clergyperson out of the compensation paid to her by the church along with any other income earned by her household. However, church-related expenses should not be paid for by the clergy. They are church expenses and are in no way related to the clergy or to her compensation. So while we have included our discussion of the reimbursement of business expenses in the section on structuring compensation, we firmly believe that *church-related expenses should have nothing to do with your compensation!*

When a clergyperson is discussing the compensation package with the appropriate board or committee, it is important for him to help them see this distinction. We believe that it is correct for a church to pay for *all* the church-related expenses incurred by the minister and that this should not be related to the minister's pay in any way. The reality is, however, that most churches are not willing or able to have an unlimited amount available to the clergyperson for reimbursement of church-related expenses. Most will approve a capped amount that may or may not be enough cover all of the church expenses incurred by the clergyperson.

The IRS rules governing the reimbursement of the minister's church-related expenses are the same rules that apply to every other employee. These rules are not unique to clergy. This generally is helpful in discussions with a church board, since many of the board members receive reimbursement from their employers for their business-related expenses and therefore are familiar with the rules.

The IRS defines business expenses as "ordinary and necessary" expenses for your job: "An ordinary expense is one that is common and accepted in your field of trade, business, or profession. A necessary expense is one that is help-ful and appropriate for your business. An expense does not have to be required to be considered necessary."[28] The IRS has very precise rules governing the reimbursement of ordinary and necessary employee business expenses. If a business or a church reimburses an employee in the wrong way, the amount reimbursed to that employee will be considered as additional compensation on which the employee must pay tax.

There are no tax consequences if the reimbursement is done through an established accountable reimbursement plan. An accountable reimbursement plan is one in which

> the expenses have a church connection,
>
> the pastor adequately accounts to the church,
>
> any excess reimbursement is returned to the church within 120 days of reim-bursement, and
>
> the reimbursement comes out of the church's funds and doesn't come from funds that reduce the minister's compensation.[29]

The following examples would not be considered accountable plans and would result in additional compensation to the pastor for any amounts reim-bursed:

> The church gives the pastor a separate check each month for $100 to cover travel and expenses. No accounting is required to the church of how the money is spent.
>
> The church gives the pastor a separate check each month for $100 to cover travel and expenses. She must turn in receipts for all amounts spent but is allowed to keep any amounts not spent.
>
> The church pays the pastor $30,000 per year. This year at the pastor's request, the church reduces the pastor's pay to $28,000 and sets the remaining $2,000 in an account to be used to reimburse his expenses. The church requires him to turn in receipts for all amounts spent. By the end of the year, he has submitted receipts and received reimbursement for $1,500. The church decides to pay him the remaining $500 as a gesture of goodwill.

The church should draft a written policy as to what expenses will be reim-bursed, how reimbursement will be made, and what is considered adequate documentation. In his excellent book *Church and Nonprofit Tax and Financial Guide*, Dan Busby provides samples of these types of policies. In addition, your denominational headquarters likely can supply you with a sample policy.

Churches that are unwilling to reimburse their pastor's church-related expenses are shifting the payment of church expenses over to the pastor. They are expecting the pastor to pay church expenses out of her compensation. When a church does this, it results in an unrealistic picture of how much it costs to operate the programs of the church. In chapters 5 and 6, we stressed the importance of financial reports that accurately reflect the true condition of the church. If many of the church-related expenses are underwritten by the pastor, the true financial condition of the church cannot be known.

If your church is unwilling to reimburse your church-related expenses, you may still be able to deduct these expenses on your individual income tax return. However, it is much more advantageous for tax purposes to be reimbursed for these expenses. Like all other employees, the pastor can only deduct unreimbursed business expenses if she itemizes her deductions, which most parsonage-dwelling clergy cannot do. Additionally, the amount of the deduction is reduced by 2 percent of adjusted gross income. Clergy face another reduction on the amount they can deduct: business expenses are prorated between taxable income and tax-free (parsonage allowance) income; only the portion of business expenses allocable to taxable income is deductible. Your tax professional will be able to assist you in handling any unreimbursed church-related expenses on your tax return.

In conclusion, ministers generally are not highly compensated; therefore, it is crucial to thoughtfully plan salary and benefits. Good stewardship requires putting the church's limited resources to the wisest use, and this often requires knowledge of the applicable laws and regulations. In frank, transparent discussions between pastor and lay leaders, the goal of structuring compensation in ways that maximize the benefit to the pastor should be foremost. When this is done, the pastor can rest in the fact that, while the compensation may not be much, it is configured in the best possible way, and the power of money can therefore be diminished.

PART THREE: PERSONAL SPENDING—DISARMING THE POWER OF MONEY BY SETTING LIMITS BEFORE YOU SPEND

Money has power in our lives when we spend what we do not have on things that we do not need. Many of us buy on impulse and at the end of the month have difficulty remembering where it all went. As a recent study entitled "The Absent-Minded Consumer" observed, "Many of us are profoundly ignorant about how much we spend, and on what we spend it."[30] And when we pay little attention to where the money goes, we tend to spend more. One reason we may choose to live in darkness when it comes to our personal spending habits is because ignorance provides a distance from the harsh reality of what might be uncomfortable to admit. Budgeting flips a light on in our personal financial lives and provides a way to disarm money's power.

Literally hundreds of books have been published on the topics of personal budgeting and personal financial planning. There are also some excellent resources available on the Internet, including free programs to help you set up and maintain a budget. Developing a personal budget can be as simple or as complex as you want it to be. We believe that a simple approach is best, because the more simple the plan, the more likely you are to stick with it. As one author on the subject noted, "Budgets are like diets: easy to start and even easier to quit."[31]

Most of us come at budgeting by examining our monthly expenses, dividing them into lots of different categories, and then comparing that with our income. With any luck, our monthly income is greater than our total average monthly expenses. We then diligently attempt to track our expenses, dividing our receipts into how much we spent on groceries versus how much on health and beauty products. After a month or two of this, we call it quits!

The problem with this approach is twofold. First, it is too detailed and cumbersome for many of us to want to continue for very long. We get lost in the details and lose sight of the big picture. Second, it focuses on expenses rather than on income without ever questioning the legitimacy of our spending habits. It simply records the details of what is already happening in our financial lives. To continue the diet analogy, Richard Jenkins observes, "The real secret to building a budget that really works isn't tracking what you spend, any more than counting calories is the secret to losing weight."[32]

The secret to a workable budget is to begin with income, asking the question, "How much of our income should be committed each month to covering our expenses?" This challenges us to think about the big picture rather than the details. It forces us to grapple with how much of our income should be set aside for retirement or saved for a major purchase rather than just hoping that something will be left over to put into savings after we pay all the bills.

So how much of our income should be allocated to spending? Several years ago, an article on budgeting by Richard Jenkins appeared on the MSN Money Web site entitled "A Simpler Way to Save: The 60% Solution." Because of its simplicity, this method has developed a cultlike following and has even been incorporated into Microsoft Money. The model recommends that just 60 percent of one's gross income be committed to monthly spending while the remaining 40 percent should be allocated to savings and discretionary spending. While the percent varies, all financial planners agree that monthly spending needs to be contained to less than 100 percent of income! The approach works like this: The pastor and her spouse realize that they have been living paycheck-to-paycheck and have contributed virtually nothing to savings or retirement. While cutting their expenses to 60 percent seems impossible to them since their student loan repayment obligation is still high, they agree to try to cut their committed expenses down to 70 percent of their gross salary from its current level of nearly 100 percent. By reducing their committed spending (for things like charitable contributions, taxes, car payments, groceries, and utilities) to 70 percent, they will be able to send 10 percent of their gross income to the church-sponsored 403(b) plan, 10 percent to an emergency fund, 5 percent to saving for a new car, and still have 5 percent for discretionary monthly spending.

The brilliance of this approach is its simplicity. There is no real need to track the details of monthly spending, as long as it falls below the amount you have designated for that purpose. It takes savings off the top, rather than leaving it to whatever might be left after all the bills have been paid. Best of all, it requires the clergyperson to live within his means and do the hard work of reducing committed spending to where it should be.

Committed Expenses and Discretionary Expenses: What's the Difference?

Much of the spending we do daily is discretionary: we can buy a latte on the way to work, or not. Committed expenses, on the other hand, are expenses that are not negotiable, since we have no choice in the short-term as to whether or not to pay for them. They include taxes (which either the church withholds for the pastor or the pastor pays in estimated quarterly installments), charitable contributions, rent or mortgage, car payments, student loan repayments, insurance, groceries, utilities, and other basic bills. The key to living within our means is to get committed expenses under control.

While we do not have a choice in the short-term about paying for a committed expense, we may have a long-term choice as to continuing it. An example of a committed expense that we can choose to eliminate if necessary would be health club dues or a premium cable TV package; we may be committed to paying for these monthly, but they can be eliminated if our committed expenses are too high. A good place to start in getting committed expenses under control is to eliminate or reduce spending on things to which we are obligated but could probably live without.

Some committed expenses are easy to eliminate, while others are much more difficult. If you find that your committed spending still exceeds your goal after eliminating the items you can live without, you may need to face some hard realities. Your house or car may be more than you can afford, your lifestyle may be more lavish than your income allows, or your impulse buying may result in steep monthly credit card payments. These types of issues could indicate an underlying problem that money will never satisfy.

The Other 40 Percent

With only approximately 60 percent of our income allocated to these committed fixed expenses, 40 percent of gross income is available for the following, at
approximately 10 percent of gross income for each:

Discretionary monthly expenses: This money is to be used for all discretionary
  expenses during the month, such as that latte on the way to work, treat-
  ing the family to a nice dinner out, going to the movies, or taking the kids
  on an outing.

Retirement savings: These are the contributions to the 403(b) plan described
  earlier in the chapter. As mentioned earlier, these contributions can be
  made automatically, so they are never even a part of the paycheck.

Emergency fund: Most financial advisors recommend keeping three to six
  months of average expenses in an emergency fund that, while separate from
  the checking account, can be quickly and easily accessed. This provides a
  cash safety net if you become ill or lose your job. If you do not have disabil-
  ity insurance, you may need to keep even more in this type of fund.

Short-term savings: It is a good idea to set aside money each month to save for
  expenses that are expected or planned but irregular, such as a summer vacation, Christmas shopping, or a new car purchase. The idea here is not to
  save long-term but to have cash when you need it for unusual expenditures.

Practical Example

Pastor Rich earns $2,000 per month in gross salary and housing allowance.
Sue, his wife, earns a gross salary of $3,000 per month in her teaching posi-
tion. Since the arrival of Abby, their first child, ten months ago, Rich and Sue
seem never to have enough cash to pay all their bills. They live in the church
parsonage and the church pays all utilities, but still there is never enough. Rich
and Sue are currently contributing nothing to their employer-sponsored
retirement plans because they can't seem to spare the money. They also have
nothing in savings and wonder what would happen if one of them became
unable to work. Their credit card carries a substantial balance from a trip they
took before Abby's arrival and from the cost of decorating a nursery. Their
combined student loan payments are substantial, as are their car payments on
a new van and a new sedan.

Rich and Sue decide to try to restrict their committed expenses to 60 percent of their gross pay. They set up their budget beginning with income (see
chart 9.1).

Next they look at savings. They agree that it is important for them to begin

Chart 9.1

Monthly Budget for Rich and Sue

Income	
Gross wages—Rich	$2,000
Gross wages—Sue	3,000
Total gross wages	5,000
Savings	
Retirement—Rich: 10 percent of his income	200
Retirement—Sue: 10 percent of her income	300
Emergency fund—10 percent of total gross wages	500
Short-term savings—10 percent of total gross wages	500
Spending	
Discretionary—10 percent of total gross wages	500
Cash available to cover committed expenses	3,000
Committed spending—60 percent	
Contributions	500
Taxes (these include amounts withheld from both Rich and Sue's paychecks for federal and state income taxes, Social Security, and Medicare)	800
Student loan payments	150
Day care	400
Monthly minimum credit card payments	100
Car payments, auto insurance, gas	840
Groceries	600
Cell phone, cable, Internet	75
Health club dues	50
Medical and dental	20
Total committed spending	3,535
Committed spending in excess of cash available	$(535)

contributing to their employer-sponsored retirement plans and to create an emergency fund. They also would like to start setting aside money for a summer vacation. They agree on 10 percent of their gross wages to be set aside for each of these purposes and want to have an additional 10 percent each month to cover their discretionary expenses. This leaves them with $3,000 to cover their committed expenses.

Rich and Sue then turn their attention to their committed monthly expenses. To their regret, they discover that they are overcommitted, spending over $500 per month more than their goal.

Since Rich and Sue are carrying a significant balance on their credit card, they should first pay off that balance before beginning to put money into an emergency fund or short-term savings. The interest rate on their credit card far exceeds any interest they would earn in a savings account. Once the credit card is paid off, they can begin putting money away.

Rich and Sue must next look at ways to reduce their committed monthly spending. Sue agrees to give up the health club, since she almost never finds time to go anymore and plans instead to walk each evening with Abby. They both agree that their spending on groceries can be reduced, since they tend to purchase a great deal of convenience food. Many of their expenses cannot be reduced, however. It becomes clear to them both that they are living beyond their means, especially with the vehicles that they have chosen. They agree to consider the possibility of selling the sedan and becoming a one-car family.

In conclusion, the real challenge with any type of budgeting plan is not tracking spending but learning to live within one's means. Having a budgeting plan that is simple to use can disarm the power of money by setting clear limits before we spend.

PART FOUR: PERSONAL GIVING—DISARMING THE POWER OF MONEY BY GIVING IT AWAY

The primary way in which an individual gains freedom from the power of money is by giving some of it away. Ordination does not change this. Being undercompensated for sixty-hour workweeks does not change this. Helping others learn how to be better givers does not change this. Money's power is not based upon how much or little one has. The monetization of value is a constant in our culture. Thus, clergy must learn the spiritual discipline of "cheerful giving" (2 Cor. 9:7) if they are to consistently help others do the same. Furthermore, in this culture it appears that the one unforgivable sin is hypocrisy. How can a pastor really call upon others to give when she herself does not?

We believe that the New Testament does not have a rule for tithing. One cannot require a tithe from one's self or from others. However, insofar as Christian ministry (ordained and lay alike) is a participation in the loving self-offering of the triune God, how can any Christian not be committed to giving? This is especially true for those who carry the burden of leadership. Clergy, like all other Christians, hold the treasure of the gospel "in clay jars" (2 Cor. 4:7). The giving of clergy is always an imperfect representation of the generosity of God, yet that is the God to which clergy are called to bear witness. We believe that increased freedom in the giving of the ordained plays a key role in helping laity find their own freedom for increased giving.

CONCLUSION

We have examined four areas in the life of the minister where money, if left unchallenged, can exert control: paying taxes, structuring the compensation package, personal spending, and personal giving. Our hope is that this discussion will serve as a good starting place to help disarm the power of money in the personal life of clergy.

DISCUSSION QUESTIONS

1. What resources does your denomination have to help clergy plan for retirement? If you are currently serving a church, are you participating fully in the retirement plan? If you are a student, do you plan to participate fully?
2. Prepare a personal budget using the 60 percent formula. Are you currently limiting your committed monthly expenses to 60 percent of your gross income? If not, what committed monthly expenses could you eliminate or reduce?
3. Prepare a money autobiography. A money autobiography is an attempt to narrate the role that money has played in a person's development from early childhood forward. Dan R. Dick of the Center for Christian Stewardship for the United Methodist Church offers an excellent example at http://www.gbod.org/stewardship/article.asp?id=11618. What did you find most surprising about the role money has played/is playing in your life?

RECOMMENDED FOR FURTHER READING

The following are published annually:
Busby, Dan. *Zondervan Minister's Tax and Financial Guide* (Grand Rapids: Zondervan)
Hammar, Richard R. *Church and Clergy Tax Guide* (Carol Stream, IL: Christianity Today International)
Worth, B. J. *Worth's Income Tax Guide for Ministers* (Nappanee, IN: Evangel Publishing House)

10

Experiencing Freedom
through Giving

Let us be very clear on two matters. First, almost all churches are dependent upon voluntary giving in order to fulfill their mission. And second, many churches do a very poor job of faithfully raising that money. We learned the level of that dependence the hard way when Sunday morning services were canceled due to weather one wintry Sunday morning. It took the better part of six weeks to get back on track due to the loss of one week's receipts. It was quite a surprise to realize that if people do not come to worship one week, they feel little obligation to make up their giving the next week. Some members certainly gave for the lost week, but not everyone. Not all church members are motivated by a sense of obligation to the local church.

THE REASONS PEOPLE GIVE

In *Money Matters: Personal Giving in American Churches*, Dean R. Hoge, Charles Zech, Patrick McNamara, and Michael J. Donahue have recognized four principal motivations for giving: "reciprocity with God; reciprocity with the religious group; giving to extensions of the self; and altruism and thankfulness." They continue: "Reciprocity is important because it is a primary motivation for financial gift giving in the United States."[1] Some churches directly teach this. God gives, and we must give in return. And then God will give some more. In this way, God seems to be bound by human giving. This is the primary principle that underlies the prosperity gospel. It is our belief that such thinking is both biblically and theologically untenable. It is theologically problematic insofar as such thinking radically changes the relationship between God and humanity. One could say that it eliminates the relationship altogether. What remains in such a construal is an automatic reflex with much more in common with magic than classical Christian faith. The favorite passage is Malachi 3:8–10. Hoge and his coauthors found few mainline Protestant churches that directly taught this motivating factor. However, they offer examples wherein church members believed that reciprocity with God is a possibility even when there is a strong pulpit ministry which denies that:

> Later we took part in a discussion in a Sunday school class. . . . The teacher put forth a rhetorical question: "What do we get when we give?" One man, who attended the class regularly, said, "We get a check mark." He meant in the Book of Life. "And someday we'll be held accountable for our lives, and we will need as many good marks at that time as we can get." He was not joking. He was totally serious, and the other class members nodded in agreement.[2]

In other words, the message of salvation by grace alone, implying the impossibility of reciprocity with God, is often forgotten when the offering plate is being passed.

Even though the motivating force of reciprocity with God may be prevalent among far too many Christians, it would still be rejected in principle by the vast majority. One cannot say the same for the second type of motivation: reciprocity with the religious group. Here the primary motivating force is the church's recognition for gifts. This is of course a bedrock principle for secular fund-raising. People give with the intention and understanding that the gift will be made public (and, in the case of large gifts, usually with tremendous fanfare). For the most part, most regular and/or pledged giving is not publically recognized within congregations.

In many if not most churches, the pastor does not know how much individual members give. We believe that one can faithfully argue the wisdom of pastors either knowing or not knowing. A lack of knowledge can spare pastors from either favoring the best givers or appearing to favor them. It may also help to dampen the reciprocity motivation. However, we believe that one can also (in spite of the dangers of its abuse) argue for pastoral knowledge of individual giving.

Giving is a (and probably *the*) primary indicator of a person's relationship with money. As we have argued throughout, money is a spiritual and theological issue. One can argue that pastors need to know how much a person gives for diagnostic reasons. If they do know, they should treat such information with great discretion and confidentiality, never sharing it with others. Once again, the power of money must never be underestimated.

However, Hoge and his coauthors note that when it comes to capital or other large gifts, recognition is much more frequently practiced. Many churches have memorial plaques on all types of church furniture, rooms, and so forth. The authors state:

> People with ambivalent feelings about peer reciprocity may make distinctions about when it is or is not defensible. Several denominational leaders with whom we discussed this issue distinguished between a capital campaign for a new church building, and annual stewardship appeals. They thought that peer recognition for large gifts for a new church building is theologically legitimate, whereas in annual stewardship campaigns it is not.[3]

We fail to understand the "theological" distinction between the two. Certainly there exists a cultural difference: it is the common practice by many congregations to recognize publicly large gifts for capital project or special appeals, whereas it is not common practice to announce the weekly contributions by individual name. Our suspicion is that the former became common practice because it is a significant motivator for giving. We will argue below that theologically, there is always a problem with lifting up the contributions of individuals over against the community. It is easy to turn a project that has the capacity to unite people into a competition that only further divides them.

Many pastors have not been very reflective at this point. Hoge and his coauthors cite a conversation with one pastor regarding the use of memorial plaques. The pastor begins:

> "You'll find no plaques here. We will do a memorial book, listing the gifts. But to have plaques really does generate the wrong motivations and reward the wrong motivations for stewardship. It does indeed pander to the wrong reason for giving—for recognition, not for generosity. Well, if we have a dedication service, we will say in the program who gave this thing or that thing. But never the amounts."
> [The authors say,] "So you are not totally against recognition, but you want to keep it subtle."
> [The pastor replies,] "Exactly. We want to keep it in line. I understand that all giving is done with mixed motivation. But you don't pander to the wrong motivation. You pander to the right one."[4]

We too recognize the difficult situations in which pastors frequently find themselves when receiving large monetary gifts. Still, it is our hope that pastors do not *pander* to any motivation.

The third type of motivating factor is giving as an extension of oneself. Many church members give because they sense the importance of the church to themselves. Some give to churches because it is what their family has "always done." Others give because they have gained a major part of their identity through such an affiliation. Hoge and his coauthors state:

> The point here is simple: Gifts to the self—including extensions of the self—are rational acts. To the donor, they are hardly felt as sacrifices at all, because the money is, in effect, paid to oneself. On the contrary, gifts to extensions of the self produce feelings of joy, not pain.[5]

This motivation does not involve reciprocity. Such givers are not looking for recognition, and quite often they have little awareness of what the gift has to do with God or the church. Instead, these givers are motivated by a sense of personal identification with the church.

We would view this motivation as, in principle, theologically neutral. It does not include an attempt to manipulate God as in the reciprocity-with-God motivation. Nor does it include the desire for public recognition as in the reciprocity-with-religious-group motivation. Instead, it reflects the psychological reality that human beings are created in relational ways. The self always includes relationships with family, friends, and institutions that have played an important role in one's life. The problem as we see it with this third motivating force is that additional reality that institutions can lose their importance to individuals. Without an ongoing vital relationship with a local church, people frequently cease to see the church as an extension of the self. At that point, giving may be reduced or ended altogether.

The final motivating force is giving out of altruism or thankfulness. This motivation could be seen as the opposite of the first type: reciprocity with God. Here the emphasis is upon what God has already done, not what God might do as a result of the gift. The problem, as Hoge and his coauthors understand it, is that this type of motivation may be the least prevalent among church members:

> The motive of giving out of gratitude no doubt exists, but we are uncertain if it is a major motive in giving, operating over long periods of time. . . . It is difficult to know how strong a motive thankfulness is. No doubt, some giving is done without the self-interest of reciprocity foremost in the giver's mind. The strength of the thankfulness motive is partly dependent on a theological vision of the gifts one is receiving from God, so we would expect it to be more prominent among theologically committed people than among the secularized or the weak in faith.[6]

We agree completely with that and would therefore add that it is important for clergy to work toward increasing this motivation among church members. But the reason for that is not in order to raise more money. It may well be the case that the other three motivating forces are much more efficient for fund-raising purposes. The human desires to secure a good future, to gain public acclamation, and to care for oneself are dominant motivational factors. The problem with them is not that they are bad per se but that they are less than what a relationship with the triune God can do in the life of a person. This chapter is an attempt to reinforce that reality and promote ways in which the motivation of thankfulness can be increased in the lives of believers.

FUND-RAISING IN LOCAL CHURCHES

One of the simple realities of congregational life is that most churches are financially dependent upon voluntary giving, including past giving (trusts and foundations are very important for many local churches).

Interestingly, this has not always been the case. In the earliest days of the United States, the financing of Christian work was quite different from what most of us experience. The disestablishment of the church from the state (state funding was the common means in Europe) caused Christians in the New World to become creative in funding religious work.[7] The common practice today is the annual pledge campaign.

Most pastors do not relish the annual giving campaign. In our experience, many if not most pastors would avoid talking about giving altogether if they could.[8] There are a number of reasons for this: (1) Money-talk does not fit one's vocational understanding (this is akin to what we saw in the first chapter), (2) there is the bad example of television evangelists who seem (and do) constantly ask for money in order to continue the ministry, and (3) some clergy have a fear of rejection by congregation members. Money is a hot topic. Some people are easily put off by money-talk. We cannot fully answer the second of the three concerns. This book is directed to lay and clergy leaders in local congregations. Continuous fund-raising talk is not the norm for those aspects of Christianity. But we firmly believe that money-talk is an important part of the vocation, and a better understanding of that may also help with the third concern. Christian leadership demands risking complaints and even rejection.

Several factors are important in understanding stewardship talk within congregational life. First and foremost is what fund-raising practices reveal about the ecclesial focus of the local church. Often theological concerns are completely abandoned in the light of the need for raising money. Congregation members are thought of and treated one way throughout the year, but when it comes to annual fund-raising, the focus shifts. As Michael O'Hurley-Pitts writes, even small word shifts reveal great differences:

> The church is a community, not a pool of "donor prospects" who, if
> alienated, can be replaced by the next direct mailing or telemarketing
> campaign for "yet-to-be-identified donors." . . . By contrast if the
> Church engages in true stewardship, where gifts are sought, the result
> will not only be more financial resources for God's ministry to the
> world, but more parishioners who are willing to give of their time and
> talent as well. The distinction between a donation and a gift is not
> merely semantic: a donation is motivated by the recognition of need;
> a gift proceeds as an offering of one's plenty set beside the poverty of
> one's soul.[9]

This is a fundamental distinction. Are parishioners members of the body of Christ who give because of transformed relationships with God and their neighbors? Or are they donors who contribute their "fair share" to the upkeep and mission of the local church? In theological terms, members of Christ's body give out of their gratitude and poverty in the light of God's quantitatively and qualitatively different gift to them. The ongoing gracious self-giving of the triune God is the proper context for understanding human giving. On the other hand, stripped of that context, "donors" give out of their abundance and desire to help.

The additional problem with a donor approach is that donors maintain control while stewards do not. Implicit in the biblical understanding of stewardship is that this world and all in it is God's creation, not ours. We have a very important place in the creation, a very high vocation within the created order, but we are not the owners of creation. We are not in final control of it. The idea of donation places the key emphasis on the voluntary nature of the gift. Donors may give, but they need not. They give where they see fit to do so. They give as much as they like to whomever they like. But if the person or organization that receives the gift no longer seems worthy, the donor may always withhold the gift in the future. The nature of the church is such that it should never accept a donation. Accepting donations is out of keeping with the character and mission of the body of Christ. Is not the acceptance of donations theologically misleading? Does it not confuse both the reality of God and who we are in relationship to God? Does it not ultimately mislead people into believing that they have a control which they do not? The necessary answer to donations is the teaching and practice of true Christian stewardship.

We want to be very clear at this point. We do not believe that one can know or completely regulate people's motivations. Christians, who are redeemed and yet still fallen, are a complicated mixture of various attitudes, motivations, and actions. Instead, we are speaking to church leaders who bear the burden of properly interpreting God's reality and what is required of those who have new life in Christ. Do the stewardship practices of Christian leaders lift up the truth of the triune God, or do they not? Do actions and teaching around fund-raising reveal the true God, or another power at work in the world? This is the crucial point. The key problem is that the fund-raising practices of many churches are not commensurate with the character of God.

A second point of concern is whether our fund-raising practices are designed to preserve an institution or to embrace the cross of Jesus Christ. This is another way to raise the question as to whether our churches are organization-focused or mission-focused. Do fund-raising practices highlight the preservation of current structures, or do they lift up a vision of God's present and future activity? An emphasis on scarcity is a sheer sign of organization-focused fund-raising.

A third point of concern is whether appeals for money are thanksgiving-based, obligation-based, or guilt-based. We are concerned that too many Christians give out of a sense of obligation and some even out of a sense of guilt.

This again should help us see how important theology is in giving. If the primary concern is raising money, then the question of motivation is not fundamental. Obligation and guilt-based giving can be quite motivating, at least in the short term. How often have we heard appeals on behalf of what others have done and how it is now the current generation's time to give? And worse, how often have we encountered Christians who give in order to fulfill some old debt? Or perhaps this is their way to atone for some hidden sin? Motivations do matter, because they reveal what we actually believe about God's character. Is God the loving one who always gives beyond what people deserve? Or is God an all-powerful entity who is best appeased by gifts?

THE DUALITY OF CHRISTIAN LIFE

John Wesley made an important distinction between having the faith of a servant versus the faith of a child of God.[10] The Christian who has a servant's faith gives out of obligation. The relationship is a remote one and perilous at times. This type of faith believes that one may be put "out of the house" if one fails to please the house's lord. A person with a childlike faith, however, rests confident in God's love. Such a person gives in joyful response to God's goodness. He does not fear that his sins or failures will cause God to reject him. His faith is marked by freedom. His giving is motivated by joyful thanksgiving. A part of the problem here may be what O'Hurley-Pitts refers to as the "duality" of the Christian life:

> Stewardship is a relationship with God that both receives and gives, making all things possible. Christian stewards recognize their gifts,

contemplate all that is in their lives, and devote themselves daily to the
conviction that they, as Christians are invited into a state of duality: as
a child of God, the Christian is gift, and as steward giver.[11]

Returning to our main theme, we note again that the power of money is an
important factor in why it is so difficult for many Christians to embrace
(against their better judgment) this duality. Unfortunately, a type of dualism is
far more common wherein sometimes we are givers and sometimes we are
gainers. This is the foundation for a type of giving that is basically obligatory:
to receive a gift obligates one to give one. It is dualism when we forget the
basic temporal and substantial relationship between the two. Giving in Christian terms is always predicated upon first receiving. That receiving changes
the very nature of whatever giving we practice. Our giving is in an entirely new
context of grace, which strips the gift of its power to obligate the recipient.

It certainly cannot be merely a matter of ignorance; God the giver is the
cornerstone of Christianity. In the Christian tradition, God is the giver of
many good gifts, and ultimately God gives God's self for the sake of the world
in the second person of the Trinity. God's giving is the epitome of sacrificial
giving. In even more radical terms, all those to whom God gives are both
unworthy of and lack gratitude for the gift: "But God proves his love for us in
that while we still were sinners Christ died for us" (Rom. 5:8) and "He was in
the world, and the world came into being through him; yet the world did not
know him. He came to what was his own, and his own people did not accept
him" (John 1:10–11).

Does money become a means by which we hide this duality from ourselves?
Does money's purchasing power grant us the illusion that what we have is primarily through our own efforts? How much avariciousness can be traced to
this forgetfulness? How much can be linked to this basic flight from reality?
Does money's power insist upon a system of obligation? Does it demand an
eternal bookkeeping that is graceless and self-perpetuates relationships
reducible to the quantification of who owes what to whom?

RECLAIMING THE DISCIPLINE OF SABBATH KEEPING

We believe that this forgetfulness is best countered through the spiritual discipline of Sabbath keeping. The regular break in the workweek gives us the
opportunity to recall and rejoice in our duality. The remembrance that the
week actually begins with our rest and not our labor is the necessary invitation
for us to imagine our lives differently. Having first rested, we work. Having
first been given, we give. Our giving is ever and always a response to having

received. In terms of the ordering of our salvation, giving falls under the category of sanctification (the imparting of righteousness) and never justification (the imputing of righteousness). True Christian giving is centered in the realization that what is most important to me has come as gift and not through personal labor.

Sabbath keeping both implies and reveals a basic reality for faithful living. That is where we can discover God. We have much to learn from Rabbi Abraham Heschel at this point:

> In technical civilization, we expend time to gain space. To enhance our power in the world of space is our main objective. . . . [Yet,] the power we attain in the world of space terminates abruptly at the borderline of time.[12]

In other words, eventually everyone dies. Here, Jesus' parable of the rich fool who loses his life in the middle of future planning (Luke 12:13–21) is important.

The parable is followed by Luke's version of Jesus' promise of anxiety-free living that does not attempt to hoard and that is quick to give. Humans dread time because of our constant labor for the things of space. This is the human tragedy: there is never enough time for most people to acquire all that they desire. Heschel has much to say in response:

> [The] higher goal of spiritual living is not to amass a wealth of information, but to face sacred moments. . . . A moment of insight is a fortune, transporting us beyond the confines of measured time.
>
> One good hour may be worth a lifetime; an instant of returning to God may restore what has been lost in years of escaping from Him.
>
> We must not forget that it is not a thing that lends significance to a moment; it is the moment that lends significance to things.
>
> [The Sabbath] is not for the purpose of recovering one's lost strength and becoming fit for the forthcoming labor.
>
> [The Sabbath] is not for the purpose of enhancing the efficiency of work.
>
> [The Sabbath] is not for the sake of weekdays; the weekdays are for the sake of Sabbath. It is not an interlude but the climax of living.[13]

We do not really keep Sabbath; instead, Sabbath keeps us. In the same way, our giving does not really keep God's mission. It does not lead beyond itself. In the words of Heschel, it gains us nothing of space. It appears to be completely unproductive. Instead, it shows us the proper way to spend time. In reality, time is *not* money. Money is completely unable to control time, as both Heschel and Jesus' parable teach. Sabbath keeping allows us to understand that faithful resting is the culmination of living, not the means to something else. In this way, the earning and purchasing self may be displaced by the giving self.

FAVORITISM AND FUND- RAISING

We have already noted three concerns regarding fund-raising: ecclesial focus, the goal, and the basis of appeal. A fourth point of concern is whether fund-raising appeals and stewardship practices are directed at the entire community or primarily to a select few. To what degree do our fund-raising practices betray the reality that against the clear teaching of the New Testament, favoritism is shown to the rich over against the poor? Such practices are strictly prohibited in James 2:1–7.

Community-focused stewardship practices are far more concerned with the character of the local congregation than with achieving particular fund-raising goals. Perhaps this is better stated by saying that a primary goal of any fund-raising appeal ought to be a strengthening of the character of Christian *koinōnia* within the congregation. We are convinced that all too often, annual fund-raising campaigns, even when financially successful, do harm to the fellowship of believers. The favoring of a few over the many is most often seen in memorial plaques, lists of top givers, and so forth. How does the public recognition of major gifts square with Christ's words (Matt. 6:1–4) from the Sermon on the Mount? Furthermore, what standards should be used in order to determine which gifts are truly worthy of public recognition? Christ seems to present a different type of measurement in lifting up the poor widow's donation (Luke 21:1–4).[14]

With this story in mind, the size of a gift can no longer be the criterion by which it is judged. Yet all too often this is exactly the way in which churches appraise financial gifts, as O'Hurley-Pitts notes:

> Because donor recognition is inevitably tied to the size of a gift, rather than the generosity with which it is given, the sacrificial offerings of the un-moneyed are automatically devalued and discounted. Where are the plaques on church walls commemorating the women who worked their fingers to the bone cleaning the church? . . . What about the laborer who gave up his vacation to help pay for a new youth worker? Or the woman on welfare who pledged a dollar a week to the building campaign?[15]

In fairness, it is far easier to quantify money than generosity. But isn't this then a premier example of the way in which money monetizes value and blinds people to those things it cannot place a price on? Is it also not the case that sometimes very large gifts are anything but generous? How munificent is the person who just gave $10,000 when her disposable income is easily in the millions?[16]

There is an additional problem with individually focused giving. This could be called the "What's in it for me?" syndrome. How is a prosperity gospel linked to individual appeals and individual benefits? Again, how does "one hand washes the other" thinking inform this? I will give and God will give back.

STEWARDSHIP AND THE MISSIO DEI

On the other hand, preaching about money can empower people to develop as disciples of Christ. When God's work is the focus, giving allows people to participate in the *missio Dei*. That is, people are empowered to become a part of what the giving triune God continues to do in the world. God's own giving must be kept primary. The first gift of God is God's self: the incarnation. This is the gift that enables and underlies all other gifts. Without this gift, any other attempt at giving fails and falls short of that which God desires for giving. Grace is what underlies all this. Money's power has primarily been known for its ability to transmute good gifts into forms of self-aggrandizement and the creation of divisions within the church between rich and poor.

Since ultimately all ministry is a participation in the activity of the triune God, we must always bear in mind what is central to God's mission. God is not primarily interested in raising money. Instead, God's passion is the salvation of God's people. The saving work of the Father, Son, and Holy Spirit is not ultimately directed toward establishing foundations, building more beautiful and larger houses of worship, or increasing clergy compensation. Instead, money-talk and stewardship drives ought to be a part of God's mission of nurturing believers and witnessing to the world. Ultimately, how the church raises and spends money is a powerful witness to good or ill. It either reveals the truth of God's kingdom or obscures it. In terms of nurturing believers, we believe that in general terms Miroslav Volf is correct that the church ought to help move people from the coercive mode (taking) to the sales mode (gaining) to the gift mode (giving).[17]

The first of these ought to be simply out of bounds for Christians, since it implies the use of various types of force to get what one wants. Unfortunately, that is not always the case. Christians who would never think to steal all too often help themselves to what is not really theirs. Volf explains:

> In this mode, we take what is not ours and what is not being offered to us. Armed with insider information, we sell our stock before it tumbles down, and the hapless buyers take the loss. Or to use a more innocent example, at work we slip a pen into our pocket and take it home.[18]

The power of money blinds many believers and keeps them from recognizing the various forms of theft that our culture frequently overlooks.

The second type of being is the "sales" mode. This is where most people, believers and unbelievers alike, find themselves. According to Volf, "The sales mode refers to the market of buying and selling. Here we give something in order to get a rough equivalent in exchange."[19] Obviously, this is a great improvement over taking. Most of us are raised with this in mind: a fair price for a fair product. The principle of reciprocity is a strong and important one. However, money's power causes us to be unable to perceive that there is more to life than this way of being. This explains well why the first two motivating forces described above are so prevalent in the church. They are demonstrations of the basic approach to living that most people take. One gets what one pays for. The only problem with the sales mode is that it is a poor substitute for the abundant life the gospel promises to people, which takes us to the third type of being.

The third sort that Volf mentions is the gift mode:

> The gift mode refers to relations between donors and recipients. Here we give favors that we don't owe and the recipients don't deserve. If recipients return favors, they do so unforced, after a time lag, and in a different form.[20]

There is a liberty implied in relationships of giving. There is no subtle (or unsubtle) implication that the favor must be returned. All true giving implies a vulnerability of "letting go." One does not anticipate receiving anything in return. The joy of giving is directly connected to that freedom. This is the freedom of leaving behind old lives of taking and/or sales. It is the freedom of finding that one has new life. "So why does giving become part of our new selves?" asks Volf. "The first and primary reason is because the God whom we worship and the Christ who dwells in us are neither takers nor getters, but givers."[21] We believe that all talk of giving in the church should ultimately have this goal: helping people move away from taking and getting to giving. Furthermore, insofar as stewardship campaigns, pledge drives, church bazaars, and the like do not have this in mind, they are less than fully reflecting the reality of the Christian God, whose nature is to give.

OVERCOMING THE BAD CONSCIENCE OF FINANCIAL APPEALS

Perhaps the greatest difficulty that clergy face here is that they themselves feel like salespeople as they attempt to function within the voluntary system of church funding. James Hudnut-Beumler notes:

[Clergy] are "peddlers in divinity," a term perhaps first applied to George Whitefield. . . . My point is that there is something about the voluntary principle of financing in the American religious context that turns every member of the clergy into a salesperson.[22]

We are convinced that if clergy are unable or unwilling to understand money matters in theological terms, they will be unable to progress beyond this sales mode. Utilizing Volf's categories, how can clergy and lay leaders challenge people to go beyond the sales mode if they themselves have not? Clergy must become convinced that within the area of financing ministry, just as in every other aspect of ministry, they are not so much salespeople with a product to sell as they are theologians with a story to tell. They are shepherds and prophets called to care for God's people and announce that Christ's lordship extends over all areas of life, including the financial area. This story can be told with gratitude and joy because the triune God truly does have authority over all other powers. Money need not dominate the lives of those who are in Christ. We believe that it is only then that the church will completely embrace the fullness of its vocation and its contemporary mission.

In this way, the goal of Christian fund-raising is discipleship itself, and not the means to fund discipleship. Thus, all practices must move toward that end, and any that do not (i.e., those practices that promote anything less than Christian living) are off-limits. Clergy and other church leaders ought not to feel any guilt that they are in some way departing from their primary work. In this culture, the subjugation of money's power to the will of God may very well be central to faithful Christian leadership. But this is exactly where much fund-raising fails. Money is all too often raised without ever questioning its domination. The money flows in, but its power is never checked by the gospel. In reality, many fund-raising practices actually strengthen the domination of money even as it is being given.

TITHING AND STEWARDSHIP

James Hudnut-Beumler contends that from 1870 to 1920, the idea of tithing was reinvented in the American church context.[23] It was then that the principle of "unified giving" first came to dominate the American religious imagination—that is, one offering taken weekly for the upkeep and mission of the church. Prior to this time, most money was raised through pew rentals and special appeals. The tithe came to prevalence during this period. As Hudnut-Beumler explains, "Tithing was attractive as a source of funding to the degree that clergy could convince themselves and others that it was a spiritual law, as unappealable as the laws of motion, force, and gravity."[24] One may trace the contemporary understanding of Christian stewardship to this point in time. The idea of a weekly offering came to dominate the way in which money was raised to support all that was necessary for the church's mission to go forward.[25] Our primary point here is to remember that the emphasis upon tithing is a modern one. Christian fund-raising has been done in a multitude of ways throughout history.

As Hudnut-Beumler shows, tithe talk has ebbed and flowed throughout the history of the church. Generally speaking, we support tithing. Both of us were raised with the idea that 10 percent of one's income is due the church. Furthermore, when one sees how small a percentage of income is given by the average American Protestant, we are even more prone to support it.[26] At the same time, we are concerned when tithing becomes the primary goal of giving in churches. We share Jacques Ellul's concern when stewardship (and in particular tithing) becomes a way of obligation fulfillment rather that the mark of joyful discipleship (see chapter 4). The tithe should never be understood as the fulfillment or completion of one's obligation to give.

We believe that tithe talk is appropriate in speaking about giving. But for it to be faithful to the character of God, it must include the following key ideas: First, it is an Old Testament concept, functioning as a mark of being a member of the community of Israel. Second, the New Testament is silent on the topic. Christ's only references to tithing are included in warnings against religious hypocrisy. Third, the radical nature of God's kingdom means that Christ is Lord over all, not simply over 10 percent of all things. Tithing must never become the means whereby we seek to establish the terms of our relationship with God. Fourth, the tithe can be a mark of commitment for Christians. It can be a spiritual discipline that reminds us of God's complete ownership and money's power that attempts to separate us from the God who loves. It may be a way in which we refuse money's power to dominate. That being the case, tithing can never be made obligatory. Ultimately, it cannot be seen as the complete fulfillment of what God calls us to give.

FROM THE HUMAN SCARCITY/PROSPERITY AXIS TO GOD'S ABUNDANCE

This redefines the context of giving. We do not need to think about money either in terms of scarcity or prosperity. Increasingly, many American congregations approach money matters from the standpoint of scarcity. Signs of this attitude are questions like "How will we continue to afford this program?"

"How will we continue to afford a full-time pastor?" The operating assumption is that there will never be as much money as there once was. Such a particular congregation has entered a period of decline. So now there is a need to scale back in order to preserve as much as possible. The focus in such thinking is upon the organization itself rather than upon God's activity. Repeatedly the conversation turns to the winners and losers in the religious economy. There can be little doubt that a tremendous shift has occurred in American Protestantism in the last fifty years. The statistics have been rehearsed constantly. We need not do that here. Needless to say, even though there are many healthy, vital mainline congregations, the traditional American Protestant denominations have lost a significant percentage of their membership in the last several decades.

Like most aspects of Christian ministry, fund-raising needs a Copernican revolution in our basic understanding.[27] That is, a paradigmatic shift in Christian understanding needs to occur. Ministry is not a matter of imitation of God's attributes but rather a participation in God's activity. Our giving is not an imitation of God's giving, nor is it a continuation of the work God began. It is, in reality, a participation in God's ongoing giving. This is the key insight that has the power to transform talk of money in the church.

DISCUSSION QUESTIONS

1. How does your church deal with financial appeals?
2. How would better Sabbath practices help you in money matters?
3. How might greater clarity concerning participating in God's mission help you in teaching and preaching about money and the church?

11

Expanding the Conversation: How to Talk about Money when *Not* Asking for It

Leading the fall stewardship campaign was often uncomfortable for me. I was asking people to pledge to God but I knew it was coming to me. . . . Money has more significance in the lives of people than almost anything else. If indeed clergy are caught up in debilitating binds over money, they are handicapped in dealing with one of the most significant spiritual problems in their own lives, and they are even more hindered in being of help to those in their congregations who likewise seek to understand what grace and forgiveness have to do with that portion of our lives that we wall off as "money."

Loren Mead

One of the problems clergy face in discussing money is the accusation that the only time they talk about it is when they need to raise it. The image of the slick television evangelist and his continuous requests for financial support is projected onto the local church pastor, and in response, many clergy shy away from talking about money any more than is absolutely necessary. Furthermore, many clergy are uncomfortable discussing money because of their assumption that money itself is corrupt. And if money is impure, then surely those who have money or have careers that generate substantial income are suspect.

We believe that when clergy refuse to engage parishioners in conversations about money that go beyond fund-raising, they miss out on a powerful opportunity to provide pastoral care. Failure to talk about money allows the believer to compartmentalize his life, to believe that this part of his life is an area over which Christ has no say. In that vacuum, the power of money grows unhindered, uninformed by the gospel. Safely tucked away from anything that might challenge it, the power of money develops and takes authority over work, leisure, relationships, and family.

When the minister's view of pastoral care is expanded to encompass issues surrounding money, however, the parishioner can be challenged to see how the power of money can be disarmed in her life. Work becomes more than just a way to make money, as the believer begins to imagine how her faith can transform her work. Compulsive spending habits, a consumer mentality, and maxed-out credit cards are confronted and brought under the lordship of Christ. Clergy who are willing to address money and its dominant role in work, marriage, family, and virtually every aspect of life can provide pastoral care that is holistic and liberating.

DISARMING THE POWER OF MONEY IN THE LIFE OF THE PARISHIONER: INTEGRATING FAITH AND WORK

In *Theirs Is the Kingdom*, Robert D. Lupton writes:

> There they sit, row after row of remarkably gifted grown-ups. Dressed in proper Sunday attire, they are waiting. Waiting for the minister to step to the microphone with words to ignite them. Hoping that this Sunday he will challenge them to more than a capital funds campaign for the new family life center. They wait, these talented ones, for words to stir them, to drive them from their comfort to challenges worthy of their best. Perhaps today they will hear the call to tasks of greater significance than their own personal success or the growth of their church.
>
> An architect, a CPA, a surgeon, and seven other professionals file down the center aisle. They bow for prayer, then dutifully fan out with the offering plates to collect a cut of the profits from the marketplace. With the exception of a CEO who reads the morning Scripture, ushering is the most noticeable role that lay leaders fill.
>
> Less visible are the real estate developers, insurance brokers, and educators who serve on church committees. But there they sit, a people with the nature and the gifts of the Divine, fully equipped with every skill and ability necessary to tackle the complex problems of the world. Although domesticated by their culture, they long for the courage to throw off the obligations of consumerism and spend themselves for the God who has called them.[1]

While most parishioners spend a significant portion of their week at work, many persons of faith see little connection between that work and their faith.

On Sunday morning, they sing hymns, read Scripture, recite liturgies, and listen to a sermon. On Monday morning, they take their places at desks, in classrooms, on assembly lines, at cash registers, on trading floors, in operating rooms, in banks. Many of them do not reflect in any meaningful way on their faith until the following Sunday. Their faith provides little in the way of wisdom, strength, or encouragement to help them cope with the challenges of their work. They drop checks into the offering plate on Sunday morning to "redeem their wealth"[2] and walk out the door, unchallenged by what they have heard to respond to "tasks of greater significance than their own personal success."[3]

In their book *Church on Sunday, Work on Monday*, Laura Nash and Scotty McLennan interviewed many persons of faith who "expressed feelings of radical disconnection between Sunday services and Monday morning activities, describing a sense of living in two worlds that never touch each other."[4] David Miller writes that many people of faith report "feeling that they live increasingly bifurcated lives, where faith and work seldom connect."[5] We believe that one of the most potent ways to disarm the power of money in the lives of parishioners is by helping them to integrate their faith and their work. As faith and work become reconnected in the life of the believer, the power of money in that believer's life is challenged.

Frequently, however, the church is silent on the topic of work. Little meaningful dialogue exists on the purpose of work. Do we work simply to make money? Is some work better than other work in God's eyes? What is the role of a Christian working in business? By and large, the church has had little to say on these issues. But in spite of the silence, a message has been heard by many members in the pew. The message may never have been spoken from the pulpit, but the point has been heard loud and clear. We believe that there are at least three unintended messages perceived by many worshipers:

1. *Sacred work is better than secular work.* Many of us who were raised in the church grew up hearing this unspoken message. As we listened to special speakers, participated in mission trips, and went off to church camp each summer, a hierarchy of work became firmly implanted in our minds. R. Paul Stevens describes the hierarchy in this way: At the top of the list are the foreign missionaries who labor unrewarded in places dangerous and unknown. Just below the missionaries are the pastors. Further down, but still acceptable, are the social workers, schoolteachers, nurses, and others engaged in helping professions. And somewhere at the bottom of the pyramid are the businesspeople, tradespeople, stockbrokers, and lawyers.[6] The implication is clear: those in "full-time Christian service" are better Christians than those who are not.

2. *Work in secular business is suspect.* Growing out of the misconception that sacred work is better than secular work is the inference that business is

particularly questionable. The church has sent the message that since those at the bottom of this list are involved in the making of filthy lucre, they are probably greedy and unethical. The church has conveyed that those working for large, multinational corporations certainly are suspect, since their employers are responsible for many of the social injustices in the world. Without a doubt, these people are at the bottom of the pyramid because they dirty themselves in the making of money. As Michael Novak observes, "Commerce is a faintly smelly enterprise, lower in dignity than other callings."[7]

3. *The only way to really serve God is through work in the church.* The natural extension of the first two unintended messages is the message that the only real way in which one can serve God is through work done in or with the church. God is pleased with Sue when she volunteers her time to work in the church food pantry, but evidently God is indifferent or less than pleased with her work from nine to five. When Bill is on a volunteer mission trip using his construction skills to build a school, he is serving God. But when Bill is using those same skills to profitably run his construction business, he is not serving God. The implication is that those who are really serious about serving God need to leave their secular work and go to seminary.

UNINTENDED MESSAGES

"How," you say, "have I *ever* sent these messages?" David Miller notes, "Whether conscious or unintended, the pulpit all too frequently sends the signal that work in the church matters but work in the world does not."[8] He describes the following experience:

> While speaking to clergy gatherings of a variety of denominations around the country, I often ask this question: "Who here prays for and commissions your teenagers as they go off on a mission trip?" Invariably, all hands go up. Then I ask: "Who here prays for and commissions your Sunday school teachers each September as the new church year starts?" Most of the hands go up again. Finally, I ask, "Who here prays for all the certified public accountants in your congregation around April 15, and who here prays for all the salespeople and those working on commission at the end of the month and end of the year when quotas are due?" Silence. Eyes drop to the ground. Usually, not a single hand is raised.[9]

Every time a church member is commissioned to perform work in the church, the message is sent that *this* work is holy in God's eyes, while work outside of church is not. The work performed from nine to five by the faithful believer in business is marginalized by the church each time it sends this message that sacred work is more important than secular work. Would the insurance salesperson, the computer programmer, the assembly line worker live his life differently if he were challenged each Sunday to see his work in the world as sacred and ordained by God? Would the purchasing agent or accountant who left her career to attend seminary have remained in business if she had been continuously reminded that her work in business was a calling?

Clergy have done little to counter the message that work in secular business is suspect. In fact, through extensive interviews with clergy, Nash and McLennan found that clergy have largely negative attitudes about business and businesspeople, including the belief that "money is bad" and "business-people are greedy."[10] They describe a deep divide between business and clergy where businesspeople "often felt ignored, disdained, or simply beyond the comprehension and experience of most clergy."[11] Rather than reaching out to equip individuals working in business with tools for integrating their faith into their work, many clergy have preferred to sit back and rant against capitalism and the social injustices brought about by multinational corporations. David Miller notes:

> Responsible theological and ethical criticism of immoral and unethi-cal business is always in order, of course. Yet clergy seem often to exhibit a presumptive and prejudicial suspicion of capitalism and mar-ketplace structures that prevents them from thinking—or talking—about the redemptive, creative, productive, ministerial and transformative possibilities in the business world and in the lives of those called to live out their Christian vocations in the marketplace.[12]

This critical stance toward business is particularly prevalent in mainline Protestant denominations whose clergy have received training at seminaries emphasizing a radicalized approach to business and whose denominational state-ments over the years have consistently demonized business. Miller continues:

> I would say that the root of the gap lies in the training that clergy receive in seminary and divinity school. Many of today's clergy were influenced by seminary faculty who are heirs of Christian socialism and advocates of liberation theology, both of which employ material-ist categories of analysis and tend to presuppose that capital structures are de facto oppressive sources of injustice.[13]

And so the believer who works in business is often left to go it alone, even though research suggests that "many Christians and Jews hunger for more support from their religious communities in relating their faith to their work lives."[14] Finding nothing on Sunday morning that helps prepare them to face the challenges of Monday, some have turned to the spirituality-at-work move-ment embodied in the books, business seminars, and retreats of people such as

Steven Covey and Deepak Chopra.[15] Others have created their own communities of Christian support within the workplace that are totally separate from the church. One recent count put such Christian faith-at-work organizations as high as 1,300, nearly all of which have developed independently of the church.[16] As Nash and McLennan observe, "Seekers can be found in every congregation and corporation, determined to embark on their spiritual journey toward vocational awareness with or without the church. The church is challenged to respond."[17]

CORRECTING THE UNINTENDED MESSAGES

The minister needs to understand the unintended messages that have been heard by those in the pew and initiate conversations within the church that will correct these messages. Dorothy Sayers wrote:

> In nothing has the church so lost Her hold on reality as in Her failure to understand and respect the secular vocation. She has allowed work and religion to become separate departments, and is astonished to find that, as a result, the secular work of the world is turned to purely selfish and destructive ends, and that the greater part of the world's intelligent workers have become irreligious, or at least, uninterested in religion. But is it astonishing? How can anyone remain interested in a religion which seems to have no concern with nine-tenths of life? The church's approach to an intelligent carpenter is usually confined to exhorting him not to be drunk and disorderly in his leisure hours, and to come to church on Sundays. What the church should be telling him is this: that the very first demand that his religion makes on him is to make good tables.[18]

As one believing CEO observes, "Relatively few churches and pastors are reinforcing the legitimacy of a call into so-called 'secular work.' I have colleagues with tremendous business influence who are starving spiritually in their local churches. There's zero feeding; there's zero reinforcing of the call they have in the marketplace."[19]

Instead of simplistically criticizing business for its many failings, the church "can offer theological insights and practical tools to equip Christians called to serve in and through the marketplace," writes David Miller. "To do anything less is to abandon millions of Christians for five-sevenths of their adult lives and to abdicate responsibility for and influence over this important sphere of society."[20] We believe that the clergyperson must not abandon the businessperson in his congregation but instead can and must provide pastoral care that applies not only to Sunday but to Monday through Friday as well.

The church needs to become the place where the faith-at-work movement is grounded. Businesspeople of faith should not have to search outside of the church for answers on how to take their faith to work. Finding ways to equip and mobilize believers in business must be one of the central areas of emphasis within the church. We believe that the minister can provide pastoral leadership that facilitates the integration of faith and work in at least four important ways:

1) praying for their parishioners' work in the world and visiting them in their workplaces,
2) preaching and teaching about faith and work,
3) providing support groups within the church that focus on work issues, and
4) challenging believers to think of their business as mission.

Praying for Parishioners' Work in the World and Visiting Them in Their Workplaces

We believe that the church should be a place in which prayers are routinely and publically offered for work performed by its members on Monday through Friday. Rather than just commissioning those in the pew for the "sacred" work they perform within the church, the minister should consider ways to ordain all believers for their daily work. Pastoral prayers can specifically seek to dedicate believers for the workweek ahead, encouraging them to see their work as more than just a paycheck but as full of possibilities for God's activity in the world. When the pastor prays for the businesswoman and her daily work, the sacred-secular divide is diminished. When the pastor blesses the work of the businessman, his work is transformed and becomes sacramental, a window through which he can see God.[21]

We believe that when the minister gets to know parishioners in their places of work, the wall between Sunday and Monday begins to crumble. David Miller calls this a "ministry of presence and listening in the work sphere." He suggests, "Clergy should go to their parishioners' places of work for short visits as regularly and naturally as they make hospital and home visits."[22] While clergy do not need to become experts in every profession, they should attempt to learn enough to provide pastoral care to members facing job-related dilemmas and ethical choices.[23] That knowledge comes best from seeing firsthand the parishioner's workplace, when appropriate. Shirley Roels writes of the importance of "enfolding" those in business in the church's embrace: "One of the best strategies for enfolding the business member involves understanding their daily business experiences."[24] While it may not always be practical to visit members at their place of work, the pastor can look for appropriate opportunities to do so. Even just arranging to meet a parishioner at her workplace

before taking her to lunch may open the conversation to matters of integration of faith and work.

Preaching and Teaching about Faith and Work

Sermons which help parishioners to grasp that their work is sacred can correct
the unintended message that secular work is unimportant; however, such sermons are not common. One survey places the number of Christians who have
never heard a sermon relating foundational biblical principles to their work as
high as 90 to 97 percent.[25] Even though research suggests that congregants are
more satisfied with their places of worship when matters of work are addressed,
there appears to be little integration occurring on most Sunday mornings.[26]
Teaching that dignifies, rather than denies, a member's identity as a businessperson can bring healing and correct the unintended messages that work
in business is suspect or that the believer must leave the world to enter full-time
Christian service.[27]

Through preaching and teaching, clergy should help believers working in
business to develop a coherent Christian understanding of the purpose of business that incorporates, rather than excludes, their faith. The minister should
challenge believers to see their work in business as a way to serve God and
neighbor, rather than simply accepting a maximization-of-shareholder-wealth
model as the sole purpose for business.

The faculty of the business school at one liberal arts college has considered
this issue and has developed a thoughtful statement on the purpose of business.
This statement draws on the work of ethicist Louke van Wensveen Siker, which
applies Richard Niebuhr's typology in *Christ and Culture* to business.[28] Rejecting
the first four types (Christ against business, Christ of business, Christ above business, and Christ and business in paradox) as problematic in one way or another,
the statement clearly sees "Christ transforming business" as a model for the biblical purpose for business.[29] The statement articulates the belief that "creation
establishes the vocation of business as good" but "profoundly broken."[30] "The
rebellion of business enthrones Mammon" and market forces.[31] However, the
image of God is still present, and Christ is at work in and through business doing
his work in the world: "Christians in business are participants by the Spirit in the
redemptive work of God. A calling into business is intrinsically a holy calling."[32]

Many people deeply desire to find meaning in their work, to feel that their
work counts for something. In contrast to the answers provided by the spirituality-at-work, self-help gurus, clergy need to help worshipers realize that
rather than *finding* meaning at work, they need to *take* the meaning with them.
When work is viewed through the eyes of our faith, we can begin to see the
office, the factory, or the store as places where God is already active. God is

already at work in the lives of our customers, vendors, coworkers, and bosses. What activity already underway in their lives would God invite us to join?

When the clergyperson purposefully integrates business-specific applications and illustrations into sermons, believers can begin to imagine ways in which their faith can transform their work. Perhaps very little changes in terms of actual practices; accountants still prepare tax returns and salespeople continue to make their calls. But a tremendous transformation of vision has occurred.

Gradually, the factory manager begins to see the factory not just as the place where a product is produced but as an opportunity to provide safe, well-paying jobs to marginalized members of the community. The teller begins to see Christ in the faces of his clients and begins to perform each financial transaction with kindness, care, and respect. The personnel manager decides to take a chance on "one of the least of these," because for the first time, he can imagine the possibilities for transformation that might occur with appropriate support, mentoring, and training. The owner begins to realize that her business provides one of the most powerful means on earth to help feed the hungry, clothe the naked, and welcome the stranger.

Providing Support Groups within the Church That Focus on Work Issues

Support groups can be facilitated by the church to help businesspersons develop meaningful strategies for integrating their faith with their work. Shirley Roels writes:

> As the alcoholic often needs AA, the businessperson needs Christian support to control the drive for personal career success, the temptations of personal greed, the lure of profit maximization, the demoralizing effect of organizational cultures of back-scratching and back-biting, the insidious corporate lie, and intoxication with work itself. . . . Might the questions and interests of a small faith-based accountability group have guided the CEO of Enron in another direction—or perhaps have guided his chief accountant, external auditor, hedgefund consultant, or investment banker? If even a few of them had had accountability groups, what might have been?[33]

We believe that when such accountability groups are located within, rather than outside, the church, businesspersons can best connect faith and work. Such groups provide a place in which business members can come together to apply biblical truths to the dilemmas faced at work. While established within the church and encouraged and supported by the pastor, these groups function best when they are led by businesspeople who are committed to the integration of faith and work.

One Church That Is Getting It Right
Redeemer Presbyterian Church, New York City

Redeemer Presbyterian Church created the Center for Faith and Work in January 2003 with the expressed purpose of equipping its parishioners to "make a difference for Christ in their respective professional fields." The Center provides programs and small groups focused on the integration of Christian faith with work that are designed to help parishioners "explore and deepen the impact of the gospel message" as it relates to their professional lives. Noting that "our lives are increasingly bifurcated, with little connection between our faith and faith community and our way of working in our careers," the center provides vocational groups to equip, connect, and mobilize professionals working in similar fields in a way that responds to God's call on their lives.[34]

The Center currently facilitates vocational groups for parishioners working in advertising, the arts, education, finance, health care, information technology, law, marketing and sales, and public service. One participant in the advertising group wrote:

> I work in advertising, which is not often considered an ethical environment, let alone a Christian one. Before joining this group, I had never met a colleague who shared my faith . . . or at least not one who admitted it. Sharing my experiences with this group and having the ability to be in Christian fellowship with others who share my profession has been a wonderful experience. When I face trials at work, I now have brothers and sisters in Christ who know what it's like to be in my situation. We pray together and advise each other, often using our own experiences to encourage. God has used this opportunity to refine me as a Christian businesswoman. I had never thought about how my performance at the office related to my faith before I took a class through the Center of Faith and Work. Now I understand that my daily activities in the workplace provide me with an opportunity to be more Christ-like by dedicating myself to the task at hand and committing to do my best.[35]

In addition to equipping believers to take their faith to work, the Center focuses on challenging participants to create "gospel-centered transformation for the common good" within their spheres of influence. The Center's director, Katherine Leary, acknowledges that the "common good" is not always simple to discern. She says that the Center seeks to provide a space in which mature believers with a deep biblical worldview and years of experience in the workplace can mentor those who are newer in the faith. Vital to those discussions is the practical mandate to be agents of change in the world. Believers are encouraged to use their influence, for example, to create a personnel policy that is more just, a product that meets a real need, a financial report with increased transparency, a production process that is more environmentally friendly, or an advertising campaign that appeals to our better nature.[36] Simply put, participants are united by "a passion for seeing the hope and love of the gospel renew the workplaces, professions, and culture of the city—which are all too often driven by greed, fear, power, and hopelessness."[37]

Challenging Believers to Think of Their Business as Mission

Finally, clergy need to open the eyes of businesspeople in their congregations to the possibilities that exist for the integration of faith and work through the burgeoning Business as Mission (BAM) movement. A recent cover story in *Christianity Today* states, "The phenomenon has many labels: 'kingdom business,' 'kingdom companies,' 'for-profit missions,' 'marketplace missions,' and 'Great Commission companies,' to name a few. But observers agree the movement is already huge and growing quickly."[38]

The Center for Applied Christian Ethics at Wheaton College has produced a helpful analysis of what Business as Mission *is* and *is not*:

> If you are using your business skills to funnel money to ministry—a common practice for linking business and mission—or, if you are using business money to fund holistic transformation, even evangelism, then you are thinking of business *for* mission. . . .
>
> If you are using your business as an avenue for evangelism—either through being a testimony in the marketplace or by funding evangelistic practices—then you are thinking of mission *through* business. . . .
>
> Business as Mission is a vision for doing business in Kingdom-enhancing ways. Practically speaking, this means subjecting every business decision, policy, and practice to the biblical values of stewardship, reconciliation, justice, dignity, and peace. Business as Mission views business as a primary institution to holistically serve peoples' needs in a way that demonstrates the reality of God.[39]

Most observers agree that Business as Mission is holistic in nature and global in outreach, seeking to create self-sustaining, profit-generating businesses located in those parts of the world where spiritual and economic need is greatest. While such businesses seek to make a profit, they are "equally concerned about the wages, the working conditions and the professional development of their workers," write Steve Rundle and Tom Steffen in their recent book *Great Commission Companies*. "GCCs do not exploit the environment or lax government oversight for short-term gain. When appropriate they even help with such things as education and health care for workers' children."[40]

Rather than relegating the business to simply a means of producing funds that can be used in the "real," spiritual ministry, Business as Mission acknowledges that the *business itself is ministry*. Similarly, the business is not simply a clever cover for missionary work in a country otherwise not open to missionaries, but the *business itself is mission*.[41] One pioneer BAM practitioner describes how, through much prayer, he came to realize that "God is quite comfortable with business . . . [and] that God was not just interested in the people's souls but also truly interested in the business itself."[42] The business can serve to bring the transforming touch of Christ into the lives of all who deal with it each day: employees, vendors, customers, lenders, and government authorities. Rundle and Steffen write:

> God is then glorified when suppliers are paid in a timely manner, customers are treated honestly and with respect, the poor receive appropriate attention, and the rich are not cheated. In many cases such behavior runs counter to the cultural status quo. Such contradictions to culture help bring clarity to Christianity and eventually confession of Jesus Christ.[43]

Examples are plentiful of BAM practitioners who have entered an economically distressed area with capital, equipment, and business savvy and created jobs, better living conditions, and an opportunity for the gospel to be heard. The Business as Mission Network, a Web site developed by Baylor business school alumnus Justin Forman, lists the twenty-five most admired BAM companies, along with current "news, resources and tools to turn good business into great ministry."[44] Forman, who began the Web site in 2006 and now has over four thousand subscribers to his digital magazine, says that he receives stories daily from people around the world who are looking to integrate business with mission.[45]

Forman states, "Some business professionals have never been asked to use their skills for more than being an usher or giving to their local church. The truth is they can do so much more. They can start businesses that could provide a way of life for people in Rwanda or India, and create an environment to share Christ."[46] But who will challenge them to think beyond their current narrow understanding of business? In a survey conducted in 2007, nearly half of respondents believed their pastor was aware of BAM, but significantly less felt that their church had an understanding of the movement (26 percent) or prayed for BAM ministries (24 percent). Perhaps most troubling, only 8 percent of those responding looked to their church as a source of information about BAM.[47]

Clergy can provide information about mission opportunities specifically designed for businesspeople to provide assistance, consulting, and business training to startup BAM companies. The church can facilitate the funding of microenterprise business development in areas of need. By sharing stories like the one described below about Business as Mission, ministers can further engage the imagination of parishioners in envisioning a new purpose for business.

One Business That Is Getting It Right
Cards from Africa—*"Beautiful Cards, Better Lives"*

Located in Rwanda, Cards from Africa is a Business as Mission enterprise that
was started in 2004 by British expatriate Chris Page. The company employs
youth who have been orphaned, many of whom work to support their younger
siblings. Cards from Africa produces handmade greeting cards featuring
unique, indigenous designs. Page writes:

> I started Cards from Africa . . . with a Rwandan artist called Gabi
> Dusabe. Both of us desired to use our different gifts and abilities to
> be a blessing to orphaned youth responsible for their younger broth-
> ers and sisters. We got paper that offices were throwing out and
> burning, and we re-pulped it, and turned it into our own hand-made
> paper.[48]

Paying wages that are two to four times higher than the local average, the company believes that the solution to the severe poverty in Rwanda is through sustainable business development. Cards from Africa placed second in the 2006
BBC World Challenge, a global competition that seeks to recognize innova-
tive, responsible, and sustainable business development.[49] The company Web
site notes:

> Today, over 90% of the country is dependent on subsistence farming
> and pressure on the land is extreme. The vast majority of the popula-
> tion struggles to scratch out a meager existence and is often not able
> to afford the education necessary to improve their situation. Rwanda's
> dependence on foreign aid, an amount higher than its business earn-
> ings, is equally unsustainable. A country's inability to choose its own
> path of development is neither dignifying nor just.[50]

Page believes that business is the only long-term solution to the poverty of
Rwanda. He writes the following about the role of business in Rwanda:

> Poverty is oppressing. I've met people in Rwanda who have lost rela-
> tives because of a sickness like malaria that could have been prevented
> with just a few dollars worth of medicine. Helping to reduce poverty
> is a very practical demonstration of God's love, and creating sustain-
> able businesses . . . [is] the way forward for Rwanda to lose the shack-
> les of poverty.[51]

In addition to making employment available to the marginalized, the company
also provides holistic care for each employee. Page writes, "We teach them for
up to an hour every morning. Sometimes from the Bible, especially on very
needed topics like forgiveness, peace and reconciliation, and sometimes on sub-

jects like AIDS, malaria, sex education, etc."[52] Cards from Africa is also committed to helping employees develop transferable business skills, as Page explains:

> The business aims to employ at least one person whose job will be to help our staff start up their own businesses. Why? Ultimately, because we don't want our staff to become dependent on Cards from Africa. So much so, we've told all non-management staff that they will only work at Cards from Africa for four years, and during those four years we will teach them as much as we can about God, themselves, others, financial management, how they can start up their own business, health, etc., and then it's up to them to implement what they learn. We view Cards from Africa as a stepping-stone to a better life, not a crutch.[53]

When asked in what ways he has seen lives changed by Cards from Africa, Page replies, "We've seen lives change holistically. Their physical needs, and those of their siblings, have been met, they're growing emotionally and spiritually, and they have hope and a purpose." Page believes that God longs for "an emerging generation of Christians who realize God is calling them into business. I look forward to the day when Christian business people in Rwanda will serve as an example to the rest of the continent because they put God and His purposes first, second and third in their business."[54]

To return to the moving words of Robert Lupton that are quoted at the beginning of this chapter, "There they sit, a people with the nature and gifts of the Divine, fully equipped with every skill and ability necessary to tackle the complex problems of the world."[55] The businesspeople in our pews have tremendous potential to carry the good news of the gospel into their many places of work. Their creativity, organizational ability, and entrepreneurial spirit provide remarkable promise for providing creative solutions to the multifaceted economic issues of our world. The challenge facing clergy today is to find ways to help these believers connect their faith with their work, to equip them to use their skills to bring about social, spiritual, and economic transformation for the kingdom through their work in business, and to provide a vision of business as a holy calling.

EXPANDING THE CONVERSATION REGARDING MONEY

We firmly believe that money's power is so great, particularly in our culture, that people profoundly need the support of the church in order to faithfully choose Christ over mammon. We return to Matthew 6:19–24 once again because many Christians do not really know where their treasure is, and thus where their heart is. Spiritual companionship can help people discern their treasure's location.

Spiritual companionship is essential in fighting money's hold. Jeannette Bakke is helpful in describing the various ways in which one can be a spiritual companion to another person.[56] Such ways include mentoring, spiritual direction, discipling, and pastoral counseling. Although certainly not the only ways, these four areas of interaction significantly cover key aspects of contemporary life. We will use her descriptions and apply them to various ways of helping people around issues of money.

Mentoring

Mentoring implies developing "particular competencies" within a given context or institution.[57] There are quite a few Christian organizations that help people gain greater money management skills.[58] The focus for these organizations is financial planning, debt management, budgeting, and so forth. Many people in the United States are deeply indebted, spending way beyond their means. In the last decade, average household credit card debt has more than doubled.[59] Our consumer culture continuously places before people the idea that we need more than what we currently have. Easy access to credit coupled with the lack of discipline in waiting has brought thousands of Christians and non-Christians alike to bankruptcy.

Christian leaders must begin with these questions: In what institution are we seeking to help people develop? What is the goal of the use of these new skills? Is the institution the American consumer culture, or is it the church? Some Christians simply want to develop as consumers, that is, they hope to be able to buy newer and nicer things. But such an attitude fails to question many of the basic cultural messages and, most importantly, fails to properly acknowledge the power of money. On the other hand, a number of organizations seek to help people better manage money in order that they can become better and more faithful givers.[60] We believe that pastors and congregations may give financial advice (if they are able), but this conversation must lead to other forms of spiritual companionship.

Spiritual Direction

A second type of spiritual companionship is spiritual direction. In this ancient art, the primary goal is to listen with another person for what the Holy Spirit would reveal. In terms of money, the ministry here would be to try to help a person discern what place money truly occupies in her life. Check registers and bank statements can reveal some things, but not the full details. In this relationship, through prayer and careful listening, we help people discern the true location of their hearts. What really does matter most to them?

An important part of spiritual direction is also to help people discern their true image of God. This must be distinguished from a person's "concept" of God. That distinction can help us understand a primary difference between discipling and spiritual direction. In part, by discipling a person, we teach him the Christian concept of God: the gracious, loving, triune God who is Father, Son, and Holy Spirit. This is primarily a matter of knowledge. By way of spiritual direction we can help a person begin to understand how well he has actually appropriated that knowledge. He may have it in his head, that is, he may conceptually understand. But does he actually and imaginatively live in accordance with that concept? How we imagine God is the God with whom we actually deal. In other words, the God of our imagination is far more powerful than the god of our ideas.

Christians know that they are not to worship money or be ruled by it. But do their lives really reflect that reality? Does the power of money actually control them? Money's power frequently distorts the reality of the triune God. Furthermore, the practices of some Christians show that they have projected the values of our consumer society onto the triune God. Does not a "You get what you pay for" mentality frequently obscure the true God's gracious reality for many people? To this way of thinking, is it not almost impossible for many to comprehend Christ's parable of the Workers in the Vineyard? In Matthew 20:1–16, the reign that Christ teaches and embodies repudiates an economics of value based upon work. The economics of Christ's kingdom stand in stark contrast to the kingdom of mammon. Spiritual direction can help a person listen to her life: What God does she really serve?

Discipling

The spiritual companionship of discipling is quite different from mentoring and spiritual direction. Actively teaching the faith provides the primary content for this form of spiritual conversation. Richard Foster offers eight steps for allowing Christ and not mammon to be one's master.[61] They provide an excellent and praxis-oriented summary of the important elements of Christian teaching regarding money.

The first of these is what we have already spent some time developing: "Listen to the Biblical writers about money."[62] God uses the Scriptures to set our imaginations free from money's power. The witness of both the Old and New Testaments helps us to understand that money is a fallen power that desires service rather than to serve. This enables us to begin to put money in a more proper and faithful perspective.

Second, Foster encourages us to consider money from a "psychological and sociological standpoint."[63] We will look at this action step in greater detail below.

The third step involves the material we have considered under mentoring. Foster reminds us that we must practice money management as disciples. In the light of the gospel, practices such as budgeting, investing, saving, and spending can never be seen as separate from Christian discipleship. All such concerns must be understood *sub specie aeternitatis,* "from the viewpoint of eternity." Christians are called to practice good money management principles in order to become free for kingdom service.

Fourth, Foster reminds us of the communal nature of the Christian faith. The economics of God's kingdom are countercultural. It is extremely difficult (if not impossible) to stand against money's power without the support of fellow believers. Therefore, we need to become part of a community of support. We best break money's hold by speaking freely of it with other struggling Christians. Money tends to isolate us into discrete earning and spending units. This is only overcome with great intention. Can there really be any doubt that it is no accident that American rugged individualism both creates and sustains the wealthiest culture in history?

Fifth, Foster reminds us of the importance of prayer: "Let us learn to pray for each other for the binding of greed and covetousness and the releasing of liberality and generosity."[64] Only God can fully release us from money's inappropriate influence. This may put us in mind of another Scripture (Matt. 17:14–20) wherein faith alone has the power to bind the powers allied against God. Prayer unites us with the one who is able to deliver people from the bondage of money.

Foster's sixth recommendation is a reminder of how money matters are treated far too seriously in our culture. As we noted in chapter 4, silence regarding money is a sign of the awe in which it is held. We can best dethrone money from its usurped throne by way of lightheartedness. Foster advises:

> So step on it. Yell at it. Laugh at it. List it way down on the scale of values—certainly far below friendship and cheerful surroundings. And engage in the most profane act of all—give it away. The powers of money cannot abide that most unnatural act of all—giving.[65]

Once again, we see that the chief way in which one is freed from money's influence is by giving it away. Ultimately, there is no more powerful way to be released from its domination.

Seventh, Foster calls us to take our stand with people rather than with money and the things it can purchase:

> There are many things we can do to declare that we value people
> above things. We can be willing to lose money rather than a friend-
> ship. We can side with the "use" of church facilities over the "preser-
> vation" of facilities. We can provide wages that respond to human
> need as well as human productivity. We can always remember that
> the child who breaks the toy is more important than the toy. We can
> give up a major purchase to feed hungry people. The possibilities are
> endless.[66]

How often do we allow things a place of value above people? Human beings, who all bear God's image, are always of far greater value than any inanimate object. Yet we frequently act contrary to that most basic affirmation of the Christian faith.

Finally, Foster advises us to stop favoring the wealthy over the poor. What the Epistle of James (2:1–7) warns against is far too evident in many Christian communities. One of the great ugly secrets of church life is how much the wealth of certain members can hold hostage the mission and ministry of a congregation. Clergy and laity alike must not allow wealth to dictate the ministry of any particular church.

Pastoral Counseling

The final type of spiritual companionship that Bakke proposes is pastoral counseling. Pastoral counseling primarily deals with identified problems. For most people the only problem associated with money is not having enough! But increasingly, clinicians are identifying money-related issues such as compulsive buying. Before we come to that, however, we want to address some of the psychological literature that deals with money issues.

James A. Knight has identified several underlying pastoral issues regarding money. The first of these are the social-psychological meanings:

> Money . . . [is] a symbol of the emotional relations between an indi-
> vidual and the other members of the group. . . . Since one of the deep-
> est of human longings is to enter fully into a shared life with others,
> money symbolizes the loving, giving and receiving that gives individ-
> uals a feeling of emotional rootedness in their community. . . . The
> proper uses of money give an individual a sense of well-being and
> emotional security, while inappropriate uses may create, as well as
> grow out of, deep emotional conflicts.[67]

Insofar as money is a primary marker for a person to understand his or her relation to the larger community, it is able to exert tremendous psychological influence. In societies such as ours, it is one of the easiest and most pervasive means of establishing the place of individuals relative to the larger group.

A second important area of influence is the depth-psychological dimensions. The first of these involves issues of anxiety and security. There is often little awareness "of the powerful effect money has on inner feelings of security," writes Knight. "In a world of turmoil and sudden change, the quest for money is motivated greatly by the desire to find something akin to a magical charm for attaining emotional security."[68] Money is often used in order to compensate for anxiety and feeling a lack of security. It does this by using its power to build self-regard. Again, Knight states:

> Money, then, is an ego supplement, and the possibility of getting rich, the idea of being wealthy, becomes an ideal. The attainment of wealth is fantasized and worked for as something bound up with an enormous increase of self-regard. Thus, the original and basic aim is not for money but for power and respect among one's fellow humans or with oneself.[69]

Finally, money and the things it can purchase are a principal means that many use to overcome fears of loss:

> The struggle to accumulate money, beyond one's reasonable needs, may be an effort to neutralize and escape a pathologic fear of impoverishment, growing partly out of a sense of isolation in today's fragmented society. [And quoting] Khalil Gibran: "Is not dread of thirst when your well is full, the thirst that is unquenchable?"[70]

Even the best-lived lives include significant loss. The natural process of aging involves a loss of health and vitality. Money is frequently used in attempts to avoid or even maintain the illusion that loss need not occur. This is especially the case with the greatest loss of all: death. Utilizing terror management theory, Sheldon Solomon, Jeff Greenberg, and Thomas Pyszczynski make the connection between overconsumption and the fear of death: "Conspicuous possession and consumption are thinly veiled efforts to assert that one is special and therefore more than just an animal fated to die and decay."[71] They believe that the accumulation of money and goods (beyond one's reasonable needs) are attempts to gather prestige. Prestige in its original sense is related to a magician's trick: an illusion by which we acquire magical power over death. In this way, money becomes the sacred means of ensuring one's immortality.[72] So deeply a part of American culture is this magical use of money that even the artwork on the American dollar shows the linkage between the pursuit of money and immortality.[73] In this light, consumerism truly can be understood as a modern religion insofar as its goal appears to be ensuring life after death.

Increasingly, clinicians are diagnosing psychological problems involving money such as compulsive buying and acquisitive desire. People who suffer from acquisitive desire are often seeking to establish their identity through possessions. They may be what were formerly described as "classic materialists." Here we observe those who appear to ascribe to the secular maxim "The one who dies with the most toys wins!"

Everyone knows at least one person who makes purchases far beyond his means. Some studies show that this materialistic impulse is a "means of self-soothing or a substitution for love and attention not received in earlier life."[74] Recommended therapies for such problems involve helping people to understand better the role of possessions in their lives by exploring the role of guilt and shame in their lives. This problem seems to be increasing in American society and could well be tied to increasing levels of wealth. As Jeffrey Kottler, Marilyn Montgomery, and David Shepard write:

> When society is diverse, diffuse, and rapidly changing, it is easier for some "emergent adults" to sort out the coming-of-age question of "who am I" with an answer of "I am what I own." . . . By midlife, most adults find that these kinds of answers to life's questions have begun to wear very thin. However individuals who have spent their early adulthood "shopping for identity" may not have developed inner resources for discovering and constructing a life that represents a commitment to the core values of one's self.[75]

Compulsive buying may be an even greater difficulty for some. People who suffer from this disorder are unable to prevent themselves from purchasing items, often things that they do not even desire to own. Ronald J. Faber defines compulsive buying as

> chronic, repetitive purchasing that occurs as a response to negative events or feelings. The alleviation of these negative feelings is the primary motivation for engaging in the behavior. Buying should provide the individual with short-term positive rewards, but result in long-term negative consequences.[76]

This is a very serious problem in that compulsive buying may be considered in the same category as kleptomania, alcoholism, or eating disorders. Pastors who encounter compulsive buyers during counseling should probably refer them to other professionals. Clergy can help, but additional aid is usually necessary.

Money issues are of course a key issue in premarital and marital counseling. Most premarital inventories include some questions regarding finances, debt, and income expectations.[77] Even though conflicts involving money often point to deeper issues, they are certainly a flashpoint for much marital strife.

Clergy and lay counselors need to encourage conversations regarding money for those about to be married.

Ultimately, these four types of spiritual companionship are complementary. Dependent upon the individual and the context, one type will be more appropriate than others. Our belief is that most clergy will be most comfortable with spending most of their time offering spiritual direction and discipling forms of companionship. Most money mentoring, we believe, should probably be done by laypeople. This is a key ministry for many businesspeople and can help to heal the secular-sacred dichotomy we often find in church. Included in that mentoring should be prayer and an adequate theological foundation so that a proper approach to money is discerned. Furthermore, most clergy lacking a clinical background should beware of spending too much time in the counseling area. If they recognize patterns of psychological turmoil, they should refer parishoners to counselors or therapists to the degree that adequate resources are available.

It is time for the church to find ways to faithfully integrate money conversations into the mainstream of church life. Faithful businesspeople are waiting to be challenged to take their faith to work. The church desperately needs the full commitment of all believers. The time for healing the breach between Sunday and Monday is long past. Furthermore, clergy have many opportunities for speaking about money separate from seeking donations. All Christians need the types of spiritual companionship that will allow them to cooperate better with all that God is seeking to do in their lives and in a broken world.

DISCUSSION QUESTIONS

1. Has your church sent any of the "unintended messages" referenced in the first part of this chapter? How might you correct such messages?
2. Select a businessperson in your church and visit her at her workplace. What did you learn by spending time with her at work?
3. How do you engage people in money conversations beyond fund-raising?

12

Conclusion

Throughout this book we have attempted to make the case that money is one of the key spiritual issues facing Christians. Both Old and New Testaments are full of texts that reference the relationship between a person of faith and money. Those texts can be grouped into certain important areas such as blessing, giving, and the relationship between money and idolatry.

Furthermore, even a brief overview of the history of the church shows how much theologians, bishops, and other leaders spoke of the relationship between money and faithful Christian living. Those pronouncements were often in the form of admonitions and dire warnings. Particularly in the early church, excessive wealth was often seen as an impediment to true Christianity. That view changed over the years as economic thought changed, but the concern never completely left. Nor, do we believe, should it.

But how one takes up the challenge of the danger of money must be understood within the full context of the Bible and the traditions that have developed around it. Therefore, a theology of money is essential. Money is powerful, and that power is best understood as one of the New Testament principalities. That means that money's tendency is away from God when divorced from the lordship of Christ. The good news is that Christians are called to and are empowered to participate in Christ's victory over all those things, including money, that would otherwise impede life as God intends it. In other words, Christians should be conscious of their use of money, so that money does not use them. They are called to the anxiety-free abundant life Christ promises. The essential discipline of that abundant living is the ability to give freely.

It is not enough for clergy to simply proclaim the promise of an anxiety-free relationship to money. They must also practice it. Many clergy experience personal anxiety in either talking about money or thinking about church finances. But properly applying a theology of money means learning how to provide leadership in the financial aspects of congregational life. We believe that in order to lead, clergy must have a basic understanding about accounting in the church. We provided the foundation for understanding fund accounting and the financial statements used by most churches.

Next, we looked in depth at the common church financial reports and statements. We sought to provide pastors with tools to quickly analyze these reports. In this way, we attempted to arm pastors with the ability to confidently understand and lead with authority in the financial matters of their churches.

Following that, we offered a larger context for budgeting in the church, one that places budgeting into an ongoing cycle of discernment, planning, and budgeting. We developed the concept that budgets are some of the most important confessional statements of what a congregation actually believes. We think that discerning God's mission can and must be both the starting and ending place of budgeting within the church.

Subsequently, we examined the critical need for financial transparency within the church. There is no place for secrecy in financial matters within the church. Money most effectively exerts its powerful influence when it is never openly discussed. We saw that financially transparent churches share information, have a comprehensive system of internal controls, actively work to prevent fraud, and foster an internal culture of openness.

Then we acknowledged the importance of disarming the power of money in the personal life of the clergyperson. We examined clergy income tax, the compensation package, personal spending, and personal giving. We asked how clergy can help others if they themselves are overwhelmed by money's power.

Ultimately, clergy must lead in fund-raising as well. We saw that such ministry for many clergy is one of their least favorite aspects of pastoring a church. The good news is that these matters are still of a spiritual nature. Adopting secular philosophies of fund-raising and the related strategies that follow them need not be the way in which clergy go about this important part of ministry. Properly understanding and encouraging faithful motivations for giving is the heart of leadership in this area.

Finally, we discussed the larger context of money-talk in the church and noted that it should not only occur during annual campaigns or other fund-raising times. We briefly examined both the *sacred-secular* and the *Sunday-Monday* divides, challenging clergy to look for ways to heal these rifts. We outlined several ways in which pastors can equip laypeople to take their faith to work and embrace their occupations as vocations from God. Furthermore, clergy can learn how to offer spiritual companionship in its various forms as they relate to money. Mentoring, spiritual direction, discipling, and counseling are all key ways in which to converse with laity. Most money-talk in the church should not involve asking for money!

In conclusion, let us return to Pastor Beth. Taking seriously the theological issues regarding money, she has sought to familiarize herself with the basic accounting and financial skills necessary to assume her role in church leadership. She knows how important money matters are and also how difficult it is to discuss them.

Pastor Beth sat down for what she knew would be a long and tense special meeting of the finance committee. The purpose of the meeting was to finally discuss the big secret that had been lurking under the surface at every meeting for the seven months Beth had been at the church—the fact that the church had borrowed, and borrowed heavily, from its building fund to support its operating fund.

Pastor Beth understood the problem. It was one she had read about but had hoped she would never encounter in a church. Since arriving at this parish, she had felt strongly that the problem needed to be faced head-on and resolved openly. But after asking some basic questions about the situation in her first days at the church, she had been wisely waiting for the lay leaders to reach the same conclusion. Finally, they appeared ready to take the difficult steps necessary to return to financial health.

Beth smiled confidently as she took out the latest set of financial reports prepared by the treasurer. She had spent some time reviewing them the previous night and had drafted a proposal that she intended to make if no one else suggested a solution.

Pastor Beth opened the meeting in prayer. In the prayer, she thanked God for the many gifts represented around the table. She acknowledged that each one there was a person of vocation. She also thanked God for bringing light into the many dark places of the world and asked that new light would be shed in that evening's meeting.

As the meeting got underway, the treasurer laid out the problem and asked for suggestions on how it could be solved. Joe, the chairperson of the finance committee, suggested that the committee quietly approach several wealthy members in confidence and ask them for special onetime gifts that could be used to replace the borrowed funds. "We don't want word of this situation getting out to the whole congregation, you know!" Joe said.

Pastor Beth cleared her throat. This was the opportunity she had been waiting for. "Joe," she stated boldly, "I have to disagree with you on this one. I think that it is important for the committee to confess to the congregation what we have done rather than to just cover it up. I believe that if we are to grow into a truly financially transparent church, we need to bring this out into the open. Furthermore, I think that unless we are open about this, money's power will continue to dominate our congregation."

"But Pastor Beth, what will people think?" gasped Helen, horrified at the idea.

"I believe that they will appreciate the candor with which the committee is dealing with the situation. The explanation as to why the committee did what it did in the past is completely understandable. There wasn't enough money to pay all the bills. The church needs to be made aware that their giving is not adequate to cover all the programs that everyone wants to have."

"But we will sound like we can't manage the church's finances!" exclaimed Joe.

"Not if we present our plan on how to fix the problem," Beth stated calmly. She then proceeded to outline her proposal. She detailed clearly a six-month strategy of increased giving and reduced expenditures that would generate sufficient excess to pay back the borrowed funds.

"Joe, you're the financial guru here, so you'll need to check out my numbers, but my calculations show that if we can increase giving by just 5 percent for the next six months and cut back on the areas of spending that I've highlighted, we can fix this thing. And I believe that the congregation will respond if we explain the situation, ask for increased short-term giving, and make a real commitment to increased financial transparency."

Joe smiled and said, "I think you are right, Pastor. It is probably better to come clean and face the problem head-on. After all, there is that verse on which you preached a few weeks ago about people who prefer the darkness because it covers up their bad deeds. Since we are a church, I guess we should be willing to open everything up to the light of day."

Beth smiled and nodded.

Notes

Chapter 1: The Problem of Money in the Church

1. A quick search on Amazon.com yields twenty-five to thirty books in print on the topic of financial stewardship and raising money for churches. There are, of course, numerous others currently out of print.

2. One of the primary research organizations in the field of church giving, empty tomb, offers the following discouraging statistics: "Overall, members donated a smaller portion of income to their churches in 2003 than in 1968. Per member giving as a percentage of income to Total Contributions declined from 3.11% in 1968 to 2.59% in 2003, a decline of 17% in the portion of income donated to the church from the 1968 base." The picture becomes even bleaker when mission giving is considered: "Benevolences, the subcategory of Total Contributions that funds the larger mission of the church beyond the local congregation, decreased 42% as a portion of income, from 0.66% in 1968 to 0.38% in 2003. The 2003 level of giving to Benevolences as a percent of income was the lowest in the 1968–2003 period. In 1968, 21¢ of every dollar donated was allocated to Benevolences. By 2003, 15¢ of every dollar went to Benevolences. Of each additional inflation-adjusted dollar donated to the church between 1968 and 2003, 94¢ went to Congregational Finances." John L. and Sylvia Ronsvalle, *The State of Church Giving through 2003* (Champaign, IL: empty tomb, 2005), 7. As we will argue later, it is the fall in benevolent giving that is most problematic from a theological standpoint. This statistic points to a profound diminishment of understanding of what God is doing in our midst.

3. "The General Assembly Council has approved the most radical restructuring of the Presbyterian Church (U.S.A.)'s mission program since 1993, as it moves to reduce the 2007–2008 General Assembly mission budget by $9.15 million. In all, 75 national staff positions in Louisville have been eliminated—most effective May 1—as well as 55 overseas mission coworker positions. Staff cuts in Louisville account for $4 million of the budget reduction, while the price tag for the overseas mission positions is $1.2 million." Jerry L. Van Marter,

Presbyterian News Service release, May 1, 2006, http://www.pcusa.org/
pcnews/2006/06244.htm.

4. David Conway, *Seminary Development News* 16, no. 1 (Spring 2003): 9. Pastors "are uncomfortable dealing with or even talking about issues of church
administration and finance. They feel unprepared for these responsibilities
and they accept them only reluctantly when there appears to be no other
choice." Ibid., 9.

5. Responding to a recent survey of what would make them "most effective as pastors," 70 percent of clergy responded that "a required course in the seminary
curriculum using a series of guest lectures by active pastors and lay church
administrators to introduce seminarians to basic financial issues and forms used
in church administration and typical challenges that may arise for a pastor
along with examples of how pastors have dealt with those challenges" would be
either "extremely" or "very helpful." *The Reluctant Steward Revisited*, ed. Daniel
Conway et al. (St. Meinrad, IN: St. Meinrad School of Theology, 2002), 58.

6. Even the largest Protestant seminaries, such as Asbury, Fuller, Princeton, and
Southwestern Baptist, offer no required or elective courses dedicated to financial ministry.

7. James A. Knight, *For the Love of Money* (New York: J. B. Lippincott, 1968),
32–33.

Chapter 2: The Bible and Money

1. Richard Foster has observed, "The truth is that it is not really difficult to discover what the Bible teaches about money. . . . The Bible is much more clear
and straightforward about money than it is about many other issues." *The Challenge of the Disciplined Life* (San Francisco: HarperCollins, 1985), 21.

2. Christopher J. H. Wright, "Sabbatical Year," in *The Anchor Bible Dictionary*, vol.
5, ed. David Noel Freedman (New York: Doubleday, 1992), 857.

3. Craig Blomberg *Neither Poverty nor Riches: A Biblical Theology of Possessions*
(Downers Grove, IL: InterVarsity Press, 1999), 44.

4. For instance: "Those who are generous are blessed, for they share their bread
with the poor" (22:9) and "Whoever gives to the poor will lack nothing, but
one who turns a blind eye will get many a curse" (28:27).

5. We have limited our discussion of material blessing to the Old Testament. This
is for the simple reason that there really are no equivalent texts in the New Testament. Craig Blomberg writes, "The New Testament carried forward the
major principles of the Old Testament and intertestamental Judaism with one
conspicuous omission: never was material wealth promised as a guaranteed
reward as either spiritual obedience or simple hard work." Blomberg, *Neither
Poverty nor Riches*, 242. The reason for this, it seems to us, is the consistent New
Testament teaching that all blessings are contained in Jesus Christ. For example: "Blessed be the God and Father of our Lord Jesus Christ, who has blessed
us in Christ with every spiritual blessing in the heavenly places" (Eph. 1:3). Of
course, the assertion that the New Testament does not have an equivalent theology of blessing is contested by many Christians, in particular, those who hold
to a "prosperity gospel." We will briefly deal with that idea in chapter 4.

6. Among the offerings stipulated in the Old Testament are burnt, peace, guilt,
thank, freewill, votive, wave, and heave.

7. Elizabeth Achtemeier, *Nahum–Malachi*, Interpretation: A Bible Commentary
for Teaching and Preaching (Atlanta: John Knox Press, 1986), 189.

8. J. Christian Wilson, "Tithe," in *The Anchor Bible Dictionary*, vol. 6, ed. David
   Noel Freedman (New York: Doubleday, 1992), 579.

9. Here, Richard Hays's four modes of appeal (rules, principles, paradigms, and
   symbolic world) in ethical argument are helpful. There are no "rules" concerning tithing in the New Testament. Instead, one can argue that giving is author-
   itatively discussed in the New Testament primarily in terms of "paradigms" and
   a "symbolic world." One sees a negative paradigm in the behavior of the Phar-
   isees. One can give (perhaps even sacrificially) and not please God. Furthermore, a new symbolic world is revealed that does not focus upon one's own
   works but looks to see the more important things that God is doing. Hays, *The
   Moral Vision of the New Testament* (San Francisco: HarperSanFrancisco, 1996),
   208–9.

10. Jouette M. Bassler, *God and Mammon: Asking for Money in the New Testament*
    (Nashville: Abingdon Press, 1991), 33.

11. Ibid., 109.

12. "Clearly, ethical issues, including the use of one's material possessions, rank
    among the major topics of prophetic rhetoric. But one has only to read in its
    entirety virtually any book of prophecy at random to see that at least as serious
    as the Israelites' ethical sins was their idolatry. Theological and ethical defec-
    tion from God's will consistently go hand in hand." Craig L. Blomberg, *Nei-
    ther Poverty nor Riches: A Biblical Theology of Possessions* (Downers Grove:
    InterVarsity Press, 1999), 70.

13. Brian S. Rosner has done a masterful job in exegeting these texts. He concludes
    his work by stating, "What do the greedy, idolaters, and believers have in com-
    mon? In each case they relate to their objects of worship in terms of love, trust
    and obedience. Thus, at the risk of blunting the affective impact of the
    metaphor, 'greed is idolatry' may be paraphrased as teaching that to have a
    strong desire to acquire and keep for yourself more and more money and mate-
    rial things is an attack on God's exclusive rights to human love and devotion,
    trust and confidence, and service and obedience." Rosner, *Greed as Idolatry: The
    Origin and Meaning of a Pauline Metaphor* (Grand Rapids: Wm. B. Eerdmans
    Publishing Co., 2007), 173.

14. A similar statement is made in Luke 16:13 at the conclusion of the parable of
    the Dishonest Manager: "No slave can serve two masters; for a slave will either
    hate the one and love the other, or be devoted to the one and despise the other.
    You cannot serve God and wealth."

15. Concerning this text and the word *mammon* in the original Greek text, Martin
    Hengel writes, "The imminence of the Kingdom of God demands freedom
    over possessions, the renunciation of all care, complete trust in the goodness
    and providence of the Heavenly Father. . . . Service of God and service of mam-
    mon are mutually exclusive: 'No one can serve two masters. . . . You cannot
    serve God and mammon (Luke 6:13 = Matthew 6:24). The Aramaic-Phoeni-
    cian word for possessions or property is clearly used here in a negative sense. .
    . . Perhaps the early church left this Semitic loan-word untranslated because
    they regarded it almost as the name of an idol: the service of mammon is idol-
    atry. Here possessions acquire a demonic character, because they are a tie to
    men and close their ears to the summons of the kingdom of God." Hengel,
    *Earliest Christianity: Containing Acts and the History of Earliest Christianity, and
    Property and Riches in the Early Church*, trans. John Bowden (London: SCM
    Press, 1986), 172.

16. Robert D. Lupton, *Theirs Is the Kingdom: Celebrating the Gospel in Urban America* (San Francisco: HarperSanFrancisco, 1989), 91.

Chapter 3: A Short History of the Church's Teachings on Money

1. Martin Hengel, *Earliest Christianity, Containing Acts and the History of Earliest Christianity and Property and Riches in the Early Church* (London: SCM Press, 1986), 232.
2. Justo L. González, *Faith and Wealth: A History of Early Christian Ideas on the Origin, Significance, and Use of Money* (San Francisco: HarperSanFrancisco, 1990), 15.
3. Clement of Alexandria, *Who Is the Rich That Shall Be Saved?* in *The Ante-Nicene Fathers*, vol. 2, *Fathers of the Second Century*, ed. Alexander Roberts and James Donaldson (Grand Rapids: Wm. B. Eerdmans Publishing Co., 1986), 595. Clement explains, "For he who holds possessions, and gold, and silver, and houses, as the gifts of God; and ministers from them to the God who gives them for the salvation of men; and knows that he possesses them more for the sake of the brethren than his own; and is superior to the possession of them, not the slave of the things he possesses; and does not carry them about in his soul, nor bind and circumscribe his life within them, but is ever laboring at some good and divine work, even should he be necessarily some time or other deprived of them, is able with cheerful mind to bear their removal equally with their abundance" (ibid.).
4. Ibid., 595.
5. Ibid., 598.
6. Cyprian of Carthage, *Treatise on Works and Alms*, in *The Ante-Nicene Fathers*, vol. 5, *Fathers of the Third Century*, ed. Alexander Roberts and James Donaldson (Grand Rapids: Wm. B. Eerdmans Publishing Co., 1986), 476.
7. Ibid. 479.
8. "The almsgiving of which Cyprian speaks is so great that people could object that it would threaten their patrimony or their children's inheritance. Cyprian himself disposed of at least a significant portion of his estate and gave it to the poor. Therefore, it probably would be wrong to interpret his emphasis on almsgiving as an attempt to widen the eye of the needle through which the rich must pass." González, *Faith and Wealth*, 127. In other words, Cyprian is not proposing an easing of the burden of wealth. One does not buy salvation, but the wealthy Christian will be expected to give away large parts of that wealth.
9. Cyprian, *Treatise on Works and Alms*, 483.
10. "The most hated sort (of wealth getting) and with the greatest reason, is usury, which makes a gain out of money itself and not from the natural object of it. For money was intended to be used in exchange but not to increase at interest. And this term interest which means the birth of money from money is applied to the breeding of money because the offspring resembles the parent. That is why of all modes of getting wealth, this is the most unnatural" ("Politics," in *The Complete Works of Aristotle*, The Revised Oxford Translation, ed. Jonathan Barnes [Princeton, NJ: Princeton University Press, 1997], 1258b).
11. John Chrysostom, *On Wealth and Poverty*, trans. Catherine P. Roth (Crestwood, NY: St. Vladimir's Seminary Press, 1984), 36 and 55.
12. Ibid., 23.
13. Focusing upon the reference to the rich man's burial (Luke 16:22), Chrysostom says, "Do not simply pass over that phrase 'he was buried,' beloved: by it you should understand that the silver-inlaid tables, couches, rugs, tapestries, all other kinds of furnishings, sweet oils, perfumes, large quantities of undiluted

wine, great varieties of food, rich dishes, cooks, flatterers, body-guards, house-hold servants, and all the rest of his ostentation have been quenched and with-ered up." Ibid., 45–46. In both the metaphor of the cargo ship and this one of burial, it seems to be the "weightiness" of the many possessions that eventually destroys the rich person.

14. Ibid., 40.
15. Ibid. 47.
16. Augustine, *The City of God*, books 8–16, trans. Gerald G. Walsh and Grace Monahan (New York: Fathers of the Church, 1952), 227.
17. Augustine, *Exposition of the Psalms 51–72*, part 3, vol. 17 of *The Works of St. Augustine: A Translation for the 21st Century*, trans. Maria Boulding (Hyde Park, NY: New City Press, 2001), 26.
18. Augustine is quick to point out that the poor may have as much trouble with money as the wealthy: "So what is it ultimately that is censured in such folk? Not the fact of possessing wealth, because good people have wealth too. What then? Note the answer carefully, for you must not disparage the rich indiscrim-inately, nor must you think yourself secure just because you are hard up. If we may not rely on riches, much less may we rely on poverty; our only reliance is on the living God." Ibid., 28.
19. Augustine, Sermon 345 in *Sermons (341–400) on Various Subjects*, in *The Works of St. Augustine: A Translation for the 21st Century*, trans. Edmund Hill (Hyde Park, NY: New City Press, 1995), 60.
20. Ibid., 62.
21. Thomas C. Oden, *Care of Souls in the Classic Tradition* (Philadelphia: Fortress Press, 1984), 97.
22. Gregory, *The Pastoral Rule*, part 3, chap. 2, *Nicene and Post-Nicene Fathers of the Christian Church*, trans. and ed. James Barmby (Grand Rapids: Wm. B. Eerd-mans Publishing Co., 1983), 25.
23. Ibid., 25.
24. Ibid. 44, 47.
25. *The Penitential of Finnian*, in *Medieval Handbook of Penance: A Translation of the Principal Libri Poenitentiales*, ed. John T. McNeill and Helena M. Gamer (New York: Columbia University Press, 1990), 92.
26. *The Penitential of Cummean*, in ibid., 105–6.
27. *An Old Irish Penitential*, in ibid., 161.
28. There can be little doubt that the deep suspicion of wealth was never shared by perhaps even the majority of Christians. The opposition to Chrysostom's preaching is a notable example. All we are arguing here is that such a universal call is increasingly muted after the late patristic period.
29. R. H. Tawney, *Religion and the Rise of Capitalism* (New York: Mentor Books, 1954), 55.
30. Ibid., 41–42.
31. Ibid., 59.
32. Ibid., 82.
33. Ibid., 79–80.
34. Walther I. Brandt, Introduction to "Trade and Usury," *Luther's Works*, vol. 45, *The Christian in Society II*, ed. Walther I. Brandt (Philadelphia: Muhlenberg Press, 1962), 239.
35. *Luther's Works*, vol. 21, *The Sermon on the Mount (Sermons) and the Magnificat*, ed. by Jaroslav Pelikan (St. Louis: Concordia Publishing House, 1956), 12.
36. Ibid.

37. Ibid., 13.
38. Kathryn D'Arcy Blanchard, "'If You Do Not Do This You Are Not Now a Christian': Martin Luther's Pastoral Teaching on Money," *Word and World* 26, no. 3 (Summer 2006): 308–9.
39. John Calvin, *Institutes of the Christian Religion*, vol. 1, ed. John T. McNeill, trans. Ford Lewis Battles (Philadelphia: Westminster Press, 1960), 719–20.
40. Ibid., 720.
41. "Away then with that inhuman philosophy which, while conceding only a necessary use of creatures, not only malignantly deprives us of the lawful fruit of God's beneficence but cannot be practiced unless it robs a man of all his senses and degrades him to a block." Ibid., 721.
42. Ibid., 723–24.
43. L. F. Schulze, "Calvin's Views on Interest and Property," *Studia historiae ecclesiasticae* 26, no. 2 (December 2000): 203.
44. W. Stanford Reid, "John Calvin, Early Critic of Capitalism, Part 1," *Reformed Theological Review* 43 (September–December 1984): 80.
45. Richard Baxter, *A Christian Directory*, cited in Leland Ryken, *Worldly Saints: The Puritans as They Really Were* (Grand Rapids: Zondervan, 1986), 58.
46. William Perkins, *Works*, cited in Ryken, *Worldly Saints*, 67
47. Ryken, *Worldly Saints*, 71.
48. John Wesley, "The Use of Money," in *The Works of John Wesley*, vol. 2, *Sermons 34–70*, ed. Albert Outler (Nashville: Abingdon Press, 1985). Outler maintains that "Wesley declines to condemn money or trade or technology. He encourages all reasonable provisions for life's 'necessaries and conveniences' for one's self and family—this, indeed, is a Christian's duty. The difference comes in his insistence on 'giving all you can'; an exhortation with so radical an implication that the ordinary conventions of generosity and philanthropy are brought into question. It is as if Wesley regarded surplus accumulation as sinful in itself or as at the least an irresistible temptation to sin" (265). We believe that even though Wesley correctly established the key Christian principles of earning, saving, and giving, the rules he created regarding them were untenable. The first and dominant response of the early Methodists (as Wesley himself admits) was to ignore the founder of the movement regarding the use of money.
49. Albert Outler, editor of *The Works of John Wesley*, vol. 3, *Sermons, 71–114* (Nashville: Abingdon Press, 1986), 238n.
50. Ibid.
51. John Wesley, "The Danger of Riches," in ibid, 229.
52. Ibid., 239.
53. Ibid., 243.
54. Ibid., 245.
55. Albert Outler observes of this sermon, "It is scarcely more than a resume of a long series of denunciations of greed and surplus accumulation, especially among professing Christians. Here, however, his tone is almost despairing. He has come to the reluctant conclusion that, over the course of fifty years, he has not been able to convert as many as fifty 'misers of covetousness.' . . . What is obvious, therefore, is the pathos of this combined denunciation and appeal: 'with dim eyes, shaking hands, and tottering feet, I give you one more advice before I sink into the dust.'" *The Works of John Wesley*, vol. 4, *Sermons, 115–151* (Nashville: Abingdon Press, 1987), 177.
56. David Hempton, "A Tale of Preachers and Beggers: Methodism and Money in the Great Age of Transatlantic Expansion, 1780–1830," in *God and Mammon:*

Protestants, Money, and the Market, 1790–1860, ed. Mark A. Noll (New York: Oxford University Press, 2002), 124.

57. Mark A. Noll, "Protestant Reasoning about Money and the Economy, 1790–1860: A Preliminary Probe," in Noll, *God and Mammon*, 271.

58. Daniel B. McGee, "Business Ethics among Baptists: A Story of Competing Visions," in *Spiritual Goods: Religious Traditions and Business Practice* (Charlottesville, VA: Philosophy Documentation Center, 2001), 222.

Chapter 4: Developing a Theology of Money

1. Jacques Ellul, *Money and Power*, trans. LaVonne Neff (Downers Grove, IL: InterVarsity Press, 1984), 15.

2. Ibid., 29.

3. Ibid.

4. See Max Weber, *The Protestant Ethic and the Spirit of Capitalism* (New York: Charles Scribner's Sons, 1958).

5. Flannery O'Connor, *Wise Blood*, in *Flannery O'Connor: Collected Works* (New York: Library of America, 1988), 64.

6. Ibid., 59.

7. Ellul, *Money and Power*, 31.

8. Ellul is certainly influenced here by one of his theological mentors, Karl Barth. Barth's primary discussion of the principalities or "Lordless powers" can be found in *The Christian Life: Church Dogmatics IV.4 Lecture Fragments* (Grand Rapids: Wm. B. Eerdmans Publishing Co., 1981), 213–33.

9. We have used the New International Version because the New Revised Standard Version's translation ("No one can serve two masters; for a slave will either hate the one and love the other, or be devoted to the one and despise the other. You cannot serve God and wealth") obscures the basic point that Ellul and we want to make. The NIV makes a clearer reference to the Authorized Version's and Revised Standard Version's use of "mammon." The NRSV's use of the lowercase "wealth" detracts from the power of the comparison.

10. Ellul, *Money and Power*, 75.

11. "Paul therefore stresses a cosmic Christology (Col 1:15–20) affirming the superior position of Christ in relation to the powers. Christ is also asserted as the ruling 'head' over the principalities and powers (Col 2:10)." Clinton E. Arnold, "Principalities and Powers" in *Anchor Bible Dictionary*, vol. 5 (New York: Doubleday, 1992), 467.

12. Daniel G. Reid, "Principalities and Powers," in *Dictionary of Paul and His Letters* (Downers Grove, IL: InterVarsity Press, 1993), 750.

13. Stephen F. Noll, *Angels of Light, Powers of Darkness* (Downers Grove, IL: InterVarsity Press, 1998), 138–39.

14. Ellul, *Money and Power*, 75–76.

15. Ibid., 77.

16. Craig M. Gay, *Cash Values: Money and the Erosion of Meaning in Today's Society* (Grand Rapids: Wm. B. Eerdmans Publishing Co., 2003), 48.

17. Ellul, *Money and Power*, 49.

18. Ibid. 17.

19. Capitalism tends to promote a practical atheism rather than a philosophical one. There is still plenty of room for a "God of the gaps." This, however, is a God who primarily comforts and blesses one's efforts. The biblical God is squeezed out of the "real world" and left to Sunday mornings or a time of crisis in which money's power is unable to save.

20. Quoted in Gay, *Cash Values*, 39.
21. We shall examine this more thoroughly in chapter 11 when we discuss the recent movement of "business as mission."
22. Abraham Kuyper, "Sphere Sovereignty," in *Abraham Kuyper: A Centennial Reader*, ed. James D. Bratt (Grand Rapids: Wm. B. Eerdmans Publishing Co., 1998), 488.
23. Ellul, *Money and Power*, 77.
24. Ibid., 89.
25. Charles Pierre Baudelaire, *The Generous Gambler*, http://gutenberg.net.au/ebooks06/0607031.txt.
26. Quoted in Gay, Cash Values, 90.

Chapter 5: Church Finance 101

1. Phil Sherman, *Religious and Other Faith-Based Nonprofits: Tax, Accounting, and Management* (Lewisville, TX: American Institute of Certified Public Accountants, 2006), 3.1.
2. *Statement of Financial Accounting Concepts No. 6* (Norwalk, CT: Financial Accounting Standards Board, 1985), par. 25.
3. The Financial Accounting Standards Board did not require nonprofit organizations to include capitalized tangible assets in their financial statements until the 1990s. With the advent of Statement of Financial Accounting Standard No. 93, churches and other nonprofit organizations that want to comply with generally accepted accounting principles (GAAP) must now present capitalized tangible assets and record depreciation on those assets. Churches still can, and most do, elect to prepare financial statements that are not in accordance with GAAP. Most accounting professionals agree that statements prepared in this manner are not as informative and are less widely accepted by outside parties, such as lending institutions.
4. *Statement of Financial Accounting Concepts No. 6*, par. 35.
5. Ibid., para. 80.
6. *Statement of Financial Accounting Concepts No. 1* (Norwalk, CT: Financial Accounting Standards Board, 1978), 4.
7. Brenda A. Cline, Winford L. Paschall, and Stephen B. Eason, *PPC's Guide to Preparing Nonprofit Financial Statements*, vol. 2 (Fort Worth, TX: Thomson Tax & Accounting, 2007), 9.9.
8. However, if using the cash basis results in financial statements that are not materially different from those prepared on the accrual basis, those financial statements can be considered to be in conformity with GAAP. For additional information, see Evangelical Joint Accounting Committee, *Accounting and Financial Reporting Guide for Christian Ministries* (Norwalk, CT: Evangelical Joint Accounting Committee, 2001), 7.
9. At the time of writing, the landmark donor-intent lawsuit *Robertson v. Princeton University* has just reached a negotiated settlement, under which Princeton will pay $100 million to Robertson family charities. The Robertson family alleged that Princeton University misused restricted contributions. This settlement reaffirms the premise that contributions made by a donor for a stated purpose must be used for that purpose alone. As an additional resource on this topic, see Frank Sommerville, "Legal Matters: Rules for Designated Gifts," *Church Report*, March 2006.
10. For an excellent guide to restricted gifts, see Dan Busby, *Donor-Restricted Gifts*

(Winchester, VA: Evangelical Council for Financial Accountability, 2006). Busby is a noted church and nonprofit expert.

11. Kathryn W. Miree, *Understanding and Drafting Nonprofit Gift Acceptance Policies* (Birmingham, AL: Kathryn W. Miree & Associates, 2003), 14.

Chapter 7: Budgeting in the Church

1. John and Sylvia Ronsvalle, *The State of Church Giving through 2003* (Champaign, IL: empty tomb, 2005), 104.
2. John and Sylvia Ronsvalle, *Behind the Stained Glass Windows: Money Dynamics in the Church* (Grand Rapids: Baker Books, 1996), 49.
3. Ibid., 108–9.
4. Robert N. Bacher, *Church Administration: Programs, Process, Purpose* (Minneapolis: Fortress Press, 2007), 94.
5. Richard J. Vargo, *The Church Guide to Planning and Budgeting* (Matthews, NC: Christian Ministry Resources, 1995), 20–23.
6. Robert Welch, *Church Administration: Creating Efficiency for Effective Ministry* (Nashville: Broadman & Holman, 2005), 160.
7. James D. Berkley, *The Dynamics of Church Finance* (Grand Rapids: Baker Books, 2000), 47.
8. Jack A. Henry, *Basic Budgeting for Churches: A Complete Guide* (Nashville: Broadman & Holman, 1995), 24.

Chapter 8: Financial Transparency in the Church

1. Robert West and Charles Zech, "Internal Financial Controls in the U.S. Catholic Church," *Journal of Forensic Accounting* 9, (2008: 29).
2. John H. McCarthy comments in the panel discussion entitled "Essentials of Church Financial Transparency: The Archdiocese of Boston Transparency Project," *Bringing Our Gifts to the Table: Creating Conditions for Financial Health in the Church*, (Philadelphia: National Leadership Roundtable on Church Management Conference at The Wharton School, June 29–30, 2006), 30.
3. World Christian Database, http://worldchristiandatabase.org/wcd/.
4. West and Zech, "Internal Financial Controls," 129–56.
5. In 2004, Villanova University established within its College of Commerce and Finance the Center for the Study of Church Management. The center's primary mission will be to provide research and training for future church leaders. The center envisions offering a masters in Catholic Church management, certificate programs in various aspects of Catholic Church management, and publications related to diocesan "best practices."

   In June 2006, in an effort to respond to a growing need within the Catholic Church to better manage its business operations, financial resources, and personnel, Boston College announced the creation of the nation's first graduate program in church management, a cooperative venture between the Institute for Religious Education and Pastoral Ministry and Carroll School of Management.

   The law school of Seton Hall University has launched a new research and teaching center to help church-related nonprofit organizations address the legal, accreditation, and management challenges they face today. The new center has been named the Seton Center for Church-Related Nonprofit Corporations. Its mission is to provide independent, scholarly legal research on issues of strategic importance if religiously related nonprofits are going to thrive in a changing, complex environment. The center's research and services will be available to religious nonprofits of any denomination, but Catholic-related nonprofits form by far the largest single group of such organizations in the United States.

6. http://www.ecfa.org/Content.aspx?PageName=WhatIsECFA.

7. Dale L. Flesher, "Control in Volunteer Organizations," *Internal Auditor* 56, no. 6 (1999): 45–47.

8. John B. Duncan and Morris H. Stocks, "The Understanding of Internal Control Principles by Pastors," *Nonprofit Management and Leadership* 14, no. 2 (Winter 2003): 221.

9. Larry E. Rittenberg and Bradley J. Schwieger, *Auditing: Concepts for a Changing Environment*, 5th ed. (Mason, OH: Thomson/South-Western, 2005), 170.

10. Association of Certified Fraud Examiners, *2006 ACFE Report to the Nation on Occupational Fraud and Abuse* (Austin, TX: Association of Certified Fraud Examiners, 2006), 55.

11. Ibid., 44.

12. W. Steve Albrecht, *Fraud Examination* (Mason, OH: Thomson/South-Western, 2003), 27.

13. Ibid., 90.

14. Robert Simons, *Performance Measurement and Control Systems for Implementing Strategy: Text and Cases* (Upper Saddle River, NJ: Prentice-Hall, 2000).

15. Albrecht, *Fraud Examination*, 89.

Chapter 9: Money in the Personal Life of the Pastor

1. Dan Busby, *Zondervan 2007 Minister's Tax and Financial Guide* (Grand Rapids: Zondervan, 2007), 26.

2. The 7.65 percent rate is made up of two separate taxes: 6.2 percent is the tax for Social Security and 1.45 percent is the tax for Medicare. The Medicare tax is levied on all wages without limit, while the Social Security tax is capped. In 2009, the maximum amount of wages subject to Social Security tax is $106,800 for both employees and the self-employed.

3. Historically, this dates back to the creation of the Social Security system in 1937. In an effort to protect the separation of church and state, states a document from the U.S. Conference of Catholic Bishops, "Congress declared clergy to be self-employed for Social Security purposes because, at that time, self-employed individuals were not covered by Social Security. They reasoned that designating clergy as self-employed would sidestep the issue of taxing the clergy" (*Diocesan Financial Issues—Compensation of Priests and the Dual Tax Status of Priests: Employees for Income Tax Purposes, Self-Employed for Social Security Tax* [Washington, DC: United States Conference of Catholic Bishops, 2002], http://www.usccb.org/bishops/dfi/dualtax.htm). When Congress later opened the Social Security program to self-employed individuals in 1955, clergy were left with the self-employed designation, which still exists today, while exempting clergy from participating in Social Security unless they chose to do so. That exemption remained until 1968, when Congress adopted its current position: all newly ordained ministers are included in the program unless they choose to opt out on the basis of religious convictions. So the self-employed status of clergy for Social Security and Medicare purposes, which results in the payment of a significant amount of taxes for most clergy, is the result of an apparent oversight by Congress.

4. Richard R. Hammar, *Church and Clergy Tax Guide* (Carol Stream, IL: Christianity Today International, 2005), 76.

5. *Publication 517: Social Security and Other Information for Members of the Clergy and Religious Workers* (Internal Revenue Service, 2006), 4.

6. Quoted in Diana B. Henriques, Andrew Lehrens, and Donna Anderson, "Religion-Based Tax Breaks: Housing to Paychecks to Books," *New York Times*, October 11, 2006.

7. Ibid.

8. Busby, *Zondervan 2007 Minister's Tax and Financial Guide*, 133.

9. B. J. Worth, *Worth's Income Tax Guide for Ministers* (Nappanee, IN: Evangel Publishing House, 2004), 39–40.

10. Ibid. The amounts paid for mortgage interest and real estate taxes on the minister's primary residence can also be deducted by the minister as an itemized deduction, as discussed later in the chapter.

11. The Clergy Housing Allowance Clarification Act of 2002 was passed in response to *Warren v. Commissioner*, the highly publicized case involving the amount of housing allowance excludible by the Rev. Rick Warren. Warren won the first round in the case, but the IRS appealed the decision. The Ninth Circuit Federal Court of Appeals in San Francisco asked law professor Erwin Chemerinsky to research the constitutionality of the clergy housing allowance rules. When Chemerinsky's friend-of-the-court brief argued that the clergy housing allowance was unconstitutional, Congress quickly passed this act and the case was dismissed.

12. Frances E. McNair, Edward E. Milam, and Deborah Seifert, "Tax Planning for Servants of God," *Journal of Accountancy* 198, no. 4 (2004): 66–67.

13. Becky R. McMillan and Matthew J. Price, *How Much Should We Pay the Pastor? A Fresh Look at Clergy Salaries in the 21st Century*, Pulpit and Pew Research on Pastoral Leadership No. 2 (Durham, NC: Duke Divinity School, 2003), response by James Hudnut-Beumler, "More Evidence of a Leaking Ship," 28, http://www.pulpitandpew.duke.edu/salarystudy.pdf.

14. Matthew J. Price, "Male Clergy in Economic Crisis: Fear of Falling," *Christian Century* 118, no. 23 (2001): 18.

15. McMillan and Price, *How Much Should We Pay the Pastor?* 16.

16. Anthony Ruger, Sharon L. Miller, and Kim Maphis Early, *The Gathering Storm: The Educational Debt of Theological Students*, Auburn Studies No. 12 (New York: Auburn Theological Seminary, 2005), 3, http://www.auburnsem.org/about/gatheringstorm.htm.

17. Ibid., preface.

18. McMillan and Price, *How Much Should We Pay the Pastor?* Response by Kenneth Carder, "Ministry as Commodity," 24.

19. Ruger, Miller, and Early, *Gathering Storm*, 12.

20. Ibid., 21.

21. Jeanette Gardner-Littleton, "The Displaced Parsonage," *Your Church Magazine*, November/December 1999, 69, http://www.christianitytoday.com/yc/9y6/.

22. J. David Epstein, *Clergy Tax* (Ventura, CA: Gospel Light, 2002), 98.

23. Busby, *Zondervan 2007 Minister's Tax and Financial Guide*, 58.

24. Karen has lost $300 in pre-tax dollars that she could have used to pay medical expenses. If Karen had reduced her salary by only $2,700, that $300 would have been paid to her as a part of her taxable wages and would have been included on her W-2 at the end of the year. Therefore, in real dollars, Karen's loss would be $300 less the amount of federal and state taxes she would have owed.

25. In 2009, high-deductible insurance meant a policy with an annual family

deductible of $2,300 and an annual single deductible of $1,150. These amounts
are adjusted annually for inflation.

26. Penelope Wang, "What Works in Retirement Planning," *Money*, October 1,
    2006, http://money.cnn.com/magazines/moneymag/moneymag_archive/2006/
    10/01/8387534/index.htm.
27. Annamaria Lusardi and Olivia Mitchell, "Baby Boomer Retirement Security:
    The Roles of Planning, Financial Literacy, and Housing Wealth," National
    Bureau of Economic Research Working Paper No. 12585, November 2006,
    22, http://www.dartmouth.edu/~alusardi/Papers/BabyBoomers.pdf.
28. Instructions for IRS Form 2106, p. 1.
29. Hammar, *Church and Clergy Tax Guide*, 279.
30. John Ameriks, Andrew Caplin, and John Leahy, "The Absent-Minded Con-
    sumer," National Bureau of Economic Research Working Paper No. 10216,
    January 2004, 3, http://www.nber.org/papers/w10216.
31. Jaclyne Badal, "Budget Help at a Budget Lover's Price," *Wall Street Journal*,
    April 29, 2007, http://online.wsj.com/public/article/SB117779856026586043
    .html?mod=sunday_journal_primary_hs.
32. Richard Jenkins, "A Simpler Way to Save: The 60% Solution," MSN Money,
    http://articles.moneycentral.msn.com/SavingandDebt/LearnToBudget/ASim
    plerWayToSaveThe60Solution.aspx.

Chapter 10: Experiencing Freedom through Giving

1. Dean R. Hoge, Charles Zech, Patrick McNamara, and Michael J. Donahue,
   Money Matters: Personal Giving in American Churches (Louisville, KY: Westminster John Knox Press, 1996), 129–30.
2. Ibid., 133.
3. Ibid., 137.
4. Ibid., 139.
5. Ibid., 140.
6. Ibid., 142.
7. "As they moved from the public sector into the private sphere, American
   churches had available two broad models for support: the private club and the
   voluntary member-supported institution. . . . Religious groups that charged pew
   rents and ostracized those who used the 'free' pews in the back of the church
   were employing a version of the private club financing. . . . Most churches in
   the first half of the nineteenth century chose to go with the second financing
   route: to offer themselves as privately supported public goods. . . . So the die was
   cast: the American churches were to be dependent on the voluntary contributions of their members." James Hudnut-Beumler, *In Pursuit of the Almighty's
   Dollar* (Chapel Hill: University of North Carolina Press, 2007), 11–12.
8. Robert Wuthnow tells a somewhat different story. In *The Crisis in the Churches*
   (New York: Oxford University Press, 1997), Wuthnow offers the following:
   "Their theological training convinces clergy that faith in God should have
   implications for all of life, including the work people do and the way in which
   they spend their money" (71). At the same time, clergy seem unable to find the
   appropriate categories to express that belief. Wuthnow states, "Yet when asked
   without prompting of any kind to talk about the relationships between faith
   and economic behavior, most pastors did not mention their parishioners' work
   at all. They talked instead about church finances, pledge drives, and the
   responsible use of money" (84). We believe that one can account for this

ambivalence regarding money-talk because most clergy lack the training to speak consistently about money in theological terms. The only money-talk that remains usually regards fund-raising. This is one of the primary reasons, we believe, that clergy are uncomfortable. They find themselves asking for more, whenever the topic arises.

9. Michael O'Hurley-Pitts, *The Passionate Steward* (Toronto: St. Brigid Press, 2002), 35.

10. See John Wesley, "The Spirit of Bondage and of Adoption," in *The Works of John Wesley*, vol. 1, *Sermons 1–33*, ed. Albert C. Outler (Nashville: Abingdon Press, 1984), 248–66.

11. O'Hurley-Pitts, *Passionate Steward*, 14.

12. Abraham Heschel *The Sabbath* (New York: Noonday Press, 1976), 3.

13. Ibid., 6, 98, 14.

14. Commentators disagree as to whether Christ's main point here is to praise the widow or to denounce religious authorities who prey upon the poor and marginal within society.

15. O'Hurley-Pitts, *Passionate Steward*, 78

16. Ibid.

17. See Miroslav Volf, *Free of Charge: Giving and Forgiving in a Culture Stripped of Grace* (Grand Rapids: Zondervan, 2005).

18. Ibid., 56.

19. Ibid., 57.

20. Ibid. Volf is not using "donor" with the same distinction we wish to assert between *givers* and *donors* in this chapter.

21. Ibid., 59.

22. Hudnut-Beumler, *In Pursuit of the Almighty's Dollar*, 229.

23. Ibid., 47–75

24. Ibid., 51.

25. "By the 1890s, the offering was everywhere becoming a weekly ritual whereby parishioners would 'present their tithes and offerings' to the Lord, which would be followed by the singing of the doxology in recognition that it was God from whom all blessings flowed." Ibid., 55–56.

26. As we noted in chapter 1, from 1968 to 2005, total contributions to mainline Protestant congregations decreased from 3.11 percent to 2.58 percent of income. This is an "absolute decline of 0.53%, or one-half percent of income donated to the church. The percent change in the portion of income donated to the church in the 38-year period was -17%." John L. and Sylvia Ronsvalle, *The State of Church Giving through 2005* (Champaign, IL: empty tomb, 2007), 19. Furthermore, there does not appear to be any prospect for change in the near future. A recent study by Mark O. Wilhelm, Patrick M. Rooney, and Eugene R. Tempel, "Changes in Religious Giving Reflect Changes in Involvement: Age and Cohort Effects in Religious Giving, Secular Giving, and Attendance," *Journal for the Scientific Study of Religion* 46, no. 2, (June 2007): 217–32, indicates that the best givers to churches are of the generation born between 1924 and 1938. These people have tended to give more to their churches as they aged. The baby boomers (those born between 1951 and 1965, in this study) have given a smaller percentage of their income, even as their income has increased. This trend is very troubling insofar as the best givers to congregations will not be replaced by similar givers. Giving to churches could drop off dramatically in the next ten years.

27. Dan R. Dick calls for just such a radical change in thinking about funding ministry in his *Revolutionizing Christian Stewardship for the 21st Century: Lessons from Copernicus* (Nashville: Discipleship Resources, 1997).

Chapter 11: Expanding the Conversation

1. Robert D. Lupton, *Theirs Is the Kingdom: Celebrating the Gospel in Urban America* (New York: HarperCollins, 1989), 87.
2. "Business as Mission: Lausanne Occasional Paper No. 59 (Lausanne Committee for World Evangelism, 2005), part 3, no. 6, section 8(a).
3. Lupton, *Theirs Is the Kingdom*, 87.
4. Laura L. Nash and Scotty McLennan, *Church on Sunday, Work on Monday: The Challenge of Fusing Christian Values with Business Life* (San Francisco: Jossey-Bass, 2001), 6–7.
5. David W. Miller, *God at Work: The History and Promise of the Faith at Work, Movement* (New York: Oxford University Press, 2007), 9.
6. R. Paul Stevens, *The Other Six Days: Vocation, Work, and Ministry in Biblical Perspective* (Grand Rapids: Wm. B. Eerdmans Publishing Co., 1999), 208.
7. Michael Novak, *Business as a Calling: Work and the Examined Life* (New York: Free Press, 1996), 53.
8. Miller, *God at Work*, 10.
9. Ibid.
10. Nash and McLennan, *Church on Sunday*, 129.
11. Ibid., 9.
12. David W. Miller, "The Sunday-Monday Gap: Called to Pew or Profit," keynote presentation at the 2005 Mid-Winter Convocation, "Living Out Our Callings in the Workplace, Luther Seminary, January 5, 2005, http://www.yale.edu/faith/downloads/sundaymondaygap.pdf.
13. Ibid.
14. Stephen Hart and David A. Krueger, "Faith and Work: Challenges for Congregations," *Christian Century*, July 15–22, 1992, 685.
15. Nash and McLennan, *Church on Sunday*, XXIV–XXV.
16. International Coalition of Workplace Ministries, http://www.icwm.net/pages.asp?pageid=25057.
17. Nash and McLennan, *Church on Sunday*, 257.
18. Dorothy L. Sayers, *Creed or Chaos?* (New York: Harcourt, Brace & Co., 1949), 56–57. Ultimately, Protestants must ask how far we have maintained the Reformation emphasis upon the sacred character of all work. In spite of a theology of work that knows better, the unintended message often is of the medieval variety, which still endorses "counsels of perfection" for those who desire to *truly* serve God.
19. Stan Guthrie, "Defining Business Success," *Christianity Today*, February 2007, 124.
20. David W. Miller, "The Faith at Work Movement," *Theology Today* 60, no. 3 (October 2003): 309.
21. Thomas K. Tewell, "Ministering to the Business Community," *Theology Today* 60, no. 3 (October 2003): 348.
22. Miller, *God at Work*, 146.
23. Hart and Krueger, "Faith and Work," 686.
24. Shirley J. Roels, "The Christian Calling to Business Life," *Theology Today* 60, no. 3 (October 2003): 365.
25. Doug Sherman, cited in Os Hillmann, "The Faith at Work Movement: Open-

ing 'The 9 to 5 Window,'" *Christianity Today Online*, http://www.christianity today.com/workplace/articles/issue9-faithatwork.html.

26. Hart and Krueger, "Faith and Work," 685.
27. Laura L. Nash, "Toward Integrating Work and Faith," *Religion and Liberty* 12, no. 6 (November–December 2002): 4.
28. See Louke van Wensveen Siker, "Christ and Business: A Typology for Christian Business Ethics," *Journal of Business Ethics* 8 (1989): 883–88.
29. Jeff Van Duzer, Randal S. Franz, Gary L. Karns, Tim Dearborn, Denise Daniels, and Kenman L. Wong, "Towards a Statement on the Biblical Purposes of Business," in *Business as a Calling: Interdisciplinary Essays on the Meaning of Business from the Catholic Social Tradition*, ed. Michael Naughton and Stephanie Rumpza (St. Paul, MN: University of St. Thomas, 2007), 18.
30. Ibid.
31. Ibid., 7.
32. Ibid., 16.
33. Roels, "Christian Calling to Business Life," 367.
34. Quotations are from the Web site of the Redeemer Center for Faith and Work, http://www.faithandwork.org.
35. Katy Sloan, "First Year in the City," *Redeemer Report*, January 2007, 3, http://download.redeemer.com/pdf/newsletter/RedeemerNewsletter-2007-01.pdf.
36. From personal correspondence between Katherine Leary and the authors, March 25, 2008.
37. Web site of the Redeemer Center for Faith and Work.
38. Joe Maxwell, "The Mission of Business," *Christianity Today* 51, no. 11 (November 2007): 24.
39. David Befus, Kenneth R. Chase, Kim Daus-Edwards, John H. Warton Jr., "Discussion: Business as Mission," Center for Applied Christian Ethics, 2004, http://wheaton.edu/CACE/resources/onlinearticles/BusinessasMissionDiscussion.htm.
40. Steve Rundle and Tom Steffen, *Great Commission Companies: The Emerging Role of Business in Missions* (Downers Grove, IL: InterVarsity Press, 2003), 41.
41. Ibid., 22.
42. Ibid., 116.
43. Ibid., 42.
44. http://www.businessasmissionnetwork.com.
45. Amanda Sawyer, "Baylor Alumnus Turning Good Business into Great Ministry," *Baylor Business Online*, 1, http://www.baylor.edu/business/index.php?id=49802.
46. Ibid., 2.
47. Kevin Ring, "Global Business as Missions: Taking the Pulse of the Movement," http://www.businessasmissionnetwork.com/2007/10/taking-pulse-of-movement-business-as.html.
48. Chris Page, "About God's Business in Africa," http://www.businessasmission network.com/2007/04/about-gods-business-in-africa-by-chris.html.
49. Tony Emerson, Sarah Childress, Jonathan Alter, and Matthew Philips, "Periscope," *Newsweek*, December 18, 2006, http://www.newsweek.com/id/44046/page/1.
50. http://www.cardsfromafrica.com/aboutus.asp.
51. From personal correspondence between Chris Page and the authors, March 31, 2008.

52. Page, "About God's Business in Africa."

53. From personal correspondence between Chris Page and the authors, March 31, 2008.

54. Ibid.

55. Lupton, "Theirs Is the Kingdom," 87.

56. Jeannette A. Bakke, *Holy Invitations: Exploring Spiritual Direction* (Grand Rapids: Baker Publishing Group, 2000), 29.

57. Ibid., 31.

58. See John W. Kennedy, "The Debt Slayers," *Christianity Today*, May 2006, 40–43.

59. Ibid., 42.

60. Gary Moore's "Financial Seminary" in Sarasota, Florida, is one such organization.

61. Richard J. Foster, *The Challenge of the Disciplined Life* (San Francisco: Harper & Row, 1985), 57–63.

62. Ibid., 58.

63. Ibid.

64. Ibid., 59.

65. Ibid., 61.

66. Ibid., 62.

67. James A. Knight, "Money," *Dictionary of Pastoral Care and Counseling*, ed. Rodney J. Hunter and Nancy J. Ramsay (Nashville: Abingdon Press, 2005), 747–48.

68. Ibid., 748. Attachment theory also helps explain the role that possession can assume in providing security. For a brief introduction to this important area, see Robert C. Roberts, "Attachment: Bowlby and the Bible," in *On Being a Person: A Multidisciplinary Approach to Personality Theories*, ed. Todd H. Speidell (Eugene, OR: Cascade Books, 2002), 174–99.

69. Knight, "Money," 748.

70. Ibid.

71. Sheldon Solomon, Jeff Greenberg, and Thomas Pyszczyski, "Lethal Consumption: Death-Denying Materialism," in *Psychology and Consumer Culture: The Struggle for a Good Life in a Materialistic World*, ed. Tim Kasser and Allen D. Kanner (Washington, DC: American Psychological Association, 2005), 134.

72. Ibid., 135

73. "Look at the back of a dollar bill. Try to find anything about the use of the dollar as a rational medium of exchange between honest traders, but you cannot. Instead, see the real power behind money: God! *In God We Trust!* Now gaze to the left of the pyramid. There are no pyramids in the United States, so clearly they are not depicted on the dollar as cultural artifacts per se. Why else would there be pyramids on the backs of dollars, except as the ultimate symbol of death-denial and the royal gateway to immortality?" Ibid., 136.

74. Jeffrey Kottler, Marilyn Montgomery, and David Shepard, "Acquisitive Desire: Assessment and Treatment," in Kasser and Kanner, *Psychology and Consumer Culture*, 160.

75. Ibid., p. 155–56

76. Ronald J. Faber, "Self-Control and Compulsive Buying," in Kasser and Kanner, *Psychology and Consumer Culture*, 171.

77. Charles W. Taylor, *Premarital Guidance* (Minneapolis: Fortress Press, 1999), 41.

Index

Abraham, 15
accounting
  accrual basis, 64–65, 91–97
  GAAP (generally accepted accounting
    principles) of, 208n3
  modified cash basis, 60–64, 87–91
  pure cash basis, 59–60, 85–87
  See also church accounting; financial issues
accounts
  assets, 55, 57
  expenses, 57, 58
  liabilities, 55–56, 57
  net assets, 56–57, 58
  revenues, 57, 58
  year-end closing of, 57–58
accrual basis accounting
  description of, 64
  example of, 64–65
Achtemeier, E., 14
"Acres of Diamonds" (Conwell sermon), 36
Activities Statement
  description of, 65
  monthly report on, 91–97
almsgiving
  Cyprian's objection to, 204n8
  medieval practice of, 27
  spiritual development through, 23
  See also giving practice
annual audits
  documented transaction trail examined
    during, 123–24
  internal vs. independent, 118
  requirements for, 118
  resources available for, 118–19
Archdiocese of Boston, 117

Aristotelian doctrine, 24
asset accounts
  description of, 55
  year-end closing of permanent, 57
Assets, Liabilities, and Net Assets-Modified
    Cash Basis Statement, 62, 87–91
assets, physical controls to safeguard,
    120–21
Augustine of Hippo, 24, 25–26
authorization procedures, 123
avarice sin, 27

Bacher, R., 103
Bassler, J. M., 15, 16
Baudelaire, C.-P., 48
Baxter, R., 32
BBC World Challenge, 188
belief systems, 128
Berger, P., 46
Bible
  Ananias and Sapphria story of the, 20–21
  on economic abundance and loss, 11–13,
    39
  on fallen power of money, 42–44, 191–92,
    197
  on giving and asking of gifts, 14–16, 19–21,
    158–59, 174
  on material blessings, 39–40
  parables of the, 169, 191
  on wealth and idolatry connection, 16–18
Blanchard, K. D'Arcy, 30
blessings. *See* material blessings
Blomberg, C., 13
boundary systems, 128–29
Brandt, W. I., 29

217

budgeting
  as act of discipleship, 115
  disarming the power of money through,
    102–3, 115
  discerning God's mission for the church
    phase of, 103–4, 106, 114, 115
  God's mission context of, 103
  importance and issues related to, 101–2
  planning for the future through, 114–15
  planning to accomplish God's work, 104–6,
    115
  three approaches to, 108–11
budgeting approaches
  incremental, 108–10
  program, 110–11
  zero-based, 110
budgets
  cash, 112–14
  finalizing the operating, 111–12
  objectives of, 106–7
  personal monthly, 154–55, 157
  software products to create, 107–8
  ten reasons for church, 107
Busby, D., 126, 137, 152
Business as Mission (BAM) movement
  Cards from Africa program of, 188–89
  description of, 186–88
Business as Mission Network Web site, 187
businesspeople
  Christian leadership of, 188–89
  correcting unintended messages to, 181–89
  critical stance toward, 179–80
  God over mammon and, 22, 41, 183,
    189–90, 203n15
  providing pastoral care to, 181–82
  See also capitalism; parishioners; secular
    work

cafeteria plans (Section 125 plans), 147
Calvin, J.
  examining financial matters according to, 7
  interest lending thinking by, 31–32
  middle ground sought by, 30–31
capitalism
  economic system of, 38–39
  material standards of living generated by,
    44–45
  monetization of value by, 45–46
  practical atheism promoted by, 207n18
  See also businesspeople
Carder, Bishop K., 143
Cards from Africa (BAM program), 188–89
cash budget
  preparing the, 112–14
  Village Church example of monthly, 113
Cash Flows Statement
  description of, 65
  monthly reports on, 91–97
  practice exercise on, 97

Cash Receipts and Cash Disbursements
    Statement
  description of, 60
  monthly reports on, 85–87
Catholic Church sexual abuse scandal,
    116–17
Center for Applied Christian Ethics
    (Wheaton College), 186
Center for Faith and Work (Redeemer Pres-
    byterian Church), 185–86
Chopra, D., 181
Christ and Culture (Niebuhr), 183
Christian community
  favoring the rich over the poor in, 193
  God chosen over mammon by, 22, 41, 183,
    203n15
  money's potential harm to, 20–21
  See also Protestant congregations; steward-
    ship
Christianity
  American attitudes regarding money and,
    35–37
  medieval period beliefs about wealth and,
    26–38
  modern period attitudes toward wealth
    and, 32–35
  new way of living under, 42–43
  Patristic period teachings regarding money
    and, 22–26
  Reformation attitudes toward wealth and,
    29–32
  relationship to money in context of, 6
  See also Protestantism; theology of money
Christianity Today, 186
Christian life
  duality of, 167–68
  Sabbath keeping in, 168–69
  See also stewardship
Christ over mammon, 22, 41, 183, 189–90,
    203n15
Chrysostom, J., 24–25
church accounting
  designated funds, 67–68
  gift acceptance policy, 69–70
  using funds in, 65–67
  See also accounting
Church and Nonprofit Tax and Financial Guide
    (Busby), 152
church financial reports
  common monthly, 75–84
  financial accounting information in, 74
  financial statements included in, 85–97
  managerial accounting information in, 74
  minister participation in, 73
  overview of financial statements and, 74
  See also financial statements
church fund-raising literature, 5
The Church Guide to Internal Controls (Vargo),
    125

Church on Sunday, Work on Monday (Nash and McLennan), 178

church-provided housing. *See* clergy housing benefits

church-related expense reimbursement, 151–53

Clement of Alexandria
warning against wealth by, 22–23
Who Is the Rich That Shall Be Saved? by, 22

clergy housing benefits
Clergy Housing Allowance Clarification Act (2002) on, 139, 211n11
maximizing to save federal income tax, 137–41
practical examples on taxes and, 138, 139–40
strategic use as compensation, 145–47
tax treatment of, 135–36

clergy sexual abuse scandal, 116–17

compensation planning
ability to pay student loans and, 143–44
church-related expense reimbursement and, 151–53
clergy housing benefits as part of, 135–41, 145–47, 211n11
considerations and issues related to, 142–43
health insurance and medical reimbursement, 147–49
negotiating an amount, 144–45
retirement contributions, 149–50, 155, 156
See also material blessings

Constantine, 24

conversations on money. *See* money conversations

Conwell, R.
"Acres of Diamonds" sermon by, 36
beliefs regarding wealth by, 35–37

Covey, S., 181

culture of openness, 129–30

Cyprian of Carthage
objection to almsgiving by, 204n8
Treatise on Works and Alms, 23

"The Danger of Increasing Riches" (Wesley sermon), 35

"The Danger of Riches" (Wesley sermon), 34

debt
Deuteronomy on cancelation of, 12–13
student, 142–44

designated funds
description of, 67–68
management tip on, 68
practice exercise on, 68

disarming power of money
budget as tool for, 102–3, 115
discussing compensation for, 142–53
integrating faith and work for, 177–79
learning the tax basics for, 131–41

personal giving for, 158–59
See also money; money conversations; power of money

discerning God's mission
budgeting process of, 103–4, 114, 115
practical example of, 106

discipling, 191–93

discretionary monthly expenses, 155, 156

documented transaction trail, 123–24

Donahue, M. J., 161

duality of Christian life, 167–68

Ellul, J.
concerns on stewardship as obligation, 174
on costs of capitalism, 45
on New Testament paradigm applied to money as power, 43–44
on power of money, 38–41
power of money solutions offered by, 47–48

embezzlement
active engagement to prevent, 126–29
estimates of widespread, 117
internal control to prevent, 119–26

emergency fund, 156

environmental problems, 45

Epstein, J. D., 146

estimated tax payments, 141

Evangelical Council for Financial Accountability (ECFA), 117

expense accounts
description of, 57
year-end closing of temporary, 58

expense reimbursement, 151–53

expenses, 57

Faber, R. J., 195

faith
communal nature of, 192
disarming power of money by integrating work with, 177–79
preaching about work and, 183–84
of servant vs. faith of child of God, 167

faith-work integration
disarming power of money through, 177–79
pastoral leadership facilitating, 182–89
preaching and teaching about, 183–84

federal income tax
description of, 133
exemption from withholding, 141
making estimated tax payments on, 141
maximizing clergy housing benefit to save, 137–41, 211n11
retirement contributions exempt from, 150
self-employment and, 134, 136

feudal system, 28

"filthy lucre" rationale, 6

finance committee
  power of money controlled by the, 102–3
  spending priorities set by, 102
Financial Accounting Standards Board, 208n3
financial issues
  budgeting in the church, 101–15
  five basic types of accounts, 55–57
  Statement of Assets, Liabilities, and Net
    Assets Modified Cash Basis, 62
  transparency, 116–30, 198, 199–200
  year-end closing, 57–58
  See also accounting; monthly reports; per-
    sonal financial issues
financial leadership
  importance of clergy role in, 3–7, 53–54
  inspiring confidence to manage, 6–10
  See also management tips
Financial Position Statement
  description of, 65
  monthly report on, 91–97
  practice exercise on, 97
financial statements
  accrual basis accounting, 64–65
  included in church financial reports,
    85–97
  modified cash basis accounting, 60–64
  overview of church financial reports and,
    74
  pure cash basis accounting, 59–60
  Statement of Activities, 65, 91–97
  Statement of Assets, Liabilities, and Net
    Assets—Modified Cash Basis, 62, 87–91
  Statement of Cash Flows, 65, 91–97
  Statement of Cash Receipts and Cash Dis-
    bursements, 60, 85–87
  Statement of Financial Position, 65, 91–97
  Statement of Revenue, Expenses, Net
    Assets changes—Modified Cash Basis,
    63, 65, 87–91
  See also church financial reports
financial transparency
  actively engaging in preventing fraud,
    126–29
  annual audit for, 118–19
  clergy sexual abuse scandal and lack of,
    116–17
  comprehensive system of internal control
    for, 119–26
  description and importance of, 117–18,
    198
  fostering internal culture of openness,
    129–30
  sharing financial information with congre-
    gation for, 119
flexible spending accounts (FSAs), 147
Form 1040 (Schedule C), 134
Form 1099-MISC, 134, 135
Form 4361, 137
Forman, J., 187

Form W-2
  employee wages reported on, 134, 135
  maximizing clergy housing benefits and,
    138, 139–40
Foster, R., 191, 192–93
403(b) plan, 149, 150, 155
Francis of Assisi, 28
fraud prevention
  internal control to help with, 119–26
  minimizing opportunity for fraud for,
    127–28
  minimizing perceived pressure for, 127
  reducing rationalization for, 128–29
fraud triangle
  overview of the, 126–27
  perceived opportunity factor of, 126,
    127–28
  perceived pressure factor of, 126, 127
  rationalization factor of, 126, 127, 128–29
The Fund Activity Report
  practice exercise for, 81–82
  step 1: learn the basics, 79–80
  step 2: prepare ahead, 80–81
  step 3: identify key indicators, 81
fund-raising
  the annual church, 165
  discipleship as goal of Christian, 173
  gift mode and, 172
  issues of concern related to, 166–67
  missio Dei facilitated through, 171–72
  overcoming barriers to financial appeals
    for, 172–73
  stewardship context of, 165–67, 170–72
  See also giving practice; tithe

GAAP (generally accepted accounting princi-
    ples), 208n3
Gay, C., 44–45, 46, 48
gift acceptance policy
  description and practical example of, 69–70
  management tip on, 70
  Robertson v. Princeton University landmark
    decision on, 208n9
gift mode, 172
giving motivation
  altruism and thankfulness as, 161
  altruism or thankfulness as, 164–65
  extensions of the self as, 161, 163–64
  large monetary gifts and recognition
    plaques as, 163
  reciprocity with God as, 161–62
  reciprocity with religious group as, 161
giving practice
  decreasing levels of, 213n26
  human scarcity/prosperity axis to God's
    abundance redefining, 174–75
  New testament on, 15–16, 19–20, 158–59
  Old Testament on, 14–15

personal, 158–59
spiritual development through, 23
See also almsgiving; fund-raising; tithe
God
  budgeting to support mission of, 103–6
  chosen over mammon, 22, 41, 183,
    189–90, 203n15
  giving and reciprocity with, 161–62
  sacrifice of, 168
God's mission
  budgeting process step of discerning,
    103–4, 106, 114, 115
  budget planning to accomplish, 104–6, 115
  correcting unintended messages related to,
    181–89
  as first budgeting consideration, 103
  fund-raising to facilitate, 171–72
  sending unintended messages related to,
    178–81
González, J., 22
Great Commission Companies (Rundle and Steffen), 186
Greenberg, J., 194
Gregory the Great, Pope
  Pastoral Rule by, 26
  on property ownership, 26–27
Guinn, J. F., 126

Habakkuk, 49–50
Hammar, R. R., 137
health insurance plans, 147–49
health reimbursement arrangements (HRAs),
  148
health savings accounts (HSAs), 148
Hempton, D., 35
Hengel, M., 21
Heschel, Rabbi A., 169
high-deductible health plan (HDHP), 148
Hoge, D. R., 161, 162, 163, 164
Holy Spirit, 20
housing allowance. *See* clergy housing benefits
Hudnut-Beumler, J., 142, 172–74

idolatry-wealth connection, 16–18
incremental budgeting, 108–10
interest lending, 31–32
internal control system
  authorization procedures, 123
  competent and trustworthy employees/
    volunteers, 125
  documented transaction trail, 123–24
  importance of creating effective, 119–20
  objectives of, 120
  physical controls to safeguard assets,
    120–21
  reconciliation controls, 124–25
  resources to help with, 125–26
  segregation of duties, 121–22

internal culture of openness, 129–30
IRS (Internal Revenue Code)
  on church-related expense reimbursement,
    151–52
  legal definition of minister by the, 133
  risk of audit by, 134
  self-employment vs. employee criteria of,
    134
  Social Security and Medicare opting out
    criteria of, 136–37, 210n3
  See also tax issues
IRS Code 1402(c)(4) section, 134
IRS Code 3121(b)(8), 134
IRS Code Section 107, 135
IRS Form 1099-MISC, 134, 135
IRS Form 4361, 137
IRS Form W-2
  employee wages reported on, 134, 135
  maximizing clergy housing benefits and,
    137, 138, 139–40
IRS Schedule C (Form 1040), 134
Israel
  God's blessings through faithfulness of,
    14–15
  wealth and authority of ancient, 12

Jenkins, R., 154
Judicatories, lowering administrative costs
  by, 5

King James Version, 6
Knight, J. A., 193, 194
Kottler, J., 195
Kuyper, A., 47

Leary, K., 185–87
liability accounts
  description of, 55–56
  year-end closing of permanent, 57
Lord's Prayer, 115
Luke, 169
Lupton, R. D., 17, 177, 189
Luther, M.
  comments on money themes by, 29–30
  examining financial matters according to, 7

mammon vs. Christ, 22, 41, 183, 189–90,
  203n15
management tips
  asset accounts, 55
  common monthly reports, 75
  designated funds, 68
  gift acceptance policy, 70
  See also financial leadership; pastoral minis-
    ters; tax tips/examples
marital counseling, 195–96
Marxism, 38–39
Massachusetts Conference United Church of
  Christ, 119

material blessings
　ancient Israel and, 12
　equating God's love with, 39–41
　ethos grounded in character of God of, 13
　New Testament on, 16–18, 20–21, 39–40
　Old Testament on, 11–15, 39
　pastoral counseling on proper place of,
　　193–96
　relationship between idolatry and, 16–18
　See also compensation planning
McGee, D. B., 36
McLennan, S., 178, 181
McMillan, B., 142
McNamara, P., 161
Mead, L., 176
medical reimbursement plans, 147–49
Medicare taxes
　description and rates of, 133
　opting out of, 136–37, 210n3
　retirement contribution exempt from,
　　150
　self-employment rates of, 136
medieval period
　almsgiving practice during, 27
　beliefs about money during the, 26–28
　distinction between modern economic
　　thought and, 28
Melchizedek, 15
mentoring (money), 190, 196, 199
Methodist movement
　attitudes toward wealth during the, 33–35
　origins and historical background of, 33–34
Miller, D., 179, 180, 181, 182
missio Dei. See God's mission
missionary work
　Business as Mission (BAM) movement on,
　　186–89
　Business as Mission Network Web site on,
　　187
　Cards from Africa program of, 188–89
modern period
　Methodist movement, 33–35
　Puritan attitudes toward wealth, 32–33
modified cash basis accounting
　description of, 60–61
　example of, 61–62
　Statement of Assets, Liabilities, and Net
　　Assets-Modified Cash Basis, 62, 87–91
　Statement of Revenue, Expenses, Net
　　Assets changes—Modified Cash Basis,
　　63, 65, 87–91
money
　American attitudes regarding Christian use
　　of, 35–37
　Aristotelian doctrine on, 24
　early Christian community's choice of God
　　over, 20–22
　medieval period beliefs about, 26–28
　modern period attitudes toward, 32–35

　monetization of value of, 45–47
　Patristic period teachings regarding, 22–26
　Reformation and attitudes toward, 29–32
　stewardship context of, 29–31, 37, 41,
　　165–67, 170–74
　See also disarming power of money; power
　　of money
money conversation expansion
　discipling as, 191–93, 199
　money mentoring as, 190, 196, 199
　pastoral counseling as, 193–96, 199
　spiritual companionship included in,
　　189–90, 199
　spiritual direction as, 190–91, 199
money conversations
　correcting unintended messages, 181–89
　discomfort of, 176–77, 212n8
　expanding the, 189–96, 198–99
　integrating faith and work, 177–79
　negotiating compensation, 144–45
　three unintended messages during, 178–81
　See also disarming power of money
*Money Matters: Personal Giving in American
　Churches* (Hoge, Zech, McNamara, and
　Donahue), 161
money mentoring, 190, 196, 199
Montgomery, M., 195
monthly reports
　description of, 75
　The Fund Activity Report, 79–82
　management tip on, 75
　Statement of Activities, 65, 91–97
　Statement of Assets, Liabilities, and Net
　　Assets—Modified Cash Basis, 87–91
　Statement of Cash Flows, 65, 91–97
　Statement of Cash Receipts and Cash Dis-
　　bursements, 60, 85–87
　Statement of Financial Position, 65, 91–97
　Statement of Revenue, Expenses, Net
　　Assets changes—Modified Cash Basis,
　　63, 65, 87–91
　The Summary of Cash Activity or the Bank
　　Reconciliation, 75–79
　The Trial Balance Report, 82–84
　See also financial issues
MSM Money Web site, 154

Nash, L., 178, 181
net asset accounts
　description of, 56–57
　year-end closing of permanent, 57, 58
net assets, 56–57
Neuhaus, R. J., 49
New International Version, 6, 207n9
New Revisited Standard Version, 6, 207n9
New Testament
　Ananias and Sapphria story of the, 20–21
　departure from Old Testament on material
　　blessings, 39–40

on fallen power of money, 42–44, 191–92, 197
on giving and asking of gifts, 15–16, 19–21, 158–59
rich fool parable of the, 169
silence on tithes in the, 15–16, 174
on wealth and idolatry connection, 16–18
Workers in the Vineyard parable in the, 191
See also Old Testament
Niebuhr, R., 183
Noll, M., 36, 37
Noll, S. F., 42–43

O'Connor, F., 40
Oden, T., 26
offerings
physical controls to safeguard, 120–21
segregation of duties related to, 121–22
O'Hurley-Pitts, M., 165–66, 167–68, 170
An Old Irish penitential, 27
Old Testament
on economic abundance and loss, 11–13, 39
on fallen power of money, 191–92
on giving and tithe, 14–15, 174
See also New Testament
Outler, A., 33–34

Page, C., 188–89
parables
rich fool, 169
Workers in the Vineyard, 191
parishioners
Business as Mission (BAM) movement promoted among, 186–89
favoring rich over poor, 193
internal control through trustworthy volunteers among, 125
praying for secular work done by, 182–83
preaching and teaching about faith and work to, 183–84
sharing financial information openly with, 119
spiritual companionship of, 189–96
unintended messages on sacred vs. secular work of, 178–79
See also businessmen; Protestant congregations
pastoral counseling
premarital and marital, 195–96
regarding financial issues, 193–96, 199
pastoral ministers
church financial report participation by, 73–97
clergy housing provided to, 135–41, 145–47, 211n11
competencies required for, 5–6
critical stance toward business by, 179–80
discomfort of talking by, 176–77, 212n8

examining financial leadership role of, 3–7, 53–54
inspiring financial confidence, 6–10
IRS legal definition of, 133
overcoming bad conscience of financial appeals, 172–73
six unique aspects of taxes for, 132–41
spiritual companionship through counseling by, 193–96
student debt of, 142–43
See also management tips; personal financial issues; unintended messages
Pastoral Rule (Gregory the Great), 26
Paul
body metaphor for church used by, 104
on "chain of benefaction" through giving, 15–16
on new way of living, 43
on power of almsgiving, 27
perceived opportunity
as fraud factor, 126, 127
minimizing the, 127–28
perceived pressure
as fraud factor, 126, 127
minimizing, 127
Perkins, W., 32–33
personal emergency fund, 156
personal financial issues
compensation planning, 142–53
learning the basics of paying taxes, 131–41
personal giving, 158–59
personal spending and setting limits, 153–58
retirement contributions, 149–50, 155
See also financial issues; pastoral ministers
personal giving, 158–59
personal spending
budgeting for, 154–55, 157
categories of, 156
committed expenses vs. discretionary, 155–58
deciding percentage of income allocated to, 154–55
giving as part of, 158–59
learning to limit and control, 153–54
personal spending budgets
example of monthly, 157
secrets to effective, 154–55
Peter, 21
power of money
Bible on the, 42–48, 191–92, 197
blindness of, 171
countering the, 48–50
Jacques Ellul on, 38–41, 47–48
monetization of value accounting for, 45–47
personal spending limits for, 153–58
theology of money to counter the, 48–50, 198

power of money (*continued*)
  See also disarming power of money; money;
    wealth
PPC's Guide to Religious Organizations (Guinn),
    126
practical examples
  accrual basis accounting, 64–65
  authorization procedures, 123
  clergy housing and taxes, 135–36, 138,
    139–40
  compensation level and paying student
    loans, 144–45
  compensation-related, 144–45, 148–49
  discerning God's mission phase of account-
    ing, 106
  gift acceptance policy, 69–70
  health insurance and medical reimburse-
    ment plans, 147–49
  incremental budgeting, 109
  internal control system, 121
  liability, 56
  modified cash basis accounting, 61
  negotiating compensation, 144–45
  personal spending, 156–58
  pure cash basis accounting, 59
  reconciliation controls, 124–25
  retirement contributions, 149
  segregation of duties, 122
  using funds in church accounting, 66
practice exercises
  designated funds, 68
  The Fund Activity Report, 81–82
  modified cash basis, 64
  Statement of Cash Flows, 97
  Statement of Financial Position, 97
  The Summary of Cash Activity or the Bank
    Reconciliation report, 79
  The Trial Balance Report, 84
prayer, 192
premarital counseling, 195–96
Presbyterian Church (U.S.A.)
  downsizing due to diminished giving
    by, 5
  restructuring of, 201n3
Price, M., 142
Princeton University, Robertson v., 208n.9
program budgeting, 110–11
Protestant congregations
  Business as Mission (BAM) movement and,
    186–89
  examining financial leadership in, 3–7
  expressing appreciation for secular work of,
    179–80
  favoring the rich over the poor in, 193
  funding crisis experienced by, 5, 213n26
  internal control through trustworthy vol-
    unteers from, 125
  preaching and teaching about faith and
    work to, 183–84

sharing financial information openly with,
    119
  unintended messages on sacred vs. secular
    work of, 178–79
  See also Christian community; parishioners
Protestantism
  on stewardship context of money, 41
  tremendous shift in giving and member-
    ship in, 175
  See also Christianity
pure cash basis accounting
  description of, 59
  example of, 59–60
  Statement of Cash Receipts and Cash Dis-
    bursements, 60, 85–87
Puritans, 32–33
Pyszczyski, T., 194

rationalization
  as fraud factor, 126, 127
  ways of reducing, 128–29
Rauschenbusch, W., 35–37
reciprocity with God, 161–62
reconciliation controls, 124–25
Redeemer Presbyterian Church (NYC),
    185–86
reducing rationalization
  belief systems for, 128
  boundary systems for, 128–29
Reformation
  attitudes toward wealth during the, 29–32
  living by faith cry of the, 50
  stewardship concept during, 29–30
Reid, D., 42
Reid, W. Stanford, 31–32
retirement contributions
  comparing types of, 149–50
  as monthly personal expense, 155, 156
Revenue, Expenses, Net Assets changes—
    Modified Cash Basis Statement, 63, 65,
    87–91
revenue accounts
  description of, 57
  year-end closing of temporary, 58
rich fool parable, 169
Robertson v. Princeton University, 208n9
Roels, S., 182, 184
Ronsvalle, J., 102
Ronsvalle, S., 102
Rundle, S., 186
Rwandan Cards from Africa program, 188–89
Ryken, L., 33

Sabbath keeping, 168–69
sacred work
  unintended message about serving God
    only through, 179
  unintended messages about secular vs.,
    178–79

Sayers, D., 181
Schedule C (Form 1040), 134
Schulze, L. F., 31
Section 125 plans (cafeteria plans), 147
secular work
  expressing appreciation for, 179–80
  providing Church support groups focusing
    on issues of, 184–86
  unintended message about serving God by
    sacred and not, 179
  unintended messages about secular vs.,
    178–79
  See also businesspeople
segregation of duties, 121–22
self-employment
  income taxes related to, 136
  IRS criteria for, 134
Sermon on the Mount, 17, 29, 170
Seton Hall University Law School, 117
Shepard, D., 195
short-term savings, 156
Siker, L. van Wensveen, 183
"A Simpler Way to Save: The 60 % Solution"
  (Jenkins), 154
Social Security taxes
  opting out of, 136–37, 210n3
  pastoral ministry income included in, 136
  retirement contributions exempt from, 150
  self-employment vs. employee, 133
Solomon, S., 194
spiritual companionship
  discipling for, 191–93, 199
  money conversation role of, 189–90,
    198–99
  money mentoring, 190, 196, 199
  pastoral counseling as, 193–96, 199
  spiritual direction for, 190–91, 199
spiritual direction, 190–91, 199
Statement of Activities, 65, 91–97
Statement of Assets, Liabilities, and Net
  Assets-Modified Cash Basis, 62, 87–91
Statement of Cash Flows, 65, 91–97
Statement of Cash Receipts and Cash Disbursements, 60, 85–87
Statement of Financial Position, 65, 91–97
Statement of Revenue, Expenses, Net Assets
  changes—Modified Cash Basis, 63, 65,
  87–91
Steffen, T., 186
Stevens, R. P., 178
stewardship
  Calvin's understanding of, 31
  concerns regarding "obligation" of, 174
  fund-raising in context of, 165–67, 170–72
  Luther's understanding of, 29–30
  Noll on Christian commitment to, 37
  Protestantism on money in context of, 41
  tithing and, 173–74
  See also Christian community; Christian life

student debt
  Auburn study on ministers and, 142–43,
    144
  compensation and ability to pay back,
    143–44
The Summary of Cash Activity or the Bank
  Reconciliation report
  step 1: learn the basics, 75–77
  step 2: prepare ahead, 77–78
  step 3: identify key indicators, 78–79
Sunday collection security, 121

Tawney, R. H., 28
tax issues
  clergy housing, 135–41, 145–47, 211n11
  federal income tax, 133, 134; 136, 137–41,
    150
  importance of understanding personal,
    131–32
  IRS legal definition of minister, 131
  making estimated tax payments, 141
  Medicare taxes, 133, 136–37, 141, 150
  opting out of Social Security and Medicare,
    136–37, 210n3
  self-employed vs. employee, 134, 136, 141
  six unique aspects of clergy, 132
  Social Security taxes, 133, 136–37, 150
  See also IRS (Internal Revenue Code)
tax-sheltered annuity plan (TSA), 149–50
tax tips/examples
  on dual-status issue, 135
  maximizing clergy housing to save on
    taxes, 138, 139–40
  planning federal withholding, 141
  planning house-related benefits and taxes,
    140–41
  self-employment income, 136
  tax treatment of clergy housing, 135–36
  See also management tips
Temple University, 36
Theirs Is the Kingdom (Lupton), 177
theology of money
  countering the power of money through,
    48–50, 198
  on how money exerts power on society,
    44–48
  Jacques Ellul on naming money's power,
    38–42
  New Testament teachings on, 42–44
  See also Christianity
*Tips for Preventing and Catching Misuse of
  Church Funds* (United Methodist
  Church), 126
tithe
  New Testament silence on, 15–16, 174
  Old Testament on mandatory, 15, 174
  stewardship and, 173–74
  See also fund-raising; giving practice
transparency. *See* financial transparency

Treasurer's Report. *See* The Fund Activity
   Report
Treatise on Works and Alms (Cyprian of
   Carthage), 23
The Trial Balance Report
   practice exercise for, 84
   step 1: learn the basics, 82–83
   step 2: prepare ahead, 84
   step 3: identify key indicators, 84
trustworthy employees/volunteers, 125
TSA (tax-sheltered annuity plan), 149–50
Tyndale, W., 7

unintended messages
   correcting the, 181–89
   about sacred vs. secular work, 178–79
   self-examination regarding sending,
     179–81
   See also pastoral ministers
unintended messages correction
   importance of pastoral role in, 181–82
   praying for parishioners' work in the world
     as, 182–83
   preaching/teaching about faith and work
     as, 183–84
   providing Church support groups focusing
     on work issues, 184–86
   Redeemer Presbyterian Church example
     of, 185–86
United Methodist Church General Council
   on Finance and Administration, 118
United Methodists, 5

Vargo, R. J., 107, 125
Villanova University, 117
Volf, M., 171, 172, 173

wealth
   American attitudes regarding Christians
     and, 35–37
   early Christian community's choice of God
     over, 20–22

equating God's love with blessing of, 39–41
medieval period beliefs about, 26–28
Methodist movement and attitudes toward,
   33–35
Patristic period teachings regarding, 22–26
Reformation and attitudes toward, 29–32
Wesley on the accumulation of, 34–35
See also power of money
Weber, M., 40
Welch, R., 109
Wesley, J.
   on accumulation of wealth, 34–35
   "The Danger of Increasing Riches" ser-
     mon by, 35
   "The Danger of Riches" sermon by, 34
   examining financial matters according to, 7
   on faith of servant vs. faith of child of God,
     167
   on the proper use of money, 33–34, 206n48
West, R., 116–17
"What's in it for me?" syndrome, 170
Wheaton College, 186
Who Is the Rich That Shall Be Saved? (Clement
   of Alexandria), 22
work
   disarming power of money by integrating
     faith with, 177–79
   preaching about faith and, 183–84
   providing Church support groups focusing
     on issues of, 184–86
   unintended messages about secular vs.
     sacred, 178–79
Workers in the Vineyard parable, 191
World Christian Database, 117
Wright, C. J. H., 12

Zech, C., 116–17, 161
zero-based budgeting, 110
*Zondervan 2008 Church and Nonprofit Tax and
   Financial Guide* (Busby), 126